NEW YORK
MID-CENTURY

NEW YORK MID-CENTURY

Post-War
Capital of Culture,
1945–1965

Annie Cohen-Solal
Paul Goldberger
Robert Gottlieb

With 447 illustrations, 159 in colour

Thames & Hudson

CONTENTS

VISUAL ARTS
ANNIE COHEN-SOLAL

INTRODUCTION

Monday, March 19, 1945. After an unusually warm day for that time of year, Peggy Guggenheim opened a new Jackson Pollock exhibition in her gallery, Art of This Century. The crowd had grown substantially in size and enthusiasm since his last show fifteen months before, but most critics still remained skeptical. "Despite his strong feeling for *matière*, he doesn't seem to be especially talented," wrote Parker Tyler in the magazine *View*,[1] and in *ARTnews*, the most legitimate art world publication of the time, Maude Riley honestly admitted, "I really don't get what it's all about."[2] Pollock's canvases, in fact, were exploring a unique territory in painting. In the 1930s he had studied with Thomas Hart Benton at the Art Students League, and was later embraced by the Mexican muralists, working closely with Social Realist David Alfero Siqueiros in his New York studio. By the early 1940s, his work reflected a rediscovery of Surrealism and the devices of "automatism" and "totemic symbolism," which were apparently a perfect match for Peggy Guggenheim, who was seen as essentially the "only prominent collector and gallery owner with both the money and the bravery (or eccentricity) to buy paintings from relatively unknown artists—even American artists."[3] Museum of Modern Art (MoMA) curator James Johnson Sweeney, who had heard about Pollock's work through his old friend the photographer and graphic designer Herbert Matter, first brought the artist to Peggy Guggenheim's attention in early 1942. But it was her advisor Howard Putzel who immediately proclaimed "genius" upon seeing Pollock's work later that year.[4]

Yet Guggenheim took time to warm to Pollock's work. Her favorite American artist at the time was William Baziotes, who had received a stamp of approval from André Breton, and Pollock's work was tentatively accepted at Art of This Century for the first time in April 1943 as part of a juried collage show. It was not until Piet Mondrian, one of the judges on the panel, voiced his opinion that the gallerist really started to pay attention. Immediately captivated by *Stenographic Figure*, "a frenetic graffiti-covered canvas,"[5] Mondrian declared that it was "the most interesting work [he'd] seen so far in America." He added, "You must watch this man!"[6] Guggenheim's hesitance to give Pollock a solo show at her gallery was finally overcome by another encouraging response from Marcel Duchamp, who walked up the five flights of stairs to the American artist's studio in July of that year and returned to the gallerist with what was for this European a glowing assessment, "*Pas mal.*"[7] Not bad.

PRECEDING PAGES: Morris Louis. Alpha Mu, 1961. Acrylic and resin on canvas, 103 × 161⁷⁄₁₆ in. (261 × 410 cm). Seattle Art Museum, Gift of Mr. And Mrs. Bagley Wright.

OPPOSITE: Jackson Pollock. Number 19, 1948, *1948. Oil and enamel on paper mounted on canvas, 30⅞ × 22⅜ in. (78.4 × 57.4 cm). Private collection. One of Pollock's first great drip paintings.*

The door was finally opened for Pollock's first solo show in November 1943. In anticipation, Guggenheim supported the artist with monthly payments and arranged for him to realize a large mural in the entry of her new apartment. With this personal and financial encouragement, Pollock worked at a furious pace, creating dynamic, Jungian-influenced canvases like *The Moon-Woman Cuts the Circle*. His iconic *The She-Wolf* (the first Abstract Expressionist work to be acquired by MoMA) was also produced at this time, a blue-and-yellow Surrealist landscape dominated by a fierce and tormented central figure, heavily outlined in black and white and seemingly impaled by a rigid red bolt that slices across the beast's back. The artist, with his brothers' support and his wife, Lee Krasner's, devotion, was struggling against his addiction to alcohol. His brilliant moments of creation would be punctuated by severe and debilitating setbacks, while shuttling between his studios in New York and Springs, near East Hampton.

Situated at its prestigious address, 30 West 57th Street, Art of This Century represented a unique territory in the city by 1945. Guggenheim and her husband Max Ernst had arrived in New York from London, via Marseilles, in 1941, and she created the space shortly thereafter,

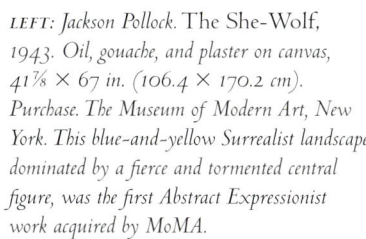

LEFT: Jackson Pollock. The She-Wolf, *1943. Oil, gouache, and plaster on canvas, 41⅞ × 67 in. (106.4 × 170.2 cm). Purchase. The Museum of Modern Art, New York. This blue-and-yellow Surrealist landscape, dominated by a fierce and tormented central figure, was the first Abstract Expressionist work acquired by MoMA.*

ABOVE: Jackson Pollock at work on a drip painting in his studio as his wife, Lee Krasner, looks on, 1950. His body hunched over the canvas, Pollock would dip his brush into a can of paint and, leaning on one leg, circle the painting in a slow, steady motion, throwing the paint with a rhythmic movement of his forearm. "My painting does not come from the easel," he said.

ABOVE: *Jackson Pollock, center, his wife, Lee Krasner, left, and an unidentified couple in his studio in Springs, near East Hampton, 1953.*

BELOW: *Jackson Pollock.* Number 25A, 1948. *Oil on canvas, 35 × 112⅜ in. (88.9 × 286.1 cm). Private collection. This is one of Pollock's major drip paintings of the time.*

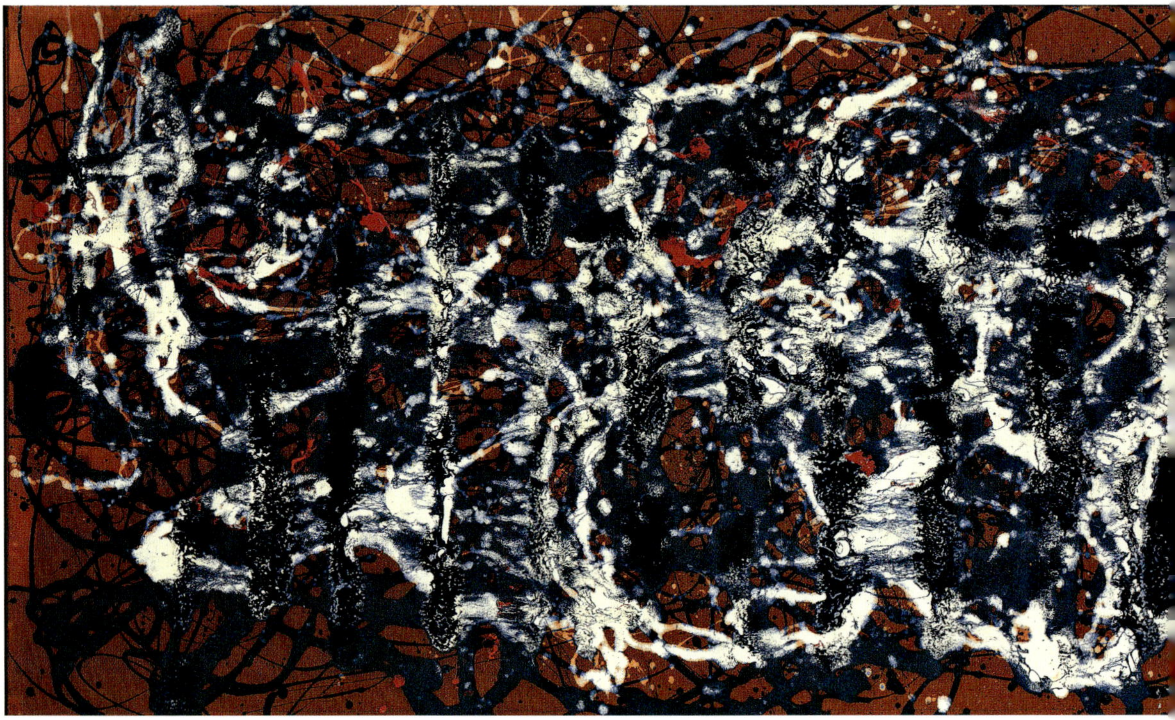

assisted by the Viennese-trained architect Frederick Kiesler. When it opened in 1942, its walls covered in pliant, undulating fabric, Art of This Century offered an opportunity for European and American artists to cross paths. It was a multidisciplinary gallery, in which Marcel Duchamp and André Breton collaborated to produce a landmark exhibition, *First Papers of Surrealism*. "She was passionately interested and had the money to make a go of it," MoMA curator Dorothy Miller said of the extravagant and unusual Peggy.[8] Living in a duplex in a double brownstone at 155 East 61st Street, she hosted fabulous parties throughout the two big floors, which were connected by an impressive spiral staircase. She also had a salon and advised the art press on new talent. "Her taste was often erratic and unsure, but she had a flair for life, a sort of smell for life, that made her recognize vitality and conviction in a picture," explained critic Clement Greenberg.[9] But her private life was often at the center of her encounters, and it was mostly women who tended to dwell on it. "Sex always seemed to dominate her conversation," Lee Krasner once commented. And Dorothy Miller recalled, "Peggy went to bed with everyone. She tried awfully hard to go to bed with Alfred Barr."[10]

To some of her colleagues, Guggenheim seemed "hostile to the general public, and very indifferent, which is not good business, if you're trying to sell pictures."[11] "I wasn't commercial," was her explanation.[12] And she didn't have to be. She had the financial

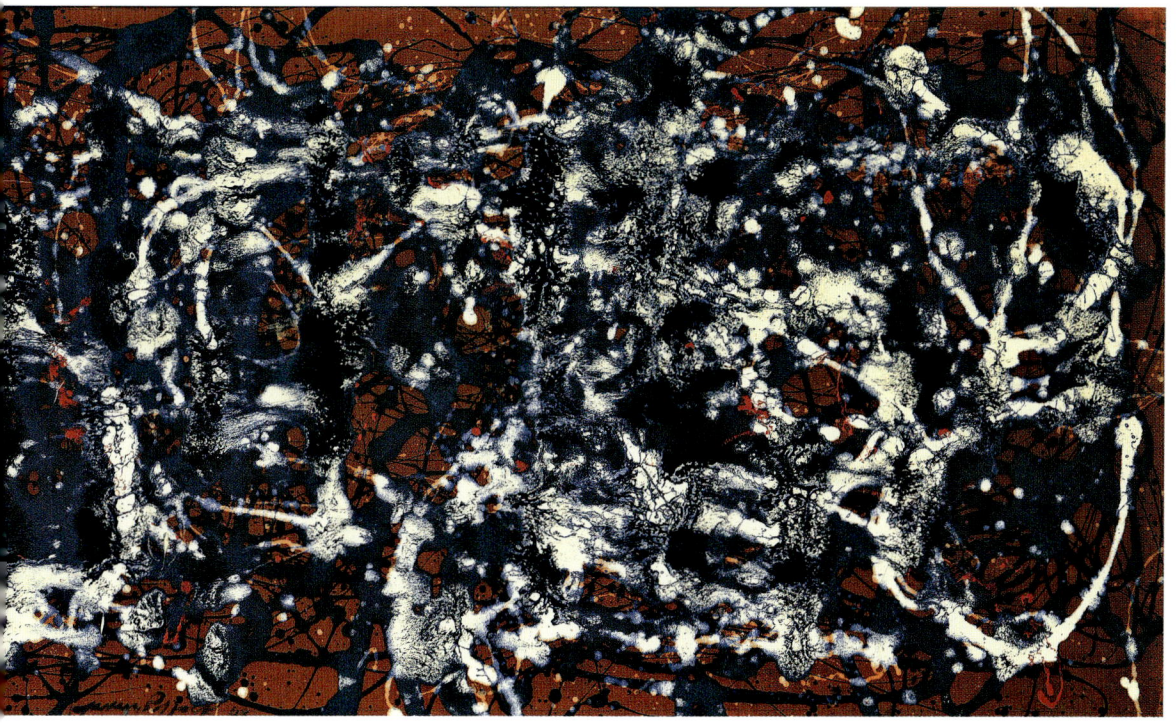

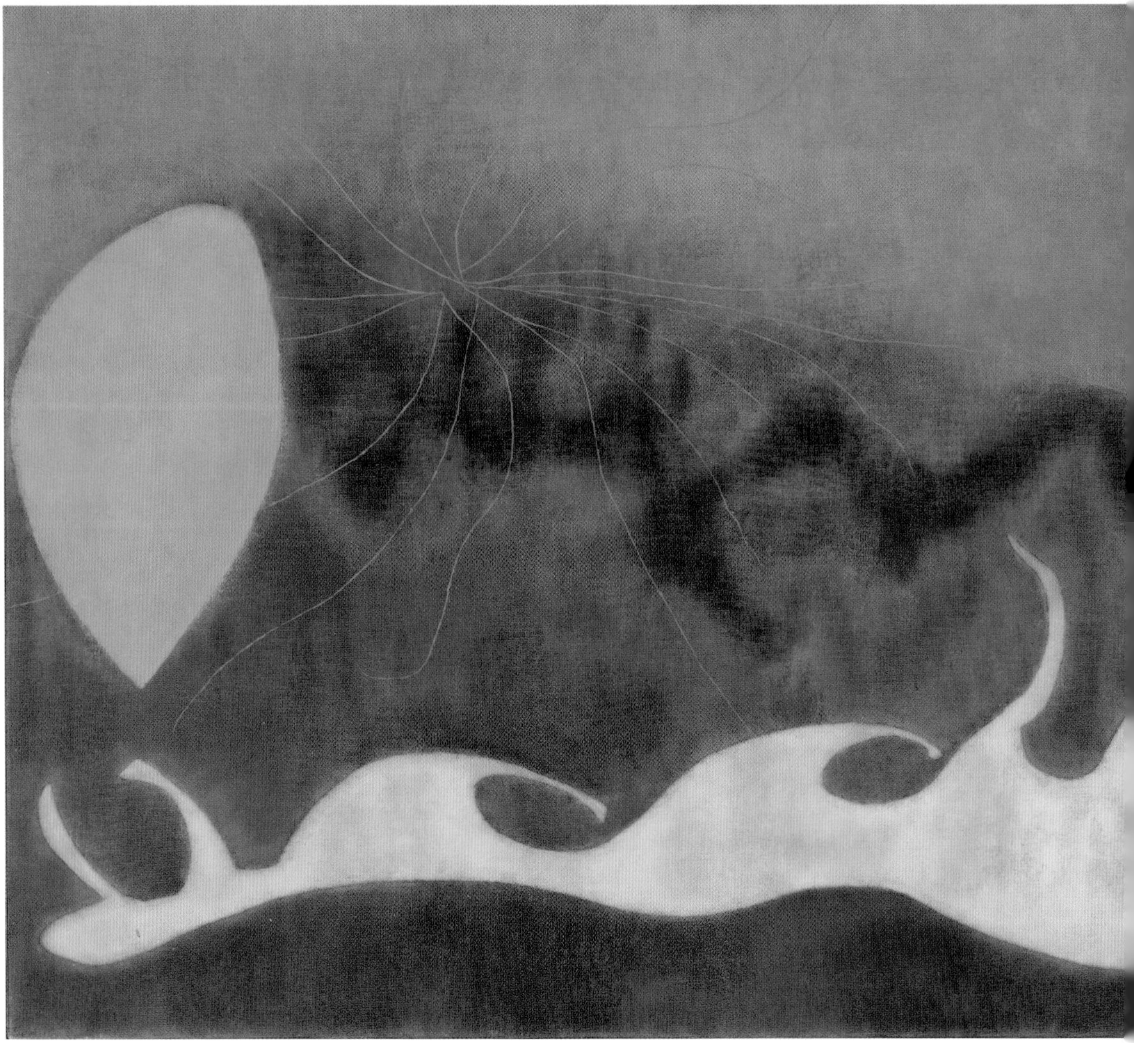

freedom to create a truly cutting-edge space and an unprecedented exhibition program. Kiesler, intending to "break down the barriers between viewers and works of art," had come up with dramatically unorthodox ideas for the presentation of Surrealist work, converging the visual arts with light, sound, and motion.[13] First, insisting on a more direct means of encounter, he took the artworks out of their frames and mounted them on "triangular floor-to-ceiling rope pulleys resembling cat's cradles."[14] The Abstract gallery had walls made of "stretched deep-blue canvas" laced to the floors and ceiling, while the floors were "painted turquoise," Peggy's favorite color.[15] The Surrealist and Kinetic galleries were similarly theatrical, featuring black floors and walls, with works by Paul Klee mounted on a mechanical belt. Other exhibitions at the gallery that shared recent developments in European art with a small, rather anxious New York audience

LEFT: William Baziotes. The Beach, *1955. Oil on linen, 36 × 48 in. (91.4 × 121.9 cm). Whitney Museum of American Art, New York; purchase 56.12. Baziotes was one of Peggy Guggenheim's favorite American artists. This cosmic seascape has echoes of the symbolism shared by French poets of the late nineteenth century and of the Surrealists' dreamlike art.*

ABOVE: Peggy Guggenheim's extraordinary Art of This Century gallery, which opened in 1942, was a multidisciplinary space in which she let the artists produce their own shows. This installation was designed by Frederick Kiesler.

included *Mark Rothko* (1944), *Alberto Giacometti* (1945), *The Women* (1945), *Hans Richter* (1946), and *Theo van Doesburg* (1946). But in 1945, was it not too early for New Yorkers at large, as indicated by the cool reaction of their guiding critics, to realize that the work of Jackson Pollock, one of the first American artists Guggenheim showed, would change the course of art history?

A few days before Pollock's January 1945 exhibition at Art of This Century, gallerist Julien Levy presented Arshile Gorky's first one-man show—an exhibit of nine paintings—in his gallery. But on the opening night, no friends of Gorky's were in sight except for André Breton and six other people. "If the audience is small, it is very distinguished," Breton declared, as pompous as always.[16] The critics who came the day before appeared to Julien Levy "stonier and more

Collector Peggy Guggenheim with a group of Surrealist artists in exile. Bottom row, left to right: Stanley William Hayter, Leonora Carrington, Frederick Kiesler, and Kurt Seligmann; middle row, left to right: Max Ernst, Amédée Ozenfant, André Breton, Fernand Léger, and Berenice Abbott; top row, left to right: Jimmy Ernst, Peggy Guggenheim, John Ferren, Marcel Duchamp, and Piet Mondrian.

unresponsive" than he had ever known them, and displayed "a kind of blind opposition" that he had "never in his career come up against."[17] To make matters worse, only two of the paintings sold, including *They Will Take My Island,* and for months after the opening, Gorky was in despair over his failure. So much so that his wife wrote that he was "paralyzed and agonized in a fever of self-criticism brought on by the suicidal attempt to see himself as others see him."[18] In *Art Digest,* Maude Riley described Gorky's work as "incoherent accident paintings" and surmised that the artist must "agonize quite a lot emotionally."[19] Clement Greenberg complained that Gorky was "relying too much on appropriations" and "had made concessions to charm," having borrowed

Armenian-born Arshile Gorky, left, was a brilliant artist who had a profound influence on Willem de Kooning and others. He stands here with de Kooning, also a European émigré, 1937. "Gorky spoke the language of painting," de Kooning said of him.

from Picasso, Miró, Matta, and early Kandinsky.[20] That reaction prompted Gorky to confront Greenberg directly. One day, meeting him by chance outside the New School for Social Research, Gorky threw down a piece of chalk right in front of Greenberg's feet and commanded, "Draw!"[21]

In the following weeks, Gorky experienced two even more difficult moments: one when a fire destroyed most of his work and another when he was forced to undergo emergency surgery for cancer. Though most of Gorky's friends considered him an extremely talented, natural artist, many confessed they found him really "hard to take."[22] With his dark moustache and somber looks, Gorky always remained a foreigner in New York; instead of trying to assimilate, he behaved in a most confrontational way. The first time he met Willem de Kooning, for instance, he told him bluntly, "You look like a truck driver!" And he often referred to sculptor David Smith as the "German sausage maker."[23] But all in all, most artists remained mesmerized by Gorky's talent. When de Kooning visited him for the first time, he climbed up the dim stairs leading to the shabby 16th Street studio and was bowled over by both the place and the art. Gorky, he said, "spoke the language of painting."[24] But the Armenian-born artist's nostalgia for a lost paradise, his struggle to become an artist, prompted him to invent myths about his identity: he claimed, for instance, that he had studied in Paris and that he had been successful there.[25] These legends evolved over the years and created many

Arshile Gorky. To Project, To Conjure, *1944. Oil on canvas, 35¾ × 46¾ in. (90.8 × 118.7 cm). Private collection. One of Gorky's most disturbing paintings and a clear assertion of his outstanding expressionist talent.*

misunderstandings, as well as recurrent professional and personal tensions with others.

Still, for years de Kooning was profoundly influenced by Gorky; he dubbed the group that Gorky formed with John Graham and Stuart Davis the "Three Musketeers."[26] In 1945, David Hare invited Gorky to spend some time in Roxbury, Connecticut. He lived in the sculptor's white clapboard farmhouse on Goodhill Road and took part in Thanksgiving dinners and New Year's Eve parties in the little village, which had recently become a haven for artists, including André Breton, who lived nearby, Yves Tanguy, George Rickey, and Alexander Calder.[27]

When Breton decided to return to France in November 1945, Roberto Matta and his wife, Patricia, gave him a farewell dinner.[28] Around the table were the Duchamps, the Kieslers, the Gorkys, and Max Ernst. When Breton insisted on playing Surrealist games after the meal, Gorky resented it. By the time the bill came, Matta and his wife had disappeared. The tensions among those artists and intellectuals who had shared so much during the war were coming to a head: Breton had estranged himself from Matta, Matta was fighting with Robert Motherwell, and Breton was leaving the United States in a rage.

ABOVE: *Arshile Gorky.* Housatonic, 1943. *Ink and crayon on paper laid down on board, 19 × 24¾ in. (48.3 × 62.9 cm). Private collection. The title refers to the Housatonic River in Connecticut, a fruitful source of inspiration for several Gorky landscapes, rendered in fields of colors.*

LEFT: *André Breton, left, with Max Ernst, just before Breton headed back to Paris in 1945. Gift of Patricia and Frank Kolodny in memory of Julien Levy, 1990.565.34, The Art Institute of Chicago.*

ISOLATION
1945–1947

"There is no past. No tradition. No roots."[29]
—W. H. AUDEN

Through the war years, even if the artists had started bonding with each other and created a community, the New York gallery world struck European visitors as hopelessly provincial. Compared to Paris, it was a desert in which the local artists remained practically invisible, gallerist Ileana Sonnabend, who was married to Leo Castelli at the time, noted. "In the 1940s, some of us woke up to find ourselves without hope," Barnett Newman later explained, "to find that painting did not really exist."[30] In a similar tone, Adolph Gottlieb remarked that "a few painters were painting with a feeling of absolute desperation. The situation was so bad that I know I felt free to try anything no matter how absurd it seemed."[31] The galleries of Peggy Guggenheim, Julien Levy, Pierre Matisse, Curt Valentin, Knoedler, and Valentine Dudensing combined did not begin to approximate Europe's vibrant art scene.

Pierre Matisse arrived in New York in 1924 and opened his gallery in the Fuller Building at Madison Avenue and 57th Street in 1931. It

This photograph was taken in 1942 on the occasion of the Artists in Exile *exhibition at the Pierre Matisse Gallery. First row, left to right: Roberto Matta, Ossip Zadkine, Yves Tanguy, Max Ernst, Marc Chagall, Fernand Léger; second row, left to right: André Breton, Piet Mondrian, André Masson, Amédée Ozenfant, Jacques Lipchitz, Pavel Tchelitchew, Kurt Seligmann, Eugene Berman.*

was not easy at first, because the rejection of French art by young American artists, which had begun in 1913 after the Armory Show, continued. "We are slightly—or greatly—victims of a fierce campaign for American modern art and naturally one reaction will be that French art will fall under attack," Pierre Matisse wrote to his family in 1931, several months after the opening of the Whitney Museum.[32] To counter this tendency, he decided to take on many of the artists who showed at Galerie Pierre, one of the most dynamic and innovative in Paris, including Balthus, Alberto Giacometti, Matta, Wilfredo Lam, and Jean Dubuffet. "In the future world," Pierre Matisse wrote, proud of his new country, "America, full of dynamism and vitality, must play a role of premiere importance."[33] His space on 57th Street gradually attracted a growing clientele; he sold several Aristide Maillol bronzes and some of the finest of his father's paintings. Then he shrewdly decided to adapt to cir-

cumstances. He began exhibiting work by other European artists, such as Joan Miró—whose career in America owed everything to Matisse—Dubuffet, Giacometti, and Raoul Dufy, and he was largely responsible for their substantial influence on young American artists. Matisse's clients represented a new breed of adventurous collector: Duncan Phillips, James Thrall Soby (co-director of MoMA), Wright Ludington, Walter P. Chrysler, Jr., and Joseph Pulitzer, Jr., and his gallery became the conduit to an education in European and American avant-garde, helping guide the direction of public opinion.

In the 1930s, German dealers, including Curt Valentin and Karl Nierendorf—two of Berlin's most perspicacious—had also taken on the New York scene and committed to presenting abstract art to the American public. At the same time, as if in a gesture of reciprocity, other spaces, run by Americans—Sidney Janis, Julien Levy, and Sam Kootz—showed European works. Completing the pre-1945 New York City gallery scene was Knoedler & Co., founded in 1846, which first showed the Hudson River School masters, followed by Ashcan School artist George Bellows and then the great expatriate artist

TOP: Curt Valentin, seen here in his gallery, ca. 1952, was, along with Karl Nierendorf, one of the best German art dealers committed to presenting abstract art to the American public as early as the 1930s.

ABOVE: An exhibition at the Nierendorf Gallery. Karl Nierendorf is reading in the background.

ABOVE: Joan Miró exhibition at the Pierre Matisse Gallery, 1963.

OPPOSITE, TOP: Alberto Giacometti exhibition at the Pierre Matisse Gallery, 1958. In the background, left to right: Standing Nude, *1958;* Bust of Yanaihara, *ca. 1957; and* Dark Head (formerly: Yanaihara), *1957: From Yanaihara's Portrait to the Dark Head. In the foreground, two busts of men and nine standing women, 1956–57.*

OPPOSITE, BOTTOM LEFT: Invitation to the Marc Chagall exhibition at the Pierre Matisse Gallery, June 1945.

OPPOSITE, BOTTOM RIGHT: Pierre Matisse posing in his gallery, 1941.

Marc
Chagall

DRAWINGS
WATER COLORS

Pierre Matisse Gallery
41 EAST 57   NEW YORK

JUNE 5 TO 23

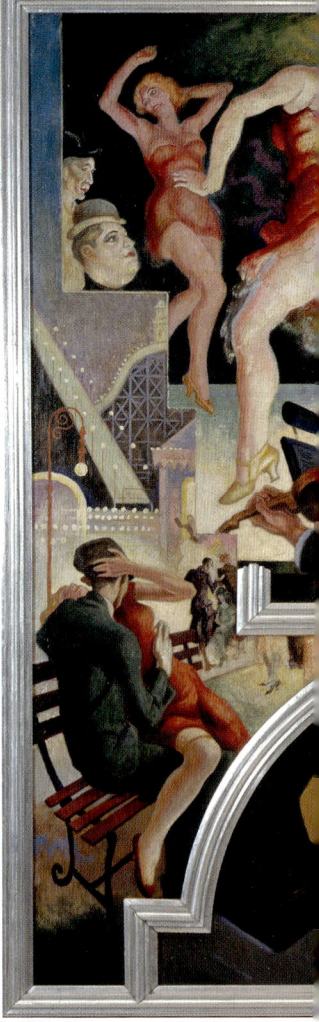

John Singer Sargent, thus building a strong list of conservative private and institutional collectors, including Andrew Mellon, J. P. Morgan, Henry Clay Frick, the Metropolitan Museum of Art, the Louvre, and the Tate. In 1924, Michael Knoedler's son, Roland, moved the gallery to 57th Street and Madison Avenue, where the art dealers were beginning to congregate.[34] That same year, Valentine Dudensing opened his gallery at 45 West 44th Street.[35] He gave Adolph Gottlieb his first solo show in 1930, and devoted subsequent shows to the likes of Henri Matisse, Piet Mondrian, and Milton Avery before the gallery closed its doors in 1948.[36]

In 1945, though, the sorry situation of the Manhattan galleries still worried artists and intellectuals alike. In an assessment of the New York art scene (the most progressive in the country) in *Horizon* magazine, critic Clement Greenberg berated the philistine United States of

his time in more dramatic terms: "Artists are as isolated in the US as if they were living in Paleolithic Europe. The isolation is unconceivable, crushing, unbroken, damning. What can fifty do against a hundred and forty million?"[37] That very question was pressing as early as February 1913, when the Armory Show opened in New York City, bringing European Modernists (such as Marcel Duchamp, Matisse, and Brancusi) to the shores of the New World for the first time. But over the next decade, Modernism, inseparable from the forceful rise of American industry, established itself throughout the country in a variety of disciplines such as design and the applied arts, penetrating American homes on a daily basis. The moment was epitomized by the creation of the Museum of Modern Art in 1929.

In 1933, at the height of the Great Depression, President Roosevelt launched a program of unexpected cultural scope and influence. Over ten years, the federal government spent $9 billion for its "New Deal," employing some eight million Americans in the Works Progress Administration alone. The most popular projects of the WPA were the nearly 1,200 public murals, veritable embodiments of democratic art. Thomas Hart Benton, the realist from Neosho, Missouri, and Jackson Pollock's teacher, became America's favorite muralist. This government intervention made the mysterious and European business of art production seem like an American story of hard times. Roosevelt's program finally stirred huge American popular cultural production and created a positive image for artists, partially erasing the then-prevalent myth of the artist as a European-trained bohemian and replacing it with that of the American workingman. In fact, without the WPA's unbiased program of autonomy, support, and public education, artists like Ad Reinhardt, Jacob Lawrence, Stuart Davis, Jackson Pollock, and Willem de Kooning might never have been encouraged to develop their respective styles. De Kooning's experience working on Fernand Léger's mural under the auspices of the WPA was a defining moment in the development of his practice, shaping the realization that he, a former house painter, was also an artist.

During the 1930s, at the height the Great Depression, President Roosevelt launched the WPA (Works Progress Administration), which employed some eight million Americans, including painter Philip Guston, here at work on his WPA mural Work—The American Way, 1939.

At the start of 1945, the sign of death hung ominously over the New York art world. On February 1, 1944, Dutch painter Piet Mondrian died in New York City, where he had emigrated just four years earlier. Active in the city's community of European artists, the abstract master had been embraced by MoMA, which acquired his vibrant and lively *Broadway Boogie Woogie* (1942–43) for its permanent collection.[38] Mondrian's passing, followed by that of his contemporary, Russian painter and theorist Wassily Kandinsky before the end of the year, signaled the end of an era. And when Arshile Gorky committed suicide in the summer of 1948, it began to seem as if the next generation was being sacrificed. Less than a decade later, Jackson Pollock's dramatic death in a car accident on August 11, 1956, was seen by many as a tragic symptom of that generation's lukewarm reception. In the first decade after World War II, New York–based artists were still fighting for recognition—with very little success. Was this long list of casualties a pure coincidence of individual destinies coming to an end at the same time or was it symptomatic of the continued marginalization of the artist in a society that was becoming richer, more powerful, and more materialistic every day?

A single institution shone as the exception to this depressing state of affairs. The community of European artists who had just emigrated to New York in the late 1930s and early 1940s were

Guston's mural Work — The American Way *graced the entrance of the WPA Community Building at the 1939 New York World's Fair.*

amazed by the Museum of Modern Art's collection and unique architecture. They all went to the museum to discover or rediscover Picasso's *Les Demoiselles d'Avignon*, Meret Oppenheim's *Object* (fur-covered cup, saucer, and spoon), and the drooping clocks in Salvador Dalí's *The Persistence of Memory*. "What was extraordinary was the modern side, the accessible side," recalled the actress Dolores Vanetti, a friend of Marcel Duchamp and André Breton. "There was this museum, this garden in the heart of the city and this modern architecture. It was like no other museum we knew."[39] MoMA also became an outpost for American artists seeking to discover the work of the European moderns, presenting such significant shows as Picasso's *Guernica* (1943), *Piet Mondrian* (1945), *Vincent*

Piet Mondrian. Broadway Boogie Woogie, *1942–43. Oil on canvas, 50 × 50 in. (127 × 127 cm). The Museum of Modern Art, New York. Mondrian's last masterpiece. The Dutch artist, who had recently emigrated from Paris to New York, evolved in a dynamic way under the influence of New York City life. His 1945 solo show at MoMA presented him as one of the key Modernist masters.*

van Gogh (1945), *Marc Chagall* (1946), *Bonnard—Picasso* (1948), *Georges Braque* (1949), *Oskar Kokoshcka* (1949), and *Paul Klee* (1950).

After the war, a number of Europeans—notably André Breton and the Surrealists, who had so profoundly influenced American artists—went home. "The refugees were around during the war," recalled sculptor Philip Pavia. "They were 'the artists'; we all looked up to them . . . with that started the nucleus. Then the refugees slowly disappeared. They went back to Europe. Then we were on our own."[40] Would the opening in 1945 of both Sam Kootz's and Charles Egan's galleries, as well as Betty Parsons's a year later, fill the void left by the Europeans' departure and radically change European visitors' gloomy perception of New York's commercial exhibition spaces? It certainly appeared not to be the case when in 1946, an observer heard that Fernand Léger was leaving for Europe, or a year later, that Matta, a major influence on Jackson Pollock, was returning to the Old World, or finally, in 1947, that Peggy Guggenheim was closing her Manhattan gallery

Contract between Betty Parsons and Peggy Guggenheim •
Betty Parsons agrees to take over Jackson Pollock's works and
interests and to sell and exhibit wherever she deems fit.She will
give him a one man show next winter.She will sell his works at
the prices set by Peggy Guggenheim and retain one third commissi
The paintings still that belong to Pollock will be paid direct
to him if sold and the ones belonging to Peggy Guggenheim will b
paid to her account when sold.ART OF THIS CENTURY,GUARANTY TRUST
CO. MADISON AVE. & 60 ST N.Y.C. From this date forward any pain
ings brought in by Pollock will be the property of Peggy Guggenh
Peggy Guggenheim will send Pollock a monthly allowance until Feb
Il next and on March I0 her contract with Pollock will expire an
Betty Parsons will hold all the paintings belonging to Peggy Gu
Guggenheim and continue to sell them irrespective of any arrange
ment Betty Parsons may make with Pollock from then on. James
Johnson Sweeney will represent Peggy Guggenheim's interets in th
matter and will come regularly to the gallery to check sales wit
Bett Parsons and to judge whether or not Pollock is living up to
his contract with P eggy Guggenheim.Herewith attached a list of
the paintings belonging to Peggy Guggenheim and a list of ,those
belonging to Pollock.

Peggy Guggenheim
May 12 1947

CI 6-0037 N Y 19
Pollock is entitled to one picture a year

ABOVE LEFT: Contract between Peggy Guggenheim and Betty Parsons regarding the transfer of Jackson Pollock's representation from Guggenheim to Parsons, May 12, 1947. At the time, Guggenheim was closing her Manhattan gallery and moving her collection to her new palace on the Grand Canal in Venice.

ABOVE RIGHT: Betty Parsons, 1960, contributed substantially to the promotion of Abstract Exressionism. Bewitched by modern art from the moment she saw the Armory show in 1913, she became a collector and an art dealer, as well as a painter.

and moving her collection to her new palace on the Grand Canal in Venice.

But on June 22, 1944, President Franklin D. Roosevelt signed the Servicemen's Readjustment Act, commonly known as the G.I. Bill, which gave unprecedented support to war veterans, opening the option to pursue higher education. Beneficiaries of this sweeping move included such New York–based artists as Jack Tworkov and Ellsworth Kelly, who took advantage of the financial support to study in Paris. Meanwhile, in New York a new group of personalities, both American and European, were reconfiguring the local map of the visual arts. Alfred H. Barr Jr., who had been chosen as the first director of MoMA in 1929, concentrated on European art, to the great distress of contemporary critics such as Clement Greenberg and Harold Rosenberg—thus the lines of a dynamic polarity were drawn. MoMA was taking only very small steps toward locally produced work until Dorothy Miller, a young, beautiful, and exceptional curator beloved by artists, initiated what became a major series of brilliant American shows. She shifted her focus not only away from European trends toward local movements, but also from the massive group shows that often represented artists with a single work each toward shows with tightly edited selections of artists, allowing each to display a greater breadth of production. One of these important exhibitions was *Fourteen Americans* (1946), which featured the work of Abstract Expressionists Arshile Gorky, Robert Motherwell, and Mark Tobey.

OPPOSITE, BOTTOM: *René d'Harnoncourt, born in Vienna, developed an early interest in art. First a collector and an antiques dealer, he became director of the Museum of Modern Art in 1949, a position he held until 1967.*

ABOVE: *Arnold Newman's 1950 photograph of Alfred Barr, surrounded by paintings, sculptures, and design objects he collected for the Museum of Modern Art, is titled* Alfred Barr and a Life's Work. *This pioneering art historian had been chosen as the first director of MoMA in 1929.*

THE SWING
1947—1949

"For some reason, '47–'48, there was a swing."[41]
—CLEMENT GREENBERG

Clement Greenberg sensed a profound shift in 1947 and 1948, particularly in the work of Mark Rothko. "He [Rothko] came under the influence of Clyff Still, I think in '47 when Still had his first one-man show at Peggy Guggenheim's gallery. . . . At that point, Rothko became more decisively abstract."[42] A certain darkness pervaded Mark Rothko's work. Influenced by the newly emigrated Surrealist painters from Europe and stimulated by his avid reading (James

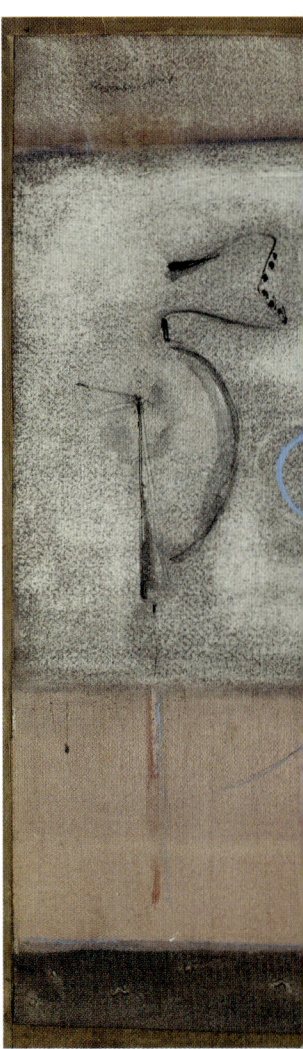

Joyce, T. S. Eliot, Sigmund Freud), he moved away from his figurative paintings of the 1930s, such as *Untitled (three nudes)* (1933–34), a weighty composition in earthy tones of brown and orange that channels equal parts Matisse and Soutine, and began exploring biomorphic forms and abstraction in the early 1940s. But the encounter with Clyfford Still was what prompted him to find his definitive abstract style and helped him to land a prestigious exhibition in 1945 at Peggy Guggenheim's Art of This Century. The mysterious dreamscapes of *Geologic Reverie* (1946) and *Vessels of Magic* (1947) soon gave way to more open expanses of color and melting forms. The artist's rich tapestries of loosely applied pigment, *Number 26* (1947) and *Number 18* (1949), for example, led directly to his Color Field works of 1950 on. The titles of Rothko's works also clearly describe his shift from representational and narrative work to canvases built around pure exploration

OPPOSITE: Mark Rothko in his studio on West 53rd Street, 1952. Born in Dvinsk (now Daugavpils, Latvia), Rothko arrived in the United States in 1913, at age ten, and became one of the leading artists of his adoptive country.

BELOW: Mark Rothko. Geologic Reverie, 1946. Watercolor and gouache on paper, 21¾ × 29¾ in. (55.3 × 75.6 cm). Gift of Mrs. Marion Pike. M.53.5. Los Angeles County Museum of Art, Los Angeles. Rothko created this work in the middle of the decade, when his aesthetics were evolving from figurative to mythological to multiform to abstract.

of color and contrast, and the boldly straightforward *Four Darks in Red* (1958) stands out as one of the strongest examples of his mature style. By 1958, the recognition of Rothko's intense, color-saturated canvases had grown immensely, and he represented the United States in the Venice Biennale. Just a few years later he was given a solo show at MoMA. But he was soon overwhelmed by personal tragedy—the separation from his wife and a serious illness—and committed suicide in 1970.

For other artists as well, the late 1940s was a rich period of transition. As Philip Pavia said, "No other moment contained so many surprises and changes, and so much shifting. The war had ended and left those of us on the Atlantic shores rich and wise." He considered

OPPOSITE: Mark Rothko. No. 6 (Yellow, White, Blue over Yellow on Gray), *1954. Oil on canvas, 94 × 60 in. (238.8. × 152.4). Private collection. The year this work was painted was one of the greatest in Rothko's career, culminating in his magnificent solo show at the Art Institute of Chicago.*

ABOVE: Mark Rothko. Untitled, *1956. Oil on canvas, 81⅞ × 69½ in. (208 × 176.5 cm). Private collection. Rothko's abstract rhetoric continued to evolve. Here colored rectangles float one on top of another.*

Sculptor Philip Pavia, a founding member and chronicler of the Club, was part of a growing avant-garde community that moved away from Surrealism toward Abstract Expressionism.

1948 a key year, "a year full of disagreements at the Waldorf Cafeteria on Eighth Street, in our Tenth Street enclave, where we had studios, and at the new Club." And he recalled, "Gorky's suicide came as a blow to the Eighth Street gang."[43] Nevertheless, some of the first positive signs came with the breakthrough exhibitions of Jackson Pollock and Willem de Kooning. Pollock's show, which opened at the Betty Parsons Gallery on January 2, 1948, was the first since Peggy Guggenheim left for Europe. It featured the earlier Jungian paintings on one side of the gallery and the new paintings of pure abstraction on the other, allowing Pollock's evolving practice to unfold before the viewer's eyes.

As Philip Pavia wrote in his journals, the forum for all the contemporary artists was on Manhattan's 8th Street. They found their studios on 10th Street, which at that time was quite an obscure neighborhood. Pavia rented a place at 90 East 10th Street between 3rd and 4th Avenues. Willem de Kooning leased a studio next door and the two shared a fire escape.[44] Pavia could hear Elaine de Kooning typing through the thin walls. Their avant-garde community, moving away from Surrealism toward Abstract Expressionism, quickly grew. The artists jokingly referred to the "Tenth Street colony" as "our club." They even had their own set of galleries—seven or eight co-op spaces—to show their work. But no one was selling much. At the time, de Kooning was "absolutely flat broke," and Milton Resnick and Franz Kline were penniless too.[45] Pavia lent them money, five or ten dollars at a time. He remembered getting a call every time they needed to pay the rent. Then he would go out and help collect funds from wealthier supporters such as critic Tom Hess.

Identifying pivotal developments in the work of the New York School, Clement Greenberg was also establishing himself as an essential voice of his generation. In his many essays during those years, he foresaw the light at the end of the tunnel: Jackson Pollock, as a "morbid and extreme disciple of Picasso's cubism and Miró's post cubism," or the constructivist sculptor David Smith as "capable of withstanding the test of international scrutiny which . . . might justify the term major."[46] He recognized that "the main premises of Western art had at last migrated to the United States, along with the center of gravity of industrial production and political power."[47] But it was on the occasion of Willem de Kooning's first solo show ever at the Charles Egan Gallery, April 12, 1948 (exhibiting black-and-white abstractions that foregrounded brushstroke, texture, and touch), that Greenberg realized that a promising phase had begun for the New York artists. In these works he saw an unprecedented encounter between abstraction and expressionism. He also noticed that a collision had taken place between the

Members of the 10th Street artists group, a
loose confederation of Abstract Expressionists,
displaying some of their works on the street
outside Milton Resnick's studio and the Tanager
Gallery, ca. 1956.

vertical and the horizontal, giving the paintings a weighty feel. "Decidedly, the past year has been a remarkably good one for American art," he stated. "Now, as if suddenly, we are introduced by Willem de Kooning's magnificent first show to one of the four or five most important painters in the country."[48] On opening night, de Kooning's show was celebrated at the Waldorf Cafeteria on 8th Street by his fellow artists, who recalled feeling a profound "sense of relief." With a show that remained "stunningly new," de Kooning had deepened the sense of the visual experience, as if he had "discovered a secret." From that day on, his position as a leader of the Abstract Expressionists became undeniable. As Philip Pavia expressed it, "Others had the look, but not as heightened as in a de Kooning painting."[49]

The ten black-and-white paintings (including *Light in August*, *Orestes*, and *Black Friday*) that de Kooning presented in his show at the Egan Gallery had all been produced in the previous year and brilliantly managed to capture a formal struggle between light and dark, as well as deeper psychological tension. The artist had built this series of tightly composed abstract black forms, bound in white, through a unique method of tracing parts of figurative drawings onto his canvases, preserving evocative shapes and turns of line that he would then work and rework with confident brushstrokes until he was satisfied. He savored the medium of painting, allowing the pigment to drip, run, or smear across the surface. In fact, one might say that a whole spectrum of painterly "color" was evident in these black-and-white works—a whirlwind of varying intensities, depths, and speeds that would continue to define his strongest works in the years to come. De Kooning, who had arrived in the United States from the Netherlands in 1926 and worked for a time designing department-store displays, became a leading Abstract Expressionist through rigorous dedication to his practice. He was finally attaining recognition and acclaim, but not without years of frustration and a fierce rivalry with Pollock, whose star had risen very rapidly. De Kooning's committed way of working, and his unapologetic personal style, which had made him a hero of his

Willem de Kooning. Black Friday, *1948. Oil and enamel on pressed wood panel, 49³⁄₁₆ × 39 in. (125 × 99 cm). Gift of H. Gates Lloyd, Class of 1923, and Mrs. Lloyd in honor of the Class of 1923. Y1976-44. Princeton University Art Museum, Princeton, New Jersey. With this and the other powerful black-and-white works in his first solo show at the Charles Egan Gallery in 1948, de Kooning asserted himself as one of the key Abstract Expressionists.*

community, turned him now into a symbol of his generation, all the more so because Pollock, involved in his struggle with alcoholism, was a difficult model to follow.

When Franz Kline, a native of industrial Pennsylvania, made his way to New York City in about 1939, he met de Kooning, Pollock, and other key figures of the nascent Abstract Expressionist movement, and his early figurative work—often incorporating urban or industrial architecture—soon gave way to abstraction. Strong compositional elements continued to define his canvases, which, starting in the late 1940s, were realized solely in black and white. Kline's *Chief* (1950), a fierce tangle of broad black strokes on a white background, demonstrates the intensity of the artist's line and his strongly decisive compositions. Color and gray tones reemerged in some of his

TOP: Franz Kline in his studio, ca. 1960.

ABOVE: Franz Kline. Cross Section, 1956. Oil on canvas, 53½ × 63 in. (135.9 × 160 cm). Promised gift of the Virginia and Bagley Wright Collection, in honor of the 75th Anniversary of the Seattle Art Museum. This work epitomizes Kline's black-and-white paintings of the period.

Franz Kline. Harley Red, 1959–60.
Oil on canvas, 82 × 67 in. (208.2 × 170.2 cm).
Private collection. This strong composition is marked
by a powerful contrast of colors.

paintings by the late 1950s, though much of his work continued to be dominated by dramatic contrasts of black and white.

Another core member of the Abstract Expressionists was New York native Adolph Gottlieb. In the 1940s Gottlieb, previously stationed in Arizona for his work on the WPA's Federal Art Project, devoted much of his painting to pictographs. A collection of invented symbols within a loose grid, Gottlieb's pictographs channeled primitive iconography as well as a range of tones associated with ancient cave paintings—ochre, olive, and beige. Works such as *The Seer* (1950), for example, even incorporated sand into the pigment, imparting an earthy texture. Gottlieb eventually expanded the scale of his canvases and his production gave way to more abstract, gestural compositions, rich in saturated pools of color.

Robert Motherwell also realized a large number of canvases in broad strokes of black and white, including his most important series, *Elegy to the Spanish Republic*, which he began in 1949; it eventually grew to more than 150 large-scale canvases. Simultaneously

ABOVE: Adolph Gottlieb, another core member of the Abstract Expressionists, in his studio, 1965.

OPPOSITE, BOTTOM: Adolph Gottlieb. The Seer, 1950. Oil on canvas, 59¾ × 71⅜ in. (151.7 × 181.9 cm). The Phillips Collection, Washington, D.C. The primitive iconography in this work is typical of Gottlieb's pictographs, but it differs in its incorporation of sand into the pigment, which imparts a more earthy texture.

ABOVE: Adolph Gottlieb. Crimson Spinning No. II, 1959. Oil on canvas, 90 × 72 in. (228.6 × 182.9 cm). Seattle Art Museum, The Jane Lang Davis Collection. When Gottlieb — a close friend of Barnett Newman and Mark Rothko — painted this series, he expanded the scale of his canvases and produced more abstract, gestural compositions, rich in saturated pools of colors.

Robert Motherwell. Elegy to the Spanish Republic #122, *1972. Oil, charcoal, and graphite on canvas, 55¾ × 76 in. (141.6 × 193 cm). Gerald Schwartz and Heather Reisman, Toronto. One of the more than 150 canvases Motherwell devoted to the horrors of the Spanish Civil War, the remarkable and moving series he began in 1949.*

monumental and poetic, these works reference the horrors of the Spanish Civil War, although more than ten years after the fact. The nostalgia of these works, expressed through looming, frieze-like patterns of black columns alternating with bulbous shapes laid heavily across a white background, seems to be for both a moment of youthful activism and peace on the Iberian peninsula. Motherwell's Columbia University professor Meyer Schapiro had encouraged him to pursue painting rather than an academic career, yet his advanced studies positioned him to become an essential spokesman for his generation.

Clyfford Still, though associated with the Abstract Expressionists, preferred to view his work as unique, particularly with respect to the European tradition. Instead, he was seeking an American sublime, delivering wide expanses of color and nuanced encounters of tone and turns of line. He famously refused to participate in group shows; his inclusion in Dorothy Miller's *15 Americans* exhibition in 1952, for instance, was conditioned on his being given his own room to display his works. His mature style, already demonstrated in *No. 2* (1949), *Untitled 1951-T,* and later *1960-R* (1960), reveals broad expanses of rich color, dramatically juxtaposed to ragged patches of contrasting pigment—clear anticipations of the Color Field movement.

Barnett Newman, who had studied together with Gottlieb at the Art Students League in the 1920s, destroyed nearly all of his early figurative paintings, deliberately developing a purely abstract practice in the 1940s. His "breakthrough" work, *Onement I* (1948), depicts a light cadmium-red vertical line bisecting a rich Indian-red background. This piece, like the rest of Newman's oeuvre, diverges from the largely gestural tendencies of Abstract Expressionism in its compositional control and precision of line—a careful sense of space that he also carried into his work as a sculptor. His *Broken Obelisk* (1963–2003), a raggedly truncated steel pillar atop a pyramidal base, has become an icon both of the artist's distinctive practice and of the American civil rights movement; an early edition of the work installed at the Menil Collection in Houston was dedicated to Martin Luther King.[50]

The opening of Sidney Janis's gallery at 15 East 57th Street—Sam Kootz's former space—in June 1948 represented another good omen

Robert Motherwell in his studio, 1962.

as the 1940s came to an end. A businessman, an avid collector, and a scholar, Janis had long been familiar with the New York scene, as well as its European precedents (a Mondrian he bought directly from the artist was only the second to be brought to the United States) and the influential émigrés active in the city during World War II. He launched his gallery with a show of work by Léger, an artist whom Janis had seen revivified by life in New York City. The first few years were challenging for the gallery; shows of work by Kandinsky, Schwitters, and Albers did not find buyers. But Janis persisted, continuing to mount exhibitions by modern and contemporary European artists: *Mondrian* (1949 and 1951), *Brancusi to Duchamp* (1951), *Early Léger* (1951), *Henri Rousseau* (1951), and *International Dada* (1953). It wasn't long before Solomon Guggenheim and Baroness Rebay discovered the gallery, acquiring three Mondrians and one Léger. In the early 1950s Janis began to mount solo exhibitions of American painters as well, including Pollock, de Kooning, Kline, Gorky, Rothko, Motherwell, and later, Philip Guston.

ABOVE: Left to right: Barnett Newman, Jackson Pollock, and sculptor Tony Smith at the Betty Parsons Gallery, 1951.

OPPOSITE: Barnett Newman. The Word II, *1954. Oil on canvas, 90½ × 70½ in. (229.9 × 179.1 cm) Private collection. Diverging from the gestural tendency of his fellow artists, Newman displays a careful sense of space that carried into his work as a sculptor as well.*

Disappointed by weak sales at the Betty Parsons Gallery, Pollock moved to Sidney Janis in 1952, opening his first solo show with his new dealer in November of that year; a second solo show followed in 1954. The drip paintings, his gesture-driven, all-over compositions, were highly visible and celebrated by the critics. On December 19, 1956, MoMA opened what had been intended to be a mid-career retrospective for the artist, who had tragically died just a few months before.

De Kooning's first solo show at the Sidney Janis Gallery in 1953 featured his fierce *Woman* series; successful solo shows in 1956 and 1959 followed. The American artists seemed to hold their own in Janis's international program. In 1961, Janis mounted *The New Realists*, his first Pop Art exhibition, after which many of this new generation of artists joined his gallery, among them Jim Dine, Claes Oldenburg, George Segal, and Tom Wesselmann. In protest, the old guard—Guston, Motherwell, Gottlieb, and Rothko—withdrew from the gallery en masse (de Kooning stayed faithful). Janis was disappointed by their departure but recognized that progress must be made, that one's eyes must always stay open. Sidney Janis continued to grace the city with his brilliant personality for the next several decades, until the memorable donation of his collection to MoMA.

Despite Pollock's and de Kooning's growing recognition, in March 1949, when Robert Goldwater, newly named editor of the *Magazine of Art*, organized a symposium entitled "The State of American Art," all participants except Greenberg still insisted that the best art originated in Paris. "There is, in my opinion," Greenberg counterattacked, "a definitely American trend in contemporary art, one that promises to become an original contribution to the mainstream and not merely a local inflection of something developing abroad. . . . I would even hazard the opinion that three or four of these artists are not only on par with, but actually ahead of the French artists who are their contemporary in age."[51] Greenberg's judgment echoed a statement Joan Miró had made in 1947 to an interviewer in Cincinnati, where he was painting a mural: "I admire much the energy and vitality of American painters. . . . They would do well to free themselves from Europe's influence."[52] This was an abnegation of Alfred Barr's credo, and the museum director was furious. A battle of ideals had begun, and Greenberg quickly challenged gallerists and most importantly, for the wider reception of American artists, journalists and the media. "It is possible that national pride will overcome ingrained philistinism and induce our journalists to boast of what they neither understand nor enjoy."[53] As if on cue, the August, 8, 1949, issue of *Life* magazine ran a profile of Jackson Pollock, provocatively entitled "Is he the greatest living painter in the United States?"

Philip Guston. Beggar's Joys,
1954–55. Oil on canvas, 72 × 68 in.
(182.9 × 172.7 cm). Private collection.
With its off-center explosion of red, orange,
pink, and blue against a field of pinkish gray,
this work is representative of Guston's foray
into pure abstraction in the mid-1950s.

Meanwhile, the artists themselves were banding closer together and in the fall of 1949 created an institution of a brand-new kind in the U.S., the Club. Its charter members paid out of pocket (five hundred dollars in "key money") to rent a loft at 39 East 8th Street. Among the original members were Ad Reinhardt, Robert Motherwell, Giorgio Cavallon, Ibram Lassaw, Landes Lewitin, Philip Pavia, Conrad Marca-Relli, and Milton Resnick.

By the late 1940s, Ad Reinhardt had moved from geometric abstraction to a more gestural form of Abstract Expressionism. He was also working as a professor at Brooklyn College, where he taught art history, specializing in Orientalism (he would later teach at Yale alongside Joseph Albers). In the 1950s, Reinhardt's work moved closer to his idea of "pure aesthetics," which included a rejection of the individualism of Abstract Expressionism and a narrowing of his palette. He began realizing his canvases in different shades of a single color: red (as in *Abstract Painting, Red*, 1952), blue (such as *Abstract Painting*, 1960–61), and ultimately black (*Abstract Painting*, 1963).

After serving in the military during World War II and then studying in Paris, Milton Resnick returned to New York in 1948, enrolling in the Hans Hofmann School of Fine Arts. In the late 1950s Resnick abandoned "impressionistic" brushwork in favor of a weightier application of pigment and flattened compositional space. His work was primarily abstract, at times almost monochrome, but

OPPOSITE: George Segal. Portrait of Sidney Janis with Mondrian Painting, *1967. Plaster figure with Mondrian's* Composition, 1933, *on an easel, 69⅞ × 56¼ × 27¼ in. (177.3 × 142.8 × 69.1 cm). The Sidney and Harriet Janis Collection, The Museum of Modern Art, New York. In this affectionate gesture, Segal celebrates the genius of gallerist Sidney Janis.*

ABOVE: George Segal poses with one of his sculptures in the Sidney Janis Gallery, 1966.

the human figure often haunted his works. In $Y + R$ (1958), for example, a wide figure in silhouette and a cluster of more agitated personages seem to emerge from the lower section of the composition, richly painted in densely applied gestural strokes of gold, green, and red.

Conrad Marca-Relli took his first art lessons as a child in Italy, where his father was assigned as a journalist. Back in the U.S. by the 1930s, Marca-Relli participated in the Federal Art Project of the WPA, where he met Willem de Kooning, Franz Kline, and John Graham. For his first solo show in New York in 1947 at the Niveau Gallery on the Upper East Side, he presented Surrealist landscapes (strongly influenced by de Chirico). He soon fell under

Willem de Kooning poses with some of his canvases during an installation at the Sidney Janis gallery, 1959, as the gallerist, in his signature bowtie, looks on.

ABOVE: *Willem de Kooning.* Two Women, *1949. Oil and charcoal on paper, 17½ × 22¾ in. (44.5 × 57.8 cm). Private collection.*

LEFT: *Willem de Kooning, right, stands with fellow artists, including Franz Kline, second from right, outside the Sidney Janis Gallery on the opening day of his exhibition, March 4, 1959.*

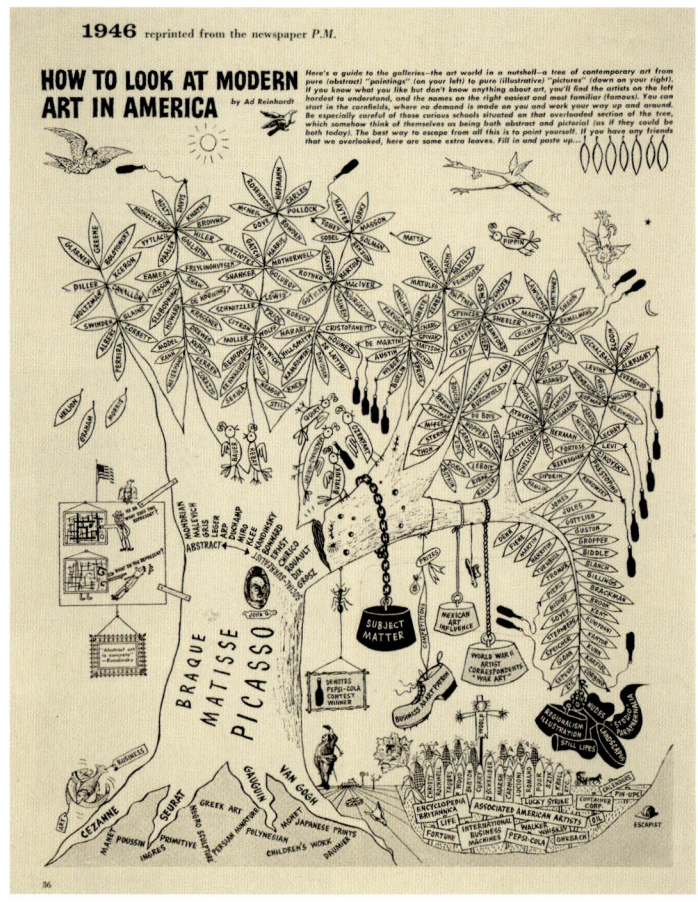

the influence of Gorky and later turned to collage. As the story goes, in the summer of 1953, while living in Mexico, Marca-Relli ran out of paint, so he started making collages. The technique can also be seen as a technical solution to problems of representing the human figure, especially in the wake of de Kooning's *Woman* paintings. In the early 1950s Marca-Relli bought a house near Pollock's in Springs, and the two became close friends. It was Marca-Relli, in fact, who identified Pollock's body after his fatal accident—a moment that inspired his large-scale collage *The Death of Jackson Pollock* (1956), a horizontal landscape of ragged pieces of flesh-colored canvas.

The Club organized three to four evening events a week (some for members only, others open to guests and outside speakers) for six years running. "Artists really felt isolated, they had no audience, nothing. It was hard for them to survive," Ileana Castelli Sonnabend reported.[54] At endless conferences, round-table discussions, readings, and parties they attempted, with others (critics, gallerists, museum curators, and collectors, as well as musicians, writers, and

RIGHT: Ad Reinhardt in his studio, 1955.

BELOW: Ad Reinhardt. Red Painting, *1953. Oil on canvas, 40 × 40 in. (101.6 × 101.6 cm). Collection of Kathy and Keith Sachs.*

OPPOSITE, TOP: Milton Resnick, seated in front of Swan, *1961.*

OPPOSITE, BOTTOM: Milton Resnick. Y + R, *1958. Oil on canvas, 67 × 68 in. (170.2 × 172.7). Private collection.*

philosophers), to define themselves. All those meetings took place in a very specific geographical context: the square block bounded by 8th Street to the south and 9th Street to the north, Broadway to the east and University Place to the west, in what was still a rather gloomy part of the East Village in the early fifties. In the company of such personalities as political theorist Hannah Arendt, composers John Cage and Morton Feldman, and playwright and critic Lionel Abel, and in the time-honored European tradition, but for the first time in the United States, artists forged a bond, a community, and, through innumerable alcohol-fueled gatherings, a sense of identity that over the years challenged the ingrained philistinism of the city of New York.

PARIS OR NEW YORK?

1950–1952

*"I wanted to see somebody come along who could match the French
so that we could stop being minor painters over there."*[55]
—CLEMENT GREENBERG

*"New York is sharp metal . . .
Everything in this city is open, accessible, approachable . . .
The various artistic groups are not at each others' throats, as they are in Paris."*[56]
—MICHEL SEUPHOR

Staging a face-off between American artists and their Parisian counterparts, in 1951 Leo Castelli curated the *Young U.S. and French Painters* show at the Sidney Janis Gallery. Many observed that the French suffered in the comparison, and "the New York painters saw themselves surpassing Paris."[57] Later that year, Alfred Barr revealed that he was becoming a convert, inviting Pollock, de Kooning, and Gorky to represent the United States at the Venice Biennale. This was also the year that de Kooning's rhythmic canvas *Excavation* won a prize in Chicago. Many saw the painting—a juxtaposition of wild organic forms and a firmly geometric compositional structure—as an echo of the hectic urban life of New York City.

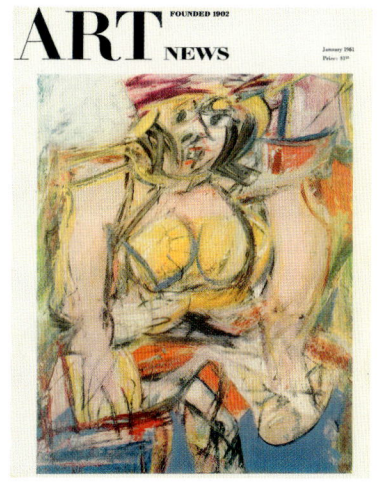

The cover of the January 1961 issue of ARTnews *featured Willem de Kooning's* Woman IV, *1952–53.*

The Club continued to grow, and soon launched the project of a group show. "We were supporting each other," recalled Conrad Marca-Relli. "There were the older artists, some of them such as Pollock who had already succeeded and others such as de Kooning who were about to succeed and who exhibited in the uptown galleries, and there were the younger ones who had never showed anything."[58] The tension between Pollock and de Kooning emerged all the more clearly, as each artist had his own critic-champion—Clement Greenberg for Pollock and Harold Rosenberg for de Kooning. Pollock lived in East Hampton and shuttled between Long Island and New York City. Some of his partisans started to consider the Club as de Kooning's camp, and Thomas B. Hess, the new editor of *ARTnews*, was sometimes blamed for "playing a power game," Marca-Relli recalled, "pushing de Kooning and trying to get rid of Jack in the number one spot."[59]

The New York artists were gaining traction but were still being ignored by many, including major institutions such as the Metropolitan Museum of Art. In response to the Met's competitive exhibition *American Painting Today, 1950,* a group of downtown artists, led by Barnett Newman, Ad Reinhardt, and Adolph Gottlieb, addressed the president of the Fifth Avenue institution in a brash open letter, published in the *New York Times* on May 22, 1950, denouncing the institution's planned show, attacking the curator's "hostility to advanced art," accusing the director of declaring "his contempt for modern painting," and regretting that "a just proportion of advanced art" would not be included in the show.[60] "We draw to the attention of those gentlemen the historical fact that, for roughly 100 years, only advanced art has made any consequential contribution to civilization."[61]

Later that year, in a small artist's studio on West 44th Street, the photographer Nina Leen struggled to assemble a group of fifteen "angry" painters for a photo shoot. On January 15, 1951, almost two months after the shoot, Leen's picture appeared in *Life* magazine with a caption that read, "Irascible group of advanced artists led fight against show."[62] Since that day, the fifteen artists who appeared in the photograph have been called "The Irascibles," one of the first groups to rebel against the establishment in the United States, a

Nina Leen's photograph of "The Irascibles" for Life *magazine, November 24, 1950. Back row, left to right: Willem de Kooning, Adolph Gottlieb, Ad Reinhardt, Hedda Sterne; center row: Richard Pousette-Dart, William Baziotes, Jackson Pollock, Clyfford Still, Robert Motherwell, Bradley Walker Tomlin; front row: Theodoros Stamos, Jimmy Ernst, Barnett Newman, James Brooks, and Mark Rothko. Missing from photo: Weldon Kees, Fritz Bultman, and Hans Hofmann.*

country in which the artist had long been regarded as a second-class citizen. In so doing, they linked their attitude to that of numerous European movements such as the Salon des Refusés in Paris, the Secession in Vienna, and the Blaue Reiter in Zurich. Smiling was the norm for celebrities in America, but the *Life* magazine photo presents a body of artists dressed in suits and ties, with exceptionally stern expressions on their faces, and exuding an attitude of refusal and contempt. In this way the group revealed their ties to the European tradition of artistic rebellion. Indeed, the photo echoes Fantin-Latour's group portrait of the avant-garde artists and writers of his time, including Whistler, Baudelaire, Manet, and himself, surrounding the portrait of their mentor in his *Hommage à Delacroix*.

ABOVE: View of the Ninth Street Show, the landmark group exhibition organized by Leo Castelli in Greenwich Village, May–June 1951.

BELOW: Poster for the Ninth Street Show.

The long march of the New York artists for recognition thus continued on its inevitable path. In May 1951 they asked Leo Castelli, a fellow member of the Club and at the time a collector and freelance curator living uptown, to hang their works in a nearby vacant space that used to be an antiques store. Organized in the most chaotic, ebullient way (there was so little space that a panoramic Pollock painting was hung vertically), this casual event will forever be remembered as the "Ninth Street Show."[63] It presented the work of seventy local artists and attracted not only the downtown crowd but also—and for the first time—the uptown crowd. Many observers reacted to its "lively manifestation of energy and accomplishment."[64] The critic Tom Hess simply stated that "a line had been crossed," signaling a "step into the larger art world whose future is bright with possibility," describing "a sudden awareness that artistic activity had achieved a critical mass and looked remarkably coherent."[65]

In 1951, French critic Michel Seuphor, who traveled to New York to visit galleries and understand the coming of age in the New World, found the most appropriate words to describe the developing situation, "New York, at its best, is a diamond giving off a thousand reflections. There are no airtight boundaries: all the artists know and frequent each other. This doesn't mean there isn't competition, only that it's not vicious. Take your place: there's room for everyone on this round world and we are all on top."[66] Sure enough, at that very moment, Dorothy Miller was preparing her *15 Americans* show at MoMA, which would be on view from April 9 to July 27, 1952.

DOWNTOWN OR UPTOWN?

1953–1955

ABOVE: Helen Frankenthaler in her New York studio, 1961.

RIGHT: Helen Frankenthaler and Robert Motherwell, 1963.

OPPOSITE: A crew installing Helen Frankenthaler's enormous Guiding Red, *1977, attesting to the increasing size of the paintings and sculptures being produced in the U.S. at that time.*

Soon the polarity between the downtown artists and the uptown gallerists was complicated by the opening of a number of new galleries in the East Village, including the Tanager Gallery at 90 East 10th, and the gradual welcoming of downtown artists into established uptown spaces, such as the Stable Gallery, which presented a thorough cross section of the New York vanguard in the Stable Annual—an overt homage to the Ninth Street Show. Clement Greenberg was doing his best to keep up with the emerging generation of Color Field, or what he later called "post-painterly abstraction," painters. Largely influenced by Ad Reinhardt, they included Sam Francis, Helen Frankenthaler, Kenneth Noland, Clyfford Still, Robert Motherwell, and Morris Louis. Gallerist André Emmerich, a European émigré like Leo Castelli, opened a new space at 18 East 77th Street in 1953, and for the next five decades he would brilliantly support all Color Field painters. A term coined by Irving Sandler in his book *The Triumph of American Painting: A History of Abstract Expressionism* (1970), Color Field painting described the

ABOVE: *Helen Frankenthaler.* Sun, Sand and Sea, *1962. Oil on canvas, 62 × 52 in. (157.5 × 132.1 cm). Private collection. Emphasizing surface over depth, the pigment rests across the picture plane like a veil, an aesthetic that had a great influence on both Morris Louis and Kenneth Noland.*

OPPOSITE, LEFT: *Morris Louis standing in front of* Untitled, *ca. 1956.*

OPPOSITE, RIGHT: *Morris Louis.* Gemini, *1962. Acrylic on canvas, 81⅞ × 27³⁄₁₆ in. (208 × 69.1 cm). Los Angeles County Museum of Art, Los Angeles.*

movement that developed out of the Surrealist-influenced gestural work of the 1940s and 1950s and moved toward quieter compositions, looser forms, and pools of color. The monochromes of Ad Reinhardt are often cited as the touchstone for this movement, which is fully articulated in the lyrical color play of Morris Louis's works such as *Alpha Mu* (1961). Helen Frankenthaler's landscape-inspired compositions and poetic use of pigment, as seen in *Seascape with Dunes* (1962), and Kenneth Noland's bold canvases such as *Turnsole* (1961).

Helen Frankenthaler, at the time married to Abstract Expressionist Robert Motherwell, realized her lyrically abstract canvases of translucent washes of color by pouring turpentine-thinned pigment directly onto a raw canvas laid across the floor. She first used the technique in her painting *Mountains and Sea* (1952), a loose, organic composition in which pools of red, green, and blue bleed into and across a warm, untreated expanse of canvas. Emphasizing surface over depth, the pigment rested like a veil across the picture plane—an aesthetic that would be highly influential on both Morris Louis and Kenneth Noland.

But Noland, a student of Josef Albers at Black Mountain College in Asheville, North Carolina, was also influenced by Ilya Bolotowsky, Paul Klee, and Matisse. Unlike Frankenthaler, he was not only committed to pure color but also pursued pure, often geometric forms. He worked in series, making subtle changes to solid abstract shapes, first the circle and later more hard-edged structures like chevrons and horizontal stripes. In 1956, Dorothy Miller selected his painting *In a Mist* (1955) for the Museum of Modern Art traveling exhibition *Young American Painters*, a canvas that reveals Noland's technique of staining as a means of realizing bold fields of color.

By gathering artists and intellectuals together and encouraging regular debates and discussions, the Club had allowed critics to join in the art world at last and enhanced their considerable influence on the art itself. Clement Greenberg, Harold Rosenberg, Thomas B. Hess, Leo Steinberg, Meyer Schapiro, Robert Rosenblum, Phillip Leider, and Max Kozloff began to play a more and more important part in the art circles. Downtown, the artists appreciated Tom Hess's clear insights and Harold Rosenberg's great writing in *ART-news*, but the "king critic of art" was Clement Greenberg, who got his start as an editor for *Partisan Review* in the forties, after the publication in that journal of his eminent essay "Avant-Garde and Kitsch." It did not take long before he became a controversial figure, however. As Philip Pavia, one of the Club's founding artists, put it, "His beliefs were remarkable, but not his choices."

Kenneth Noland in his studio at the Chelsea Hotel, 1963. A student of Joseph Albers at Black Mountain College, he remained committed to pure colors in geometric forms.

Obsessed by art, "Clem" was always searching for new talent, visiting artists' studios and developing dialogues with some of them. He was equally close to the gallerists; in 1950, for instance, he and Meyer Schapiro curated the *Talent* show at the Kootz Gallery, and in 1951, when Tibor de Nagy opened his new gallery with former *View* editor John Bernard Myers as its director, Greenberg suggested mounting a show of "Clem's list." Greenberg may have been a master at circulating his own opinions, but if he thought a group of artists showed promise one day, he might change his mind the next. Many artists started resenting him, feeling

Kenneth Noland. Turnsole, *1961. Synthetic polymer paint on canvas, 94 ⅛ × 94 ⅛ in. (39 × 39 cm). Blanchette Hooker Rockefeller Fund. The Museum of Modern Art, New York. Noland made subtle changes to solid abstract shapes, especially the circle.*

that it was he who had pushed them to produce abstract work. Greenberg's devotion to abstraction and opposition to figuration contributed to a split in the group of downtown avant-garde artists, and anti-Greenberg sentiment was what bonded Tenth Street and its inhabitants. "All references to Clem and to Pollock and to what first brought Abstract Expressionism to public attention disappeared," recalled Hilton Kramer. "Tenth Street was anti-Clem. His name was dirt there."[69]

The de Kooning-led faction, supported by Harold Rosenberg, was decidedly larger, made up of artists who still took Picasso's synthetic period as a reference point and worked with the human figure. The opposing faction, led by Greenberg and Pollock, were viewed as more radical, pushing formal extremes. The two groups continued to mix at the Club, but there was never any doubt to which side each belonged. By the fall of 1952, the downtown group, feeling that "Clem" had created a "suffocating academy," made him, as well as anyone associated with him, feel unwelcome. According to painter Friedel Dzubas, "Greenberg was first the spokesman for us, the second generation of Abstract Expressionists," and though he was "very respected" when he first started, he later "became an enemy."[70] In the same manner, Greenberg supported Pollock for a long time, until the artist made a return to the figure. After Pollock's November 1952 show at the Sidney Janis Gallery, critic and artist

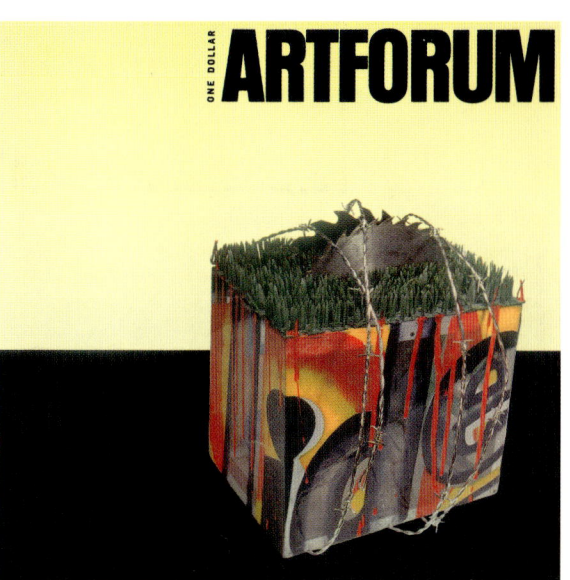

became estranged. Greenberg did not review any of Pollock's shows from 1952 to 1954.

In December 1952, Harold Rosenberg's first major article in *ARTnews*, "American Action Painters," heralded the public face of a rivalry between the two critics. Rosenberg provided an intellectual alternative to Greenberg. "Finally, someone has challenged Pope Clement," was the consensus downtown.[71] "The American painter," Rosenberg wrote, "found a new function for art as the action that belonged to himself. At a certain moment in time, the canvas thus began to appear to one American painter after another as an arena in which to act—rather than a space in which to reproduce, redesign or 'express' an object. What was to go on the canvas was not a picture, but an event," he stated.[72]

The rivalry between the two Jewish intellectuals of the same generation, with the same training and the same *zeitgeist,* kept the art world entertained for almost ten years. Well over six feet tall, with a memorable black mane, Rosenberg always towered above the crowd and was often referred to as "the lion of Judah." Furthermore, he was a "verbal magician," whereas Greenberg painfully stuttered a bit in those years, even if his writings remained brilliant, as shown in the following excerpts from his response to Rosenberg's article:

"The very flavor of the words 'action painting' had something racy and demotic about it—like the name of a new dance step—that befitted an altogether new and American way of making art." Greenberg goes on to admit that "avant-garde critics have a special weakness for the opaquely profound. . . . What is there about art writing that encourages this sort of thing? What is there in the people who read art writing that makes them tolerate it? Why is art writing the only kind of writing in English that has lent itself to Existentialist and Phenomenological rhetoric? What is there about modern art itself that leads minds like Herbert Read's and Harold Rosenberg's astray?"[73]

"Clem" opposed many more of his colleagues, including Fairfield Porter, who stated that Greenberg seemed to "think that the artists today must give up the figure. Because the figure has been done and nothing new remains."[74] To this Greenberg retorted, "Mr. Porter is being captious when he tries to pin 'value' down to its meaning as 'worth.' What difference does it make? He knows what I mean. Everything in a work of art has worth; the question is how much. . . . I happen to find de Kooning's *Women* pictures inferior by and large to his previous work, but that's an *ad hoc* judgment that has nothing to do with anybody else's figure paintings, not even Mr. Porter's."[75]

Apart from the Greenberg/Rosenberg rivalry and the Greenberg/
Porter disputes, during those years intellectual figures had many
opportunities to voice support for the artist. Meyer Schapiro,
a revered academic art historian, published "Style," a long essay
about Hegel's influence on art criticism, in 1953; the lectures he
gave at the New School for Social Research as well as at New York
University were wildly popular and very influential for local artists. Schapiro often visited the Hansa Gallery, and managed to
convince de Kooning, who was about to give up, to keep working
on *Woman I.* Harold Rosenberg, Elaine de Kooning, and Tom Hess
slowly became a triumvirate so powerful that they started influenc-
ing curators, collectors, and artists. Hess was wealthy, urbane, educated, and well liked by all sides. In 1955, interviewing twenty-five
artists for "Recent American Painting" in *ARTnews*, he noticed with
pleasure how often Schapiro's name had come up in the painters'
references. Another brilliant academic was Erwin Panofsky, whose
essay "Meaning in the Visual Arts," published in *Magazine of Art*, was
edited by yet another scholarly titan, Robert Goldwater. In addition to the critics and the academics, local poets such as Edwin Orr
Denby came to the rescue of the artist.

> The sidewalk cracks, gumspots, the water, the bits of refuse,
> They reach out and bloom under arclight, neon light— . . .
> These pictures, sat on by the cats that watch the slums,
> Are a bouquet luck has dropped here suitable to mortals.[77]

Artists Robert Rauschenberg and Jasper Johns, who by 1953
(when still in their twenties) had come to New York City from
Texas and South Carolina, respectively, worked in two lofts (one
on top of the other) in a building on Pearl Street, at the foot of

Manhattan, experiencing parallel trajectories, as Braque and Picasso had in Paris before them. A voracious, brilliant, enlightened, genial, and exultant wanderer, Rauschenberg paced the streets in all kinds of ways, documenting his "observations" with implacable fieldwork, blithely plunging into the urban chaos as he scavenged for raw materials, besotted with the "constant, irrational juxtaposition of things that I think one only finds in the city."[77] At the time, he was prowling the streets in search of objects to use in his developing *Combines* series (1953–64). He had realized his series *Red Paintings* in the early 1950s, partly as a parody of the Abstract Expressionists, partly as a step toward his work in the *Combines*, as these vermilion monochromes often incorporated found elements, such as doilies, photographs, and newspaper clippings, and became more and more collage-like and three-dimensional. "In the broadest sense," curator Paul Schimmel recently commented, "what began as highly personal, poetic and private autobiographical works increasingly became performance oriented—more theatrical, interdisciplinary, environmental, and with a broader sweep." In the mid-sixties, Rauschenberg moved from hand-painted canvases to a method of mechanical reproduction: silk screen.

Jasper Johns, a shyer, more introverted personality, worked nights in a bookstore in order to be able to go on painting. It was Rauschenberg who convinced him to become a full-time artist and encouraged his explorations. Together they made a living designing department-store display windows. But their styles were quite different. In 1954, Johns destroyed all of his previous work, realizing his first "mature" painting in the mid-1950s. *Flag* (1954–55) is a work of newspaper collage and encaustic painting that introduced what would become one of the primary motifs of his ongoing practice. Soon thereafter he produced, again in encaustic, a series of canvases of numbers, letters, maps, and targets (also career-long motifs), some of which included plaster casts of the body. The lower half of a face, for example, is repeated four times in a sort of architectural frieze above a blue-and-yellow target in the work *Target with Four Faces* (1955). Johns's dry, restrained delivery, his enigmatic use of symbols and color, combined with a sensuous, painterly surface, yielded canvases that, according to MoMA curator Kirk Varnedoe, witnessed a juxtaposition of "concrete literalness and painterly abstraction."[78] His appropriation of bold, everyday imagery became a key reference point for Pop Art, and his method of systematic repetition would be at the core of Minimalism.

"Jasper's loft was always immaculate, white, and nothing out of place," noted their mutual friend Rachel Rosenthal. "Bob's was full of objects, multicolored, chaotic and jumbled."[79] This

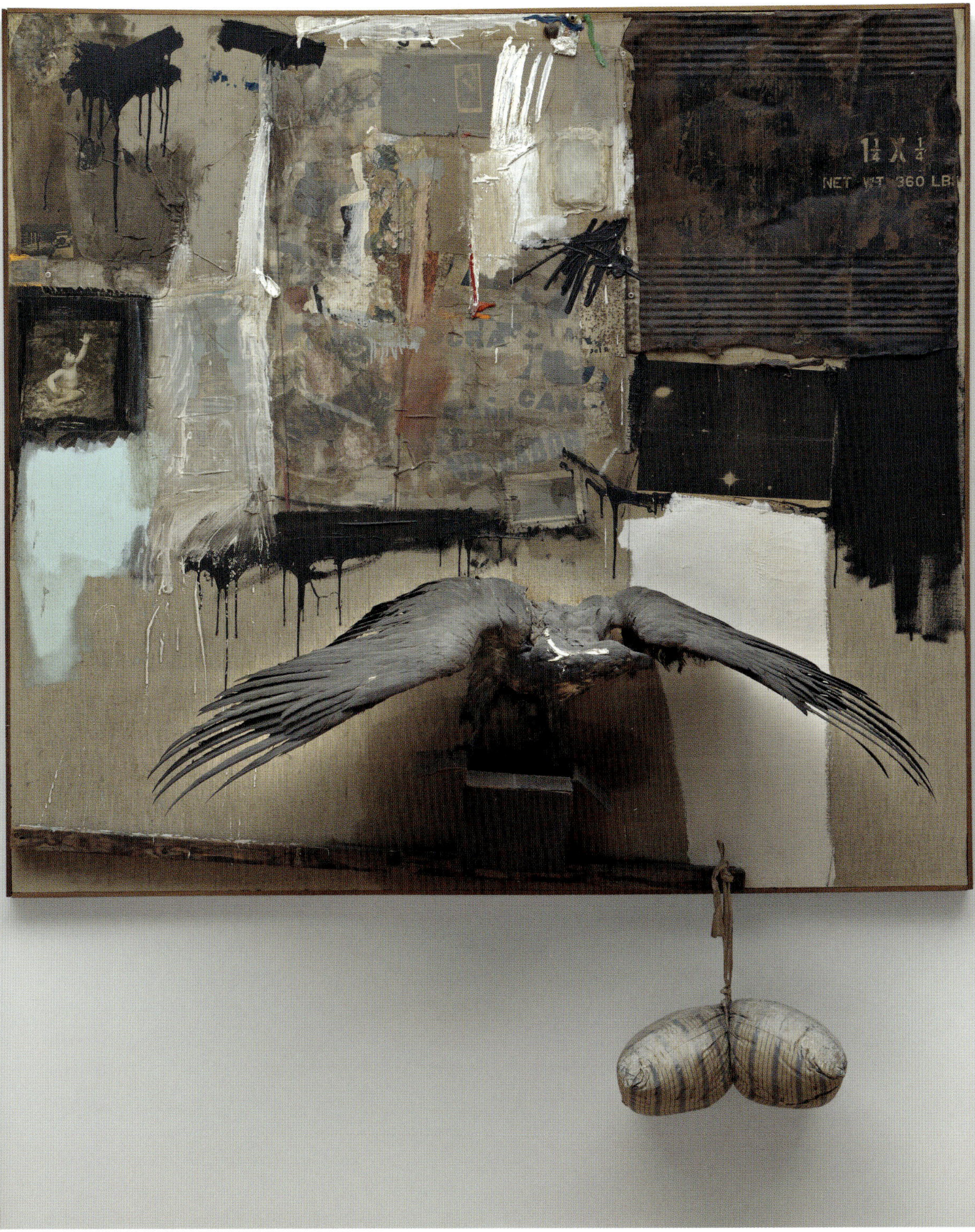
1¼ X ¼
NET WT 360 LB

complementary contrast between two spaces and two personalities struck everyone, and Rauschenberg was the first to admit his attraction to his friend's world: "I was so envious of [Jasper's] working materials: there was warm bee's wax, it smelled so good. My place smelled like the streets."[80]

For his part, Rauschenberg recalled the isolation of those unique years—with distinct irony: "Nobody cared about [Jasper's] work and nobody cared about my work. So we had a very exclusive club. We had great times. . . . What brought us together was that we were *not* doing Abstract Expressionism. That's what made our group of two people a threat to the Abstract Expressionists!"[81]

Though not yet well recognized downtown, Rauschenberg and Johns enjoyed the energy of New York City. "I felt very rich in being able to pick up Con Edison lumber from the streets and whatever the day would lay out for me to use in my work," Rauschenberg recalled. "In fact, so much so, that sometimes it embarrasses me that I live in New York City, as though I'm a guest here. . . . I was in awe of the painters; I mean I was new in New York, and I thought the painting that was going on here was just unbelievable. I still think that Bill de Kooning is

OPPOSITE: Robert Rauschenberg. Octave, *1960. Oil on canvas with assemblage (wood, paper, fabric). 77½ × 42¼ in. (196.9 × 107.3 cm). Promised gift of the Virginia and Bagley Wright Collection, in honor of the 75th Anniversary of the Seattle Art Museum.*

BELOW: Robert Rauschenberg, left, and Jasper Johns at home on Pearl Street, where they worked in neighboring studios. "Jasper's loft was immaculate," while "Bob's was full of objects, multicolored, chaotic and jumbled," their friend Rachel Rosenthal said.

one of the greatest painters in the world. . . . But I found a lot of artists at the Cedar Bar [the Abstract Expressionists' hangout, located on Cedar Street near the Club] were difficult for me to talk to. . . . There was something about the self-assertion of Abstract Expressionism that personally always put me off, because at that time my focus was as much in the opposite direction as it could be. I was busy trying to find ways where the imagery and the material and the meanings of the painting would be not an illustration of my will but more like an unbiased documentation of my observations, . . . literally of my excitement about . . . the city."[82] A veritable synergy formed around Rauschenberg; the first to support him were not the postwar painters but two composers, John Cage and Morton Feldman, as well as choreographer Merce Cunningham. Rauschenberg's encounter with the AbEx "clique," when it finally came, was extremely intense.

It was only natural that the young Robert Rauschenberg, a great fan of de Kooning's, would come knocking on the Abstract

Expressionist's door shortly after he showed his first series of *Woman* paintings at the Sidney Janis Gallery. Requesting a drawing from the downtown giant, the young Texan artist was signaling a shift in sensibility—and power. Rauschenberg was planning not to preserve the work, but to rub it out. "I know what you're doing," de Kooning declared, but still accepted the young artist's request.[83] In what Rauschenberg described as an agonizing afternoon, de Kooning slowly leafed through several portfolios of his works on paper, finally choosing a "fleshy drawing for sacrifice." A work, he said, that would be "very hard to erase."[84] With this gesture, Rauschenberg announced that the Abstract Expressionist movement as a whole was not an insurmountable obstacle any longer and that the way was free for his own generation of artists.

OPPOSITE: Jasper Johns. Thermometer, 1959. Oil on canvas with thermometer, 51¾ × 38½ in. (131.5 × 97.8 cm). Seattle Art Museum, Partial and promised gift of Bagley and Virginia Wright, in honor of the museum's 50th year. Another masterwork by an artist whose talent expressed itself in colored draftsmanship.

BELOW: Jasper Johns playing skee-ball in Dillon's Bar on University Place in Greenwich Village as his friends look on, 1959. Left to right: artists Bill Giles, Anna Moreska, and Robert Rauschenberg, choreographer Merce Cunningham, and composer John Cage.

RIGHT: Cedar Tavern closing, 1963. In the center is poet Frank O'Hara; sculptor Abram Schlemowitz, glass in hand, is in the right foreground. The bar, which had been located on Cedar Street since the turn of the century, reopened a year later several blocks away.

BELOW: New Year's Eve party at the Club, December 31, 1958. Left to right: art critic Michael C. D. MacDonald, artist Nancy Ward, art critic Harold Rosenberg, co-founder of the City Lights bookstore Peter D. Martin, and artists Franz Kline, Ted Joans, and Jimmy Cuchiara.

NEW YORK AS A MAGNET
1956–1958

*"It wasn't so much America that attracted me as New York as a magnet.
I used to dream of New York when I was a child."*[85]
—LEO CASTELLI

In the late fifties, the city of New York became home to the nation's 135 largest companies and the hub of a consumer market that had absolutely no equal in the world. The ideal metropolis for businessmen seeking a well-rounded life, New York acted as a demographic magnet, in good part thanks to the development of its museums, concert halls, theaters, and eventually its few contemporary art galleries. Progressively, New York was becoming a *locus* in which all the threads of many complex trajectories were being woven together and in which the veritable intrigue had just but started. After the emigration from Europe of many Jews who, in New York, became artists, gallerists, critics, academics, or museum curators, it was now the turn of American artists born around the country (Rauschenberg in Texas; Cy Twombly in Virginia; Johns in Georgia) to join the city that would soon become the cultural center of the Western world. And many great collectors rose to the occasion.

Son of a "well-to-do" Cleveland attorney, and a Harvard graduate, Philip Johnson met Alfred Barr in 1929, the year he was named director of MoMA. Barr immediately became the young architect's art mentor. "All I had was enthusiasm," Johnson recalled, "Alfred had the knowledge and the ability to communicate that changed my life."[86] When Barr planned the opening of the museum, Johnson's passion for architecture influenced the scope of the project, and architecture became one of the departments of this highly innovative institution. He was appointed MoMA's architectural curator in 1930, and soon started working on his first show, *Modern Architecture: International Exhibition*, which opened in 1932. As seminal as that exhibition turned out to be, Johnson's contribution to MoMA greatly exceeded it, as at heart he was a collector, and such a generous one that "when no one else would buy new art for the museum and the trustees could not be coaxed, it was always to Johnson that Barr turned."[87]

As a trustee of the museum from 1957 on, Johnson donated or provided funds for more than 2,200 works of art, including Jasper Johns's *Flag* (1954–55), Warhol's *Gold Marilyn Monroe* (1962), and Rauschenberg's first *Combine* painting, *First Landing Jump* (1961), as well as architectural material and the Jan Tschichold collection of

typography. In 1954, with help from art dealer David Whitney, his partner, Johnson began work on a monumental project, his famous Glass House in New Canaan, Connecticut, which stimulated his own collecting, as the architect always considered art and buildings as an ensemble. As the Glass House lacked walls for hanging work, Johnson created an underground art gallery that was, in the architect's words, "a demonstration of how to show pictures at maximum effect."[88] His concept for showing a large quantity of paintings was inspired by a dry cleaner's or coat-check hanger system. Starting with Abstract Expressionists Rothko and Franz Kline at one end and ending with Minimalists Frank Stella, Richard Artschwager, Donald Judd, Lee Bontecou, Dan Flavin, and Robert Morris at the other, works were hung on individual screens that revolved with the push of a button. "The special fun of collecting for me," Johnson admitted, "is to buy the kids before they get expensive."[89] Thanks to Johnson, MoMA's

OPPOSITE, TOP: *Poster for an exhibition of Frank Stella's paintings at the Castelli Gallery, 1962.*

OPPOSITE, BOTTOM: *The underground art gallery at Philip Johnson's Glass House, with its ingenious system of revolving screens.*

ABOVE: *Frank Stella.* Ouray, *1962. Copper oil paint on canvas mounted on masonite, 25 ½ × 25 ½ in. (64.8 × 64.8 cm). Private collection, courtesy of Guggenheim Asher Associates. One of the sixteen paintings in the* Copper Paintings *series. According to the artist, "The copper pictures . . . represent the extreme — the limit — to which I could take the shaping."*

collection was enriched by cutting-edge works that he usually scouted outside of any conventional categories and well before anyone else. He sometimes donated the works only years later, when public consensus had finally caught up.

And then came flamboyant collectors. Robert and Ethel Scull were perceived, at times, as the most flashy early collectors of the New York postwar avant-garde. Others considered them simply blatant social climbers. Born on the Lower East Side to Russian immigrant parents, Scull ran a taxi service, later called Scull's Angels, that he started with a share of the taxi business he inherited from his father-in-law. His first purchase was a "dubious Utrillo," but slowly, as he tired of being perceived as "new money" around town, Scull fell in love with the idea of being "a big collector," thus acquiring the visibility and the prestige that he needed in order to enhance his image.[90] With his impeccable eye and strategic ambition, and the advice of dealer Richard Bellamy, by November 1966 his collection consisted of 260 paintings, 35 sculptures, and 300 drawings. After buying mostly

Abstract Expressionists, including de Kooning, Kline, Rothko, and Newman, the Sculls turned their interest to Pop artists, with whom they soon began to socialize.

Living in a lavish apartment on Fifth Avenue filled with Mies van der Rohe and Charles Eames furniture and John Chamberlain and Walter De Maria sculptures, its white walls hung with paintings by Tom Wesselmann, Andy Warhol, James Rosenquist, Frank Stella, and Jasper Johns, Bob and Ethel became Leo Castelli's best customers, amassing the largest group of Jasper Johns paintings in the world, including *Out the Window* (1959), *Target with Four Faces*, and *Map* (1961). An ideal client, Scull would arrive at the gallery with wads of cash, ready to pay up front, whereas other collectors asked for time. The Sculls' ascent to power was not always welcome; they were resented for their aggressive, blunt behavior, especially by artists whom they took advantage of like vampires. Author Tom Wolfe profiled them as "the folk heroes of every social climber who ever hit New York."[91]

In a dramatic and unexpected move that stunned the art world, Scull auctioned off his collection at Sotheby's on October 18, 1973, just before announcing that he was divorcing Ethel. The sale brought in over $2 million, set a record price for Jasper Johns's

OPPOSITE, TOP: George Segal. Portrait of Robert and Ethel Scull, *1965. Oil on canvas, plaster, wood chair with cloth, 96 × 72 × 72 in. (243.8 × 182.9 × 182.9 cm). Aichi Prefectural Museum of Art, Nagoya, Japan.*

OPPOSITE, BOTTOM: Robert and Ethel Scull, in the foreground, with, from left, artists James Rosenquist, George Segal, and Andy Warhol, ca. 1963.

BELOW: The entryway and living room of Robert and Ethel Scull's New York apartment. Jasper Johns's Target, *1958, is on the right and* Ethel Scull 36 Times, *1963, Andy Warhol's first commissioned portrait, can be seen through the adjacent doorway.*

Roy Lichtenstein's I Can See the Whole
Room, *1961, is the focus of this photograph of
collectors Burton and Emily Tremaine's living
room; it is one of the* Tremaine Pictures
series by photographer Louise Lawler, 1984.

Double White Map (1965), which sold for $240,000, and heralded the
arrival of contemporary American art on the market.[92]

Though very different from the Sculls, Burton and Emily
Tremaine became their rivals nonetheless, especially over the best
work of Jasper Johns. The heiress to a mining fortune, Emily
Tremaine was born in Montana and grew up in Santa Barbara. Her
first major acquisition—in the middle of the Depression—was
Braque's *The Black Rose* (1927) for $3,250.[93] Advised by her cousin
Chick Austin, director of the Wadsworth Atheneum in Hartford,
who organized the first Surrealist show in America and with
Lincoln Kirstein brought Balanchine and classical ballet to the
U.S., Emily married Burton Tremaine, an East Coast businessman
and an active partner in collecting great art. As a collector, she was
bold, brilliant, and intuitive, and, according to art historian Robert
Rosenblum, her collection was "so museum worthy that it alone
could recount to future generations the better part of the story
of 20th century art."[94] It included many first-class paintings, from
such key Modern works as Robert Delaunay's *Premier Disque* (1913–
14) and Mondrian's *Victory Boogie Woogie* (1942–44) to masterpieces
of Abstract Expressionist and contemporary American art, such as
Jasper Johns's exceptional *Three Flags* (1958) and Frank Stella's *Luis
Miguel Dominguin* (1960).

In 1947, the Tremaines exhibited their collection at the Atheneum, featuring work by Alexander Calder, Matta, and Mark Tobey, as well as a selection of European artists. In 1962, the couple discovered Warhol and immediately bought no less than fifteen works that year, including *Big Campbell's Soup Can with Can Opener (Vegetable)* and *Marilyn Diptych.* The exhibition of their collection was one of the first mounted by the young gallerist Larry Gagosian after he moved to New York. The sale of Johns's *Three Flags* to the Whitney Museum for $1 million in September 1980 further fueled the spiral of speculation for contemporary American art on the market that had begun with the Scull sale.[95]

A French couple, Dominique and John de Menil, settled in Houston in 1941, where John had a senior position at Schlumberger, his in-laws' energy company. The de Menils frequently visited New York, and met three key figures who shaped their collecting: Father Marie-Alain Couturier (responsible for Matisse's Chapel of the Rosary at Vence and Le Corbusier's Notre-Dame-du-Haut at Ronchamp); Greek dealer Alexander Iolas; and designer and curator Jermayne MacAgy. Their collection started with Surrealism and step-by-step grew to include Medieval and Byzantine objects, Russian icons, African sculpture, Modern art, and Abstract Expressionism. Thanks to their oldest daughter, Christophe, a designer, they discovered contemporary

Jasper Johns. Three Flags, 1958. Encaustic on canvas, 30⅞ × 45½ × 5 in. (78.4 × 115.6 × 12.7 cm). Whitney Museum of American Art, New York. This iconic piece of art—Johns's third inspired by the American flag—owes much to its surprising technique: "One night, I dreamed I painted a large American flag," he said, "and the next morning I got up . . . and bought the materials to begin it. . . . Then I had in my head this idea of something I had read or heard about: wax encaustic."

American artists such as Warhol, Johns, Rauschenberg, Twombly, and Chamberlain. In 1964, the de Menils, champions of civil and human rights, commissioned eight murals from Rothko and in 1971 installed them in a specially designed octagonal building by Philip Johnson—the Rothko Chapel—which remains an homage to all religions and all radical thinkers. In front stands Barnett Newman's monumental sculpture *Broken Obelisk*, a tribute to justice and truth. In order to share their collection with the public, Dominique de Menil commissioned a museum building from Renzo Piano, which was inaugurated in 1987, and added a Twombly gallery in 1995 to exhibit their extensive collection of that artist's works.

In addition to MoMA and the Whitney Museum, another New York institution unexpectedly opened its doors to local contemporary artists during those years. As early as 1944, the widow of banker Felix Warburg turned over her six-story, fifty-room Gothic-style mansion at the corner of Fifth Avenue and 92nd Street to the Museum of Jewish Ceremonial Objects. Soon afterward, the board transformed the museum's mission, making it one museum among others and downplaying its religious character. With the guidance of such key art world figures as Meyer Schapiro, the board then voted to rename it the Jewish Museum, mount exhibitions of contemporary art, and even show the work of gentile artists. Subsequently, with the financial support of such contemporary

Collectors Dominique and John de Menil were born in France and emigrated to Houston in 1941, where they founded one of the most beautiful private art museums in the country.

John Chamberlain on the roof of a building, holding one of his sculptures over his head, 1960s.

collectors as Ben Heller and Albert and Vera List, the museum set out to "fill a gap in the New York art world by emphasizing the work of younger or otherwise unacknowledged artists."[96] In July 1962, Alan Solomon, who had recently left his position as Chair of Art History at Cornell University, was appointed its new director. He quickly made it clear that he would dedicate himself to the city's artists. Solomon had his finger on the pulse of the New York scene, mounting a Rauschenberg retrospective in 1963 and a Johns retrospective in 1964.

Back in the gallery world, Leo Castelli and his rich wife Ileana divorced in 1957; he decided to convert their daughter's bedroom in a brownstone at 4 East 77th Street into a gallery. Within a few months, Castelli gave twenty-seven-year-old Jasper Johns his first solo show. An immediate success for both artist and gallerist, the show turned Johns into an overnight celebrity, making the cover of Tom Hess's *ARTnews* and enjoying unusual recognition when Alfred Barr bought three paintings for MoMA's permanent collection at the opening. In a show at the Jewish Museum, Castelli had been mesmerized by Johns's *Green Target* (1955). In his desperate search for the new, this would be the historic moment that he would call his "first epiphany"; everything in this encounter was a revelation to Castelli. The bond between

ABOVE: *Leo Castelli in his gallery at 4 East 77th Street, looking at Robert Rauschenberg's* Retroactive I, 1964.

Castelli and Johns would last until the gallerist's death.[97]

Over the next four decades, the gallerist transformed the status of the artist in New York City by creating monthly stipends for them. He convinced the leading academics, including Leo Steinberg, Robert Rosenblum, and Fairfield Porter, to write about his artists' works, and he set up functional links with the museums of the city by relentlessly promoting his artists at home and abroad through an astute system of satellite galleries, for which he selected the very best collections. Castelli was attacked for "digging the graves" of the Abstract Expressionists and their supporters, including Greenberg and Rosenberg. The opposition of the old generation of painters long remained fierce: Rothko called the new post-Dada artists "charlatans and young opportunists," and Esteban Vicente proclaimed: "If that is painting, I'll stop!"[98]

OPPOSITE, TOP: The New York art world converges at the Robert Rauschenberg Retrospective *at the Jewish Museum, 1963. Standing, left to right: Sherman Drexler, Claes Oldenburg, Richard Lippold, Merce Cunningham, Robert Murray, Peter Agostini, Edward Higgins, Barnett Newman, Robert Rauschenberg, Perle Fine, Alfred Jensen, Ray Parker, Friedel Dzubas, Ernst van Leyden, Andy Warhol, Marisol, James Rosenquist, John Chamberlain, George Segal; kneeling, left to right: Jon Schueler, Arman, David Slivka, Alfred Leslie, Tania, Frederick Kiesler, Lee Bontecou, Isamu Noguchi, Salvatore Scarpitta, Allan Kaprow.*

ABOVE: Jasper Johns. Green Target, *1956. Encaustic and newspaper collage on board, 9¼ × 9¼ in. (23.5 × 23.5 cm). Private collection. Castelli was so captivated by a version of this work when he first saw it at a group show at the Jewish Museum that he came to call it his "first epiphany." The artist plays with the illusion of depth created by concentric circles, preventing the eye from focusing on one point of the painting.*

WHIRLWINDS & HAPPENINGS
1959–1961

"A walk down 14th Street
is more amazing than any masterpiece of art."[99]
—ALLAN KAPROW

The art world was full of excitement in the late 1950s. Leo Castelli was imposing a new pace on the New York gallery scene and making important innovations in how it functioned. Castelli's thirst for "epiphanies" forced an aesthetic of urgency and constant change. He had a keen sense of how to use the new international events that

were getting organized such as the Venice Biennale and the Basel Art Fair to create an ongoing party where collectors, artists, critics, and gallerists enjoyed themselves while developing the art market. Castelli's vast network of contacts, which he had been cultivating for more than twenty years, gave him access to precious "inside information." Acting as a dynamic mediator between the art market and the institution, Castelli had positioned himself perfectly, epitomizing the dealer as entrepreneur.

In the late fifties, Allan Kaprow, who had studied with Hans Hofmann and later at the New School under John Cage, was beginning to create his Environments and Happenings. In 1959, he presented *18 Happenings in 6 Parts* at the Reuben Gallery, a series of multimedia participatory events featuring the involvement of the general public as well as fellow artists such as Rauschenberg and Johns. The year before, Kaprow had published the essay "The Legacy of Jackson Pollock," expressing disappointment with "the *suggestion* through paint of our other senses." Heralding his innovative, artist-driven theatrical events, Kaprow declared, "We shall utilize the specific substances of sight, sound, movements, people, odors, touch. Objects of every sort are materials for the new art."[100] Performance art had arrived. While Kaprow was experimenting and extending the artist's means of engaging with the public, a new type of dealer, perhaps best represented by Dick Bellamy, was exploring innovative ways of presenting artists.

Richard Hu Bellamy was a cult figure, central to New York's art circles for several decades. Born in Cincinnati, the son of a Chinese mother and an American father, he arrived in New York City in the early 1950s. Some five years later, he was asked to become director of the Hansa Gallery when it moved from East 10th Street to Central Park South. Although he had no previous gallery experience, he had a strong interest in, and a personal connection with, the Hansa artists. A cooperative undertaking that had quickly made its name after opening downtown in the winter of 1952, all of the gallery's founders had studied with Hans Hofmann, including Allan Kaprow, Alfred Leslie, George Segal, Richard Stankiewicz, Jean Follett, Robert Whitman, and Jan Müller. Other cultural activities took place in the space; Clement Greenberg, for instance, gave several talks there in the early 1950s.

RIGHT: Jim Dine performs in his happening Car Crash *at the Reuben Gallery, 1960.*

BELOW: Jim Dine, center, performing in Allan Kaprow's The Big Laugh *at the Reuben Gallery, 1960.*

LEFT: A scene from Carolee Schneeman's happening Meat Joy, *1964.*

BELOW: The cast of Claes Oldenburg's Circus: Ironworks/Fotodeath, *Reuben Gallery, 1961. Standing, left to right: Gloria Graves, Carl Lehmann-Haupt, Olga Adorno, Pat Oldenburg, Marilyn Jaffee, Judy Tersch, Claire Wesselmann, Chippy McClellan, Lucas Samaras; seated, left to right: Edgar Blakeney, Max Baker, Tom Wesselmann, Claes Oldenburg, Henry Geldzahler, Clifford Smith.*

OPPOSITE, TOP: Poster for the Green Gallery's first group show, 1960. Richard Bellamy Papers, 11.B.28. The Museum of Modern Art Archives, New York.

OPPOSITE, BOTTOM: This 1962 installation at the Green Gallery presented works by Claes Oldenburg, Philip Wofford, and Richard Smith, as well as Yayoi Kusama's soft sculpture Accumulation No. 1.

Hansa was intended to be a provisional space where young artists could show their work, develop a sort of club dynamic, and not necessarily worry about sales until the critics and uptown galleries took notice. "They wanted their work to reach the largest public that they could," Bellamy explained. But the need for the gallery persisted, and the artists' commitment to it grew exponentially. Gallery decisions were made by a democratic, parliamentary system (the artists even decided the prices of their works). In time, however, many of the artists were taken on by established galleries, and Hansa closed its doors in 1959.

In 1960, backed by collector Robert Scull, Bellamy opened the Green Gallery with a solo show by sculptor Mark di Suvero. The next program featured work by Bellamy's discovery Lee Lozano, as well as George Segal and Jack Tworkov. Claes Oldenburg's soft sculptures were first shown at the gallery, as were Donald Judd's cadmium red light sculptures and Morris Louis's rich Color Field canvases.

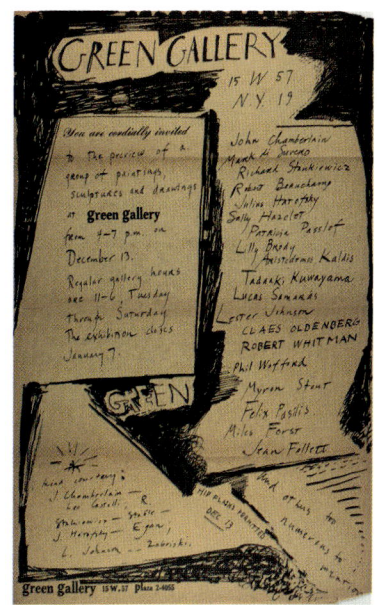

Bellamy spent his nights and weekends in artists' studios, had an impeccable eye, and acted fast. But slow sales prompted Scull to withdraw his funding in 1965, and the gallery was forced to close. Bellamy was able to place several of his artists with Leo Castelli, who had always been ready in the wings, closely following Bellamy's program with particular appreciation for Minimalists Dan Flavin, Donald Judd, and Robert Morris. After the close of the Green Gallery, Bellamy continued to show young artists and advise collectors; his impact on contemporary art, through his shows at the Green Gallery and the artists and work that he quickly embraced and effectively presented, was invaluable.

ABOVE: Robert Morris. Untitled (Tangle), *1967. 1-inch-thick felt, dimensions variable; museum installation 116 × 106 × 58 in. (294.6 × 269.2 × 147.3 cm). The Museum of Modern Art, New York. "Random piling, loose stacking, hanging, give passing form to the material. Chance is accepted and indeterminacy is implied since replacing will result in another configuration," Robert Morris said. His use of industrial felt in this work explores the weight of the material as an unpredictable way to shape art.*

OPPOSITE: Dan Flavin. "Monument" 1 for V. Tatlin, *1964. Fluorescent lights and metal fixtures, 96 × 23⅛ × 4½ in. (243.8 × 58.7 × 10.8 cm). The Museum of Modern Art, New York. This is the first in a series of thirty-nine "monuments" to the Russian artist Vladimir Tatlin.*

Claes Oldenburg. Giant BLT
(Bacon, Lettuce, and Tomato
Sandwich), *1963. Vinyl, kapok
fibers, painted wood, and wood,
32 × 39 × 29 in. (81.3 × 99.1
× 73.7cm). Whitney Museum of
American Art, New York. Gift of
The American Contemporary Art
Foundation Inc., Leonard A. Lauder,
President. Composed of nineteen
separate parts, the sandwich must be
reassembled each time it is exhibited.*

NEW YORK AS A *LOCUS*
1962–1965

"More and more middle-class youth set out on an artistic trek which leads them inevitably to New York, the nation's center for art education, museums and art sales."[101]
—Dore Ashton

For years Castelli and his friend Alan Solomon planned shows at the Jewish Museum, discussed art, literature, and girls, and embarked on a daunting new challenge to guarantee American artists a visibility that they had never experienced. After her divorce from Castelli, Ileana remarried and she and her new husband, Michael Sonnabend, opened a gallery in Paris, where they tirelessly fought for their American heroes.

Inspired by new marketing strategies, they hired creative designers to launch advertising campaigns in European art magazines and found potential collectors in Germany, Italy, Great Britain, and Northern Europe. The Sonnabends' move not only expanded the reach of Castelli's gallery, essentially becoming its satellite, but most

important helped put New York and its artists on the international map. The awarding of the Golden Lion to Rauschenberg at Venice's 1964 Biennale was the consequence of a hard fight against both ingrained French supremacy and Italian provincialism.

By the fall of 1964, the art press was consumed with Pop Art, and innumerable articles discussed whether or not Pop was a new art, and whether or not it could last: "What Is Pop Art?" "Anti-Sensibility Painting." "Pop Art Sells On and On—Why?"[102] Indeed, many saw Pop as "primarily a collector's movement," and the 1960s would soon reveal the growing audience, as well as the growing market, for contemporary art.[103] Pop Art emerged in the United States in the late 1950s as an artistic movement hinged on the appropriation of images from popular culture. Advertisements, increasingly present in the postwar American visual landscape, were incorporated by Pop artists, as were methods of mechanical reproduction. Hailed by the *New York Times* as the "Svengali of Pop," Castelli became its leading champion, astutely using his personal charisma.[104] And among the movement's key figures were Roy Lichtenstein, Jim Dine, Robert Indiana, James Rosenquist, Claes Oldenburg, Tom Wesselmann, Larry Rivers, and Andy Warhol.

LEFT: James Rosenquist in his studio, standing next to Paint Brush, 1964.

BELOW: James Rosenquist. White Bread, 1964. Oil on canvas, 54 × 60 in. (137.2 × 152.4 cm). National Gallery of Art, Washington, D.C. In contrast to Rosenquist's earlier work, in this major painting the colors are brighter and representational depiction is tending toward abstraction.

James Rosenquist. World's Fair Mural, *1963–64. Oil on hardboard,
240 × 240 in. (609.6 × 609.6 cm). Collection of the Frederick R.
Weisman Art Museum of the University of Minnesota, Minneapolis.
Gift of the artist. Created for the New York Pavilion at the World's Fair,
this mural, composed of overlapping sections of billboard advertisements,
presents a lively patchwork of American life. Uncle Sam's hat signals
patriotism, the moon references the space race, carnival peanuts and soda pop
hint at the events of the fair, the car conveys flash and speed, and so on.*

OPPOSITE: *Roy Lichtenstein.* Girl with Piano, *1963. Oil on canvas, 68 × 48 in. (172.7 × 121.9 cm). Private collection. This stunning work was inspired by comic books and may well be a Pop Art homage to Renoir's* Two Young Girls at the Piano.

ABOVE: *Roy Lichtenstein.* Look Mickey, *1961. Oil on canvas, 48 × 69 in. (121.9 × 175.3 cm). Dorothy and Roy Lichtenstein, Gift of the Artist, in Honor of the 50th Anniversary of the National Gallery of Art 1990.41.1, Washington, D.C. This is the first painting in which Lichtenstein employed cartoon imagery and indicated his fascination with printed mass media.*

RIGHT: *Roy Lichtenstein straightening one of his paintings in his studio, 1959.*

Jim Dine in his studio, 1963. A key figure of the Pop Art movement, he first gained renown for his happenings and subsequently for his paintings, drawings, sculptures, and assemblages of everyday objects.

Through the 1950s, Lichtenstein painted canvases with vaguely Americana themes, at times experimenting with the Abstract Expressionist style. He presented his first solo show in New York in 1951 (at the Carlebach Gallery), but it wasn't until January 1961 that he made his first semi-abstract works incorporating cartoon figures. *Look Mickey*, painted in the summer of 1961, executed without a hint of expressionism, is based on an image appropriated from the book *Walt Disney's Donald Duck, Lost and Found* in his children's Little Golden Books collection. To give it the look of printed mass media, he appropriated the Benday dot patterns that make up all magazine and newspaper images. In this work, the dot pattern was created with a plastic-bristle dog-grooming brush dipped in oil paint and pressed onto the canvas. In later works, he devised a stencil process to generate the Benday dots, before ultimately turning to silk screen. His works of the early 1960s feature large-scale images of foodstuffs and household objects: *Cherry Pie* (1962), *Standing Rib* (1962); comic book–style images of American melodrama: *Crying Girl* (1964), *In the Car* (1963); parodies of Abstract Expressionists: *Yellow Brushstroke I* (1965); images appropriated from All-American Men of War comics and DC Comics' Girls' Romances and Secret Hearts: *Blam* (1961), *Girl with Ball* (1961).

Jim Dine's first works after moving to New York in 1958 were his Happenings of 1959–60—chaotic theatrical events that took place in environments he created and in which he performed. In this period he also started making drawings, paintings, sculptures, and assemblages of common, everyday objects. His work of the 1960s features clothing and domestic objects—bathrobes, ties, and toothbrushes—as well as artists' materials, such as palettes and paintbrushes, realized in a harried, almost aggressive hand.

Before turning to painting, Tom Wesselmann studied at Cooper Union to become a cartoonist. De Kooning was a key reference point for Wesselmann in the development of his work based around the figure. His early works presented the figure in small collages of torn paper, fabric, and found materials. These *Little Great American Nudes* collages show "Wesselmann working through the influence of Willem de Kooning via Jasper Johns' targets, flags and alphabets, fusing the hand-drawn sensuality of the former with the easy access of the latter's cool neutrality."[105] He soon transitioned into harsher, more monumental works such as *Great American Nude #44* (1963). By the late 1960s, Wesselmann shifted his focus from

common domestic items and popular advertising to an increasingly present eroticism.

Originally trained as a jazz saxophonist, Larry Rivers studied at the Hans Hofmann School of Fine Arts from 1947 to 1948. His work was initially influenced by Abstract Expressionism, but after seeing a Bonnard retrospective at MoMA, he quickly shifted toward figurative compositions. Described as contrarian and iconoclastic, Rivers was not afraid of appropriating sacred art-historical subject matter, as seen in his magisterial *Washington Crossing the Delaware* (1953), which echoes Emmanuel Leutze's heroic painting of the subject in the Metropolitan Museum. For the most part, however, his work anticipated the rise of Pop Art in its appropriation and deconstruction of images from commercial mass media in combination with

Jim Dine. Five Feet of Colorful Tools, *1962. Oil on unprimed canvas surmounted by a board on which painted tools hang from hooks, 55 ⅝ × 60 ¼ × 4 ⅜ in. (141.2 × 152.9 × 11 cm). The Sidney and Harriet Janis Collection. The Museum of Modern Art, New York.*

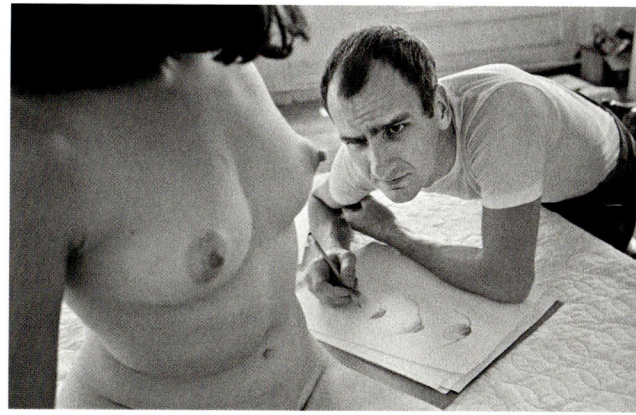

LEFT: Tom Wesselmann. Great American Nude # 44, 1963. *Acrylic and paper collage on board with radiator, telephone, coat, and door, 81⅛ × 106¼ × 12½ in. (206 × 269.9 × 31.8 cm). Private collection.*

ABOVE: Tom Wesselmann drawing a nude model, ca. 1963.

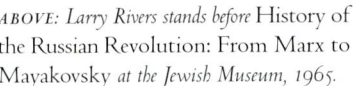

ABOVE: Larry Rivers stands before History of the Russian Revolution: From Marx to Mayakovsky *at the Jewish Museum, 1965.*

RIGHT: Larry Rivers. Washington Crossing the Delaware, *1953. Oil, graphite, and charcoal on linen, 83⅜ × 111⅜ in. (212.4 × 283.5 cm). The Museum of Modern Art, New York. In his appropriation of sacrosanct art-historical subjects, Rivers anticipated the Pop Art movement.*

the incorporation of found objects. It also demonstrated a fluency with material and content, drawing on visual, literary, musical, and performing arts vocabularies.

In January 1964, Andy Warhol, who had been struggling as an illustrator for years, moved to 231 East 47th Street, a powder-blue building at the corner of Lexington Avenue that he owned and called the Factory. Surrounded by his team of "Superstars"—Brigid Polk, Ultra Violet, Baby Jane Holzer, Edie Sedgwick, Viva, Ingrid Superstar, International Velvet, Billy Name, Ondine, Paul America, Nico, Candy Darling, Holly Woodlawn, and Jackie Curtis, among many others—in a space entirely covered with silver wallpaper, he

pioneered a new form of continuous and collective production with his silk screens, presented his band of outsiders as artists, and launched the cult of the celebrity. "It was a very dark place," recalls gallerist Ivan Karp. "There was one very bright light on in this living room area, which was very well decorated with fine, elegant furniture and beautiful paintings with a generally surrealistic character."[106]

Two years earlier, in June 1962, the gallerist Irving Blum had offered Warhol his first solo exhibition at the Ferus Gallery in Los Angeles. Blum plunged into the deep end by daring to show the entire *Campbell's Soup Cans* series: thirty-two rigorously identical canvases, each 16 x 20 inches, presented in the form of a "cool, clean, distant image" on which the only variable was the type of soup indicated on the label (Black Bean, Vegetarian Vegetable, Chicken Broth, Beef and Carrots, Tomato); in all, an absurd and grandiose poetic evocation of everyday America.[107] "When I saw the *Campbell's Soup Can* series in his New York studio," Walter Hopps, Blum's colleague at Ferus, recalled, "I said to Warhol, 'I absolutely must take your work and show it in Los Angeles!' And Andy, who had never been to California, got all excited: 'California—that's Hollywood!' he said, sitting amid a stack of magazines scattered across the floor so chaotically that you couldn't move about the room."[108]

A collector of Jasper Johns's drawings, Warhol wanted to show at Castelli. But Leo, fearing that his work would rival Roy Lichtenstein's, refused to add Warhol to his stable of artists. Ileana Sonnabend recognized Warhol's potential and promoted him. She recalled her admiration for the "very beautiful drawings of shoes, Coke bottles, and airmail stamps," as well her empathy for Warhol's feeling of isolation in the city. "He told me he had no friends. I used to call on him regularly and we'd go to an arcade on Forty-second Street filled with odd characters, like the gentleman who wore a very elegant tuxedo and made fleas dance on a large green baize, like in a gambling club."[109]

In January 1964 Sonnabend mounted a show of Warhol's *Death and Disaster* series in her Paris gallery, calling it *Death and Americans*, a true masterstroke. She landed a knockout punch for Pop Art and simultaneously overcame the French audience's sensitivity to it. "Why does Warhol affect us?" asked critic Alain Jouffroy. "We find ourselves submerged in pure tragedy. . . . Ripped from the context of the mainstream press, from the indiscriminate flood of information broadcast in every direction and at all times, his images become sacred icons in a godless world."[110] The American expatriate poet John Ashbery gave the artist a precious compliment: "This is a decisive step in the history of Pop Art. . . . With Warhol, his most recent art has become unmistakably polemical, or as the French say, *engagé*."[111] By inscribing his variations on pain around Marilyn Monroe, Jackie Kennedy, or Elizabeth Taylor, or in *Tunafish Disaster* and the *Electric Chair* series, by "dramatizing the breakdown of commodity exchange," by probing the "open sores in

BELOW: Andy Warhol stands amid his towering installation of Brillo box sculptures at the Stable Gallery, 1964.

OPPOSITE: Andy Warhol. Big Campbell's Soup Can with Can Opener (Vegetable), 1962. Casein and graphite on linen, 72 × 52 in. (182.9 × 132.1 cm). Private collection.

OVERLEAF: Andy Warhol and actors shooting a scene for Warhol's film Camp at the Factory, 1965. Participants include Warhol, left; Jane Holzer, lying on the couch; dancer Paul Swan, seated with back to camera; Philip "Fu-Fu" Smith, seated at center in railroad cap; Mario Montez, seated behind Jane Holzer; filmmaker/actor Jack Smith, standing at right.

American political life," Warhol unveiled a "stark, disabused, pessimistic vision" of his country, in a phase of *peinture noire* that he would never return to again.[112]

With his white wig and extravagant looks, Warhol was subversive about the conventionality of the American way of life. His art was a social critique of the hypocrisy he perceived and attacked. "You see houses everywhere, the green lawns with the sprinklers, the jungle gyms in the backyards, the kids riding their bikes to school, the mailman coming by with a smile, a woman unloading bags of groceries from her station wagon, and you can't help but think, 'This is the real America.' But then you start learning the details. You find out the nice man who always had an extra piece of gum to give you has gone completely off his rocker and killed his wife, that the ex-minister of the church you grew up in is now a big drunk who's totaled three cars . . . that your best friend's parents who were always so great are getting a divorce . . . that the girl you had a crush on in elementary school is now a religious fanatic. . . . Nobody in America has a normal life."[113]

ABOVE: Andy Warhol, right, poses with Robert Indiana in the Warhol studio, 1964.

BELOW: Warhol standing between two of his portrayals of Marylin Monroe, ca. 1964.

Andy Warhol. Jackie (The Week That Was), *1963. Silkscreen ink on synthetic polymer paint on canvas, 80 × 64 in. (203.2 × 162.6 cm). Private collection. One of the many Warhol works devoted to President Kennedy's assassination in November 1963, echoing his "stark, disabused, pessimistic vision" of the United States.*

Andy Warhol. Flowers, 1964. *Synthetic polymer paint and silkscreen ink on canvas, 85 × 84 in. (215.9 × 213.4 cm). The source of Warhol's* Flowers *paintings was a series of color photographs of hibiscus blossoms that appeared in the June 1964 issue of* Modern Photography. *The photographer was Patricia Caulfield, editor of the publication.*

By the time Castelli took Warhol on in late 1964, the artist was producing his "celebrities" paintings and had ceased to be at his best. Warhol's first exhibition at Castelli opened on November 21, 1964; it presented his *Flowers* paintings, a rather softened mode in comparison to the Paris exhibition. Had Castelli missed Warhol's core message? As the critic Thomas Crow wrote, "Warhol came to produce his most powerful paintings by dramatizing the hollowness of the consumer icon: that is, events in which the mass-produced image [served as] the bearer of desires were exposed in their inadequacy by the reality of suffering and death."[114]

Andy Warhol, surrounded by his Flowers *paintings, at the Factory, East 47th Street.*

In 1965 the United States Congress created the National Endowment for the Arts, an independent agency of the U.S. government with a mission to support, primarily financially, worthy artistic endeavors. At last, the New York art scene was not only validated but funded by the government of the very country that had so coolly received its work just a few years before. "In the sixties," sociologist Diana Crane observed, "art collecting became a profitable, if risky, investment."[115] Still, the general public did not seem the least bit interested in contemporary art, and it wasn't until the legendary Scull sale in October 1973 that prices for contemporary American artists started picking up and have been climbing ever since.

The most definitive change in the art world in 1965 was a seemingly minor one, meriting only brief mention in the *New York Times*. It was a change in the day of gallery openings—from Thursday to Saturday. "Openings were always difficult," Ivan Karp once admitted. "We found ourselves in the gallery with the artist, the artist's girlfriend, and some other buddies, maybe."[116] The new policy went into effect on Saturday, May 21, 1965. In time, it allowed the contemporary art world to expand its audience and establish a community of followers, who would exchange notes on shows they saw around 57th Street or in the Village, or later in SoHo and Chelsea.

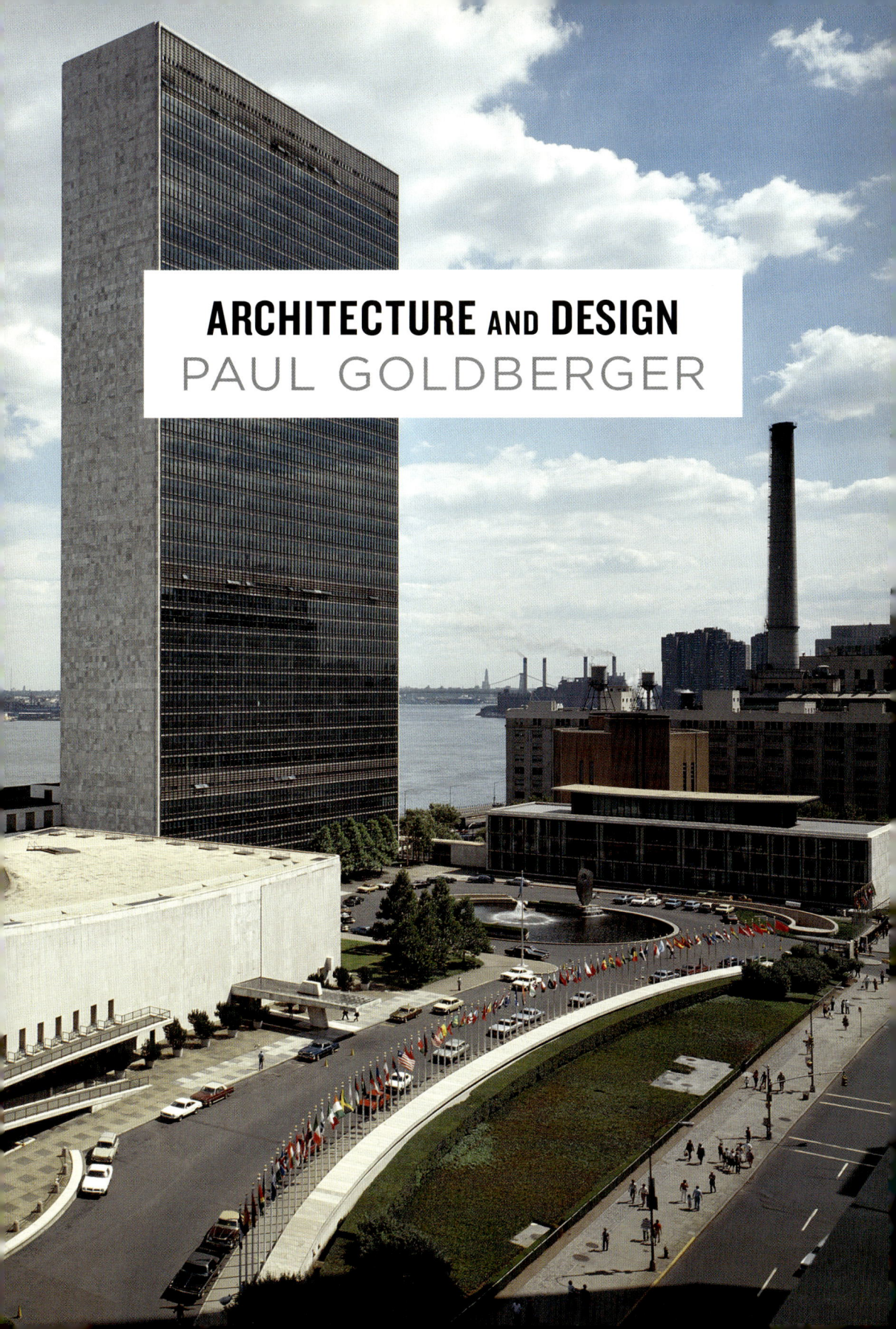

ARCHITECTURE AND DESIGN
PAUL GOLDBERGER

ARCHITECTURE

New York commanded the world in 1945. With London, Tokyo, and Berlin severely damaged and Paris dispirited by years of Nazi occupation, it was poised to become the preeminent city of the second half of the twentieth century. Its architecture and design, however, reflected neither the glorious history of a great European city nor the promise of the future that the world's confidence in it would suggest. The rest of the world may have been prepared to locate the United Nations in New York—a decision that was made in 1946, although the site was not chosen and the buildings were not finished until the early 1950s—but New York itself was not yet ready to be the beacon of the new in architecture and design, even though it had presented a compelling image of the future in its World's Fair of 1939. Wallace K. Harrison's Trylon and Perisphere and Norman Bel Geddes's Futurama exhibition in the General Motors Pavilion suggested that a clean, sleek, streamlined new world was just around the corner.

Like the rest of the United States, New York has always had an attitude toward Modernism that could be described as ambivalent at best. The city's architecture in the immediate postwar period was conventional, and cautious, driven more by economics than by any larger vision. The exuberance that gave rise to New York's great buildings of the 1920s and 1930s, the years that formed the city's iconic skyline, was long gone. The Depression and the war had been more than enough to put at least a temporary end to the zestful competitiveness that had yielded such high-rise buildings as Yasuo Matsui and H. Craig Severance's Bank of Manhattan Building, Clinton & Russell's Cities Service Tower, Raymond Hood's Daily News Building and Rockefeller Center, William Van Alen's Chrysler Building, and Shreve, Lamb & Harmon's Empire State Building. These buildings largely defined the modern skyscraper in New York, and therefore in the world. But by 1945, the Jazz Age, and its accompanying Art Deco and Art Moderne architecture, was clearly over.

What would replace it? Paradoxically, even as New York's power and prominence in the world grew, its architecture reflected a kind of hesitation, as if architects wanted to distance themselves not only from the spirited buildings New York had built in the twenties and thirties but also from the austere European Modernism that had become architecture's avant-garde. The International Style, as Henry-Russell Hitchcock and Philip Johnson named it in their

PRECEDING PAGES: The United Nations Headquarters, 1950, on the East River, with the General Assembly in the foreground and the Secretariat in the background, designed by an international group of architects, planners, and engineers led by Wallace K. Harrison, who served as the director of planning.

OPPOSITE: Completed in 1958, Mies van der Rohe and Philip Johnson's bronze-and-glass Seagram Building was more than the epitome of the International Style; its elegant form became a symbol of New York's postwar aspirations.

From the air, Stuyvesant Town and Peter Cooper Village, 1947, resembled a Modernist abstraction. Like many large-scale postwar high-rise housing developments, they owed a debt to Le Corbusier's "tower in the park" schemes from the 1920s.

celebrated 1932 book and exhibition at the Museum of Modern Art, wasn't truly international, as its manifestations in the United States in 1945 were scarce indeed. Raymond Hood's Daily News and McGraw-Hill buildings, finished in 1930 and 1931, were among the few skyscrapers in New York that had clearly been influenced by the International Style; the same could be said of Philip Goodwin and Edward Durell Stone's original building for the Museum of Modern Art, completed in 1939 (see page 29). There were many prewar apartment houses and shop interiors that also reflected a Modernist sensibility, and apartment towers like the Majestic and the Century, by Irwin Chanin, married a kind of commercial, streamlined Art Moderne style to the classic glamour of New York high-rise living. William Lescaze, a celebrated Swiss architect, relocated to New York and built several handsome modern townhouses that broke crisply with the urban fabric of nineteenth-century New York brownstones. But his most prominent building—indeed, the most important early International Style skyscraper in the United States—was the headquarters of the Philadelphia Saving Fund Society in the rival city of Philadelphia.

Little had been built during the war—Mayer & Whittlesey's 240 Central Park South apartment building, finished in 1940, was one of the few structures of note from those years—and so in 1945, at the beginning of the postwar period, New York looked quite a bit like it had looked in 1939, its architecture dominated not by modern buildings but by traditional ones. New York has always had an eclectic sensibility, and its architects, when they were not displaying Jazz Age gusto, tended toward classical, Renaissance, and Georgian designs. Historical styles were often freely interpreted, not to say mixed and matched, but to one degree or another the influence of the architecture of the past was almost always visible in what New York built in the years before the war.

After 1945, however, that connection to the past was harder to sustain. The postwar world was different, and even if architects had not yet figured out how different it was going to be and how they were going to express that difference, it was hard not to feel that elaborate classical or Italian Renaissance designs were not quite as convincing as they had been before the war. And ornate buildings were expensive in any event. So the architecture of the late 1940s in New York was mostly a kind of hybrid of modern and traditional, masonry buildings that were plainer and less elaborately detailed than their prewar predecessors. The career of the architect Emery Roth exemplifies the change: Roth went from designing apartment houses like the San Remo and the Beresford, with elegant Renaissance detailing crowned by ornate towers, completed a dozen years before the war, to buildings like the Normandie and 880 Fifth Avenue, finished a few years after—still grand, still built of masonry, still formal in tone, but devoid of the opulent details and elaborate crowns that had made the prewar buildings so distinctive. They were typical of many apartment buildings that went up in the late forties, an architectural style that might be thought of as stripped-down classicism, produced as their architects tiptoed into Modernism.

Most of what was built in those years was housing, which the city desperately

The city gradually began to adopt Modernism with the completion of projects such as the Look Building in 1950 by Emery Roth & Sons. The façade's mix of white brick and ribbon windows served as a bridge between prewar masonry and postwar glass.

needed after the war; huge complexes of high-rise towers like Stuyvesant Town and Peter Cooper Village, built by the Metropolitan Life Insurance Company in 1947, brought hesitant Modernism into a new realm. These developments, and numerous others that were built in those years, consisted of red brick slabs set in open space, loosely recalling architect Le Corbusier's "tower in the park" visionary schemes of the 1920s. In New York, Le Corbusier's ideas were diluted into buildings that were conventional in almost every way but their placement—not directly on the street as New York buildings always had been, but in diagonal rows set in wide-open space.

Office construction began more slowly than housing after the war, and there was no call for the very tall towers that had created the skyline before the war and continued to define it for at least another decade. Architects tiptoed into Modernism here, too. Emery Roth's sons, Richard and Julian, who took over their father's firm after his death in 1948, built it into a major presence in New York, beginning with masonry office buildings featuring horizontal strip windows and rounded corners like the Look Building of 1949, then moved in stages through the 1950s to the glass towers that by the 1960s would change the streetscape of Park Avenue and much of the rest of midtown Manhattan. But they produced little of architectural distinction; as with housing, quantity seemed to matter more than quality on the architectural front in New York in 1945, and for quite some time thereafter.

In the early 1950s, however, two major projects brought a level of architectural sophistication to the city that had not been seen since the early thirties: the United Nations complex, produced by

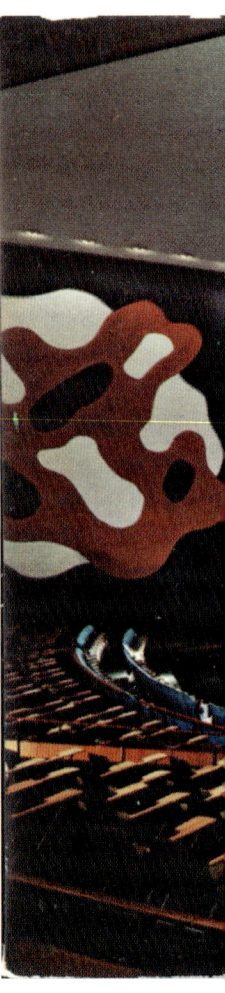

ABOVE: The ceiling of the Trusteeship Council Chamber, designed by Danish architect Finn Juhl in 1952, is a light and vibrant solution for concealing mechanical equipment.

RIGHT: A large, circular auditorium with seating for 850 people, the General Assembly Hall's dramatically canted, semicircular ribbed walls and shallow dome directed the audience's focus onto the Speaker's chair. The mural is by Fernand Léger.

an international committee of architects working under Wallace K. Harrison, and Lever House, the glass skyscraper on Park Avenue by Gordon Bunshaft of Skidmore, Owings & Merrill. When the United Nations was finished in 1950, the unusual, swooping geometric form of the General Assembly Building together with the austere glass slab of the Secretariat Building (see pages 126–27) gave New York the architectural symbol of a new age that it had been lacking—"the long-awaited, triumphant realization of interwar-era Modernist architecture and urbanism," Robert A. M. Stern was to write years later.[1] It was not, to be sure, the pure expression of Le Corbusier's ideas that the architect, who served on the United Nations Board of Design, had hoped for. Though Le Corbusier's sketches had a greater impact on the final plan than the proposals of any other architect, it was highly compromised by the challenges of achieving consensus among the new organization's administration and the committee of architects who constituted the Board of

Design. In addition to Le Corbusier, the group included the Brazilian architect Oscar Niemeyer, Nikolai Bassov of the Soviet Union, and Matthew Nowicki of Poland, among others. The group was contentious, and Harrison, whose official title was Director of Planning for the United Nations, often had trouble holding it together. Le Corbusier was both its most famous member and its most forceful personality, and he and Harrison clashed often, despite the fact that many of the proposals that Harrison made as alternatives to some of Le Corbusier's schemes were themselves derivative of the French architect's ideas.

Whether because of Le Corbusier's imposing presence or because the committee shared his views of Modernism, there was consensus on the basic idea of the United Nations plan, which was to place the offices in a tall glass skyscraper, and meeting and social functions in smaller buildings at the base. No one other than the critic Lewis Mumford seemed to be troubled by the fact

that this configuration made the United Nations bureaucracy and not its assembly hall in effect the dominant symbol, perhaps quite appropriate for the twentieth century but troubling nevertheless. Mumford took further issue with the specific design of the tower, calling the skyscraper an outmoded form designed to maximize land values, and he noted that small floors vertically arranged tended to discourage the easy interactions among employees that occur in horizontally configured office spaces. And if a long, narrow glass slab was going to be built, Mumford wrote in *The New Yorker*, then at the very least it should have been oriented in an east–west direction, not north–south as the Secretariat Building was, so as to spare one of the long sides the impact of the strong western sun in the afternoon.[2]

Mumford anticipated the energy-conscious concerns that would affect architecture a generation after the UN was built. And Le Corbusier did not entirely disagree with him. One of the elements of Le Corbusier's proposals that Harrison rejected was his suggestion that the western façade of the Secretariat have brise-soleils, or concrete grills, which would have blocked the most intense summer sun. And like Mumford, Le Corbusier was never fully comfortable with the site of the United Nations, tightly squeezed between midtown Manhattan and the East River. It was too constrained, he felt, but for a different reason than Mumford. Le Corbusier wanted a more open site not to avoid putting offices in a high-rise tower but to allow even more open space around the tower. He envisioned the UN as an example of a twentieth-century urbanism of slab towers and sculpted architectural forms that would stand not on streets but in open space. To put the UN headquarters "in the very shadow of the skyscrapers of Manhattan is inadmissible," the architect said, and he made it clear that he favored a suburban site.[3] Ultimately he had no choice but to accept the Manhattan site, and he rationalized that the UN headquarters would be less a model city than a "Battle-Post," a compact modern base from which the organization would connect to the rest of the world.

For all its symbolic power as a work of modern architecture, however, the United Nations complex was not in itself enough to embolden the city's architects and real estate developers; their innate sense of caution, not to mention the determination of New York developers to maximize every square foot of rental space, still dominated the city's architectural sensibility. But the UN's presence did create a subtle challenge to New York's architectural culture, and it marked the beginning of a series of attempts, many of them successful, to break out of the standard New York architectural mold.

OPPOSITE: Lever House, completed in 1952 by Gordon Bunshaft of Skidmore, Owings & Merrill, was the first glass-curtain-wall skyscraper on Park Avenue. An abstract composition of two glass slabs, its lightness stood out dramatically amid the masonry structures that were then its neighbors.

RIGHT: Philip Johnson and Mies van der Rohe, the architects of the Seagram Building (see page 128), also took charge of designing Seagram's executive offices in the new building. This office was furnished with the Brno chair, the Barcelona chair, and the Barcelona table, all designed by Mies van der Rohe.

BELOW: Philip Johnson designed the Four Seasons restaurant in the Seagram Building, including the Grill Room. A sculpture by Richard Lippold hangs over the bar. Mark Rothko was commissioned to paint a series of murals for the restaurant. He completed the paintings, known as the Seagram murals, but withdrew from the commission.

Bunshaft's Lever House, the first glass tower built in New York for commercial purposes, was finished two years after the UN, and it demonstrated that Modernism was capable of an elegance, even a refinement, that most New Yorkers had not experienced. The design, a vertical glass slab that appeared to float over a horizontal slab with an open, public ground floor, seemed, even more than the UN, to represent lightness amid New York's heavy masonry cityscape. And more than any other building of its time it suggested that the postwar world of American corporate architecture would be creative, open, and full of light. Though some critics were disappointed by certain elements of the building, such as the quality of the open ground floor, which was originally to have had a garden designed by Isamu Noguchi, or the way in which the building's vertical slab was turned away from Park Avenue, leaving an odd spatial void in the street wall, its status as the most architecturally ambitious postwar office building in New York could not be denied. Only a handful of buildings of equal distinction followed it, however, and as midtown Manhattan was remade through the 1950s, most of the new structures were banal glass office towers that represented economy and practicality more than imagination.

Philip Johnson, left, Ludwig Mies van der Rohe, and Phyllis Lambert, who oversaw design and construction on behalf of her father, Samuel Bronfman, the head of Joseph E. Seagram & Sons.

The most stunning exception to this trend was the Seagram Building by Ludwig Mies van der Rohe and Philip Johnson, which went up diagonally across Park Avenue from Lever House and was finished six years later. A tower of bronze and glass set back from the street on an expansive, inviting plaza, Seagram was elegant in its materials, serene in its proportions, and sumptuous as a presence in the cityscape—the building that more than any other epitomized the potential of the International Style to rise to the level of the sublime. If it had a certain coolness, that could be thought to represent the sensibility of the postwar American corporation—surely as important a factor in shaping New York in the years after 1945 as any other. As expressed in Seagram, this corporate quality was vastly more exalted than in its architecturally less distinguished neighbors. And the extraordinary Four Seasons restaurant by Johnson on the ground floor became the benchmark for modern restaurant design in the same way as the tower was seen as the Platonic version of an International Style skyscraper.

There were no equivalents at the Seagram Building to the compromises made at Lever House. Mies van der Rohe was far more attuned to the subtleties of the urban context than Bunshaft had been, and the owners of the Seagram liquor empire, the Bronfman

family, were determined to spare no expense. Phyllis Lambert, the daughter of chief executive Samuel Bronfman, was an architectural connoisseur (she later became an architect in her own right) and she made the building a personal project, from choosing the architect to observing every detail of design and construction. Her father had initially selected a lesser architect, Charles Luckman, to build the Seagram headquarters, and it was only a disapproving letter from his daughter, who was then living in Paris, that led him to discharge Luckman and invite Lambert to return across the Atlantic and take charge of selecting a more eminent practitioner. Her efforts were to good purpose: though the period brought several other distinguished tall buildings, including One Chase Manhattan Plaza, 140 Broadway, and the Pepsi-Cola Building, all by Skidmore, Owings & Merrill, CBS by Eero Saarinen, and the Kips Bay Plaza and Silver Towers housing complexes by I. M. Pei, no postwar New York skyscraper ever achieved the degree of international acclaim that the Seagram Building did.

OPPOSITE: One Chase Manhattan Plaza, designed by Gordon Bunshaft of Skidmore, Owings & Merrill, 1961.

LEFT: Sculpture by Jean Dubuffet, commissioned for One Chase Manhattan Plaza.

ABOVE: Pepsi-Cola Building (later Olivetti Building, later 500 Park Avenue), also designed by Gordon Bunshaft of Skidmore, Owings & Merrill, 1960.

OVERLEAF: 140 Broadway, 1967, is another Gordon Bunshaft building. In the foreground is Isamu Noguchi's sculpture Cube, *1968.*

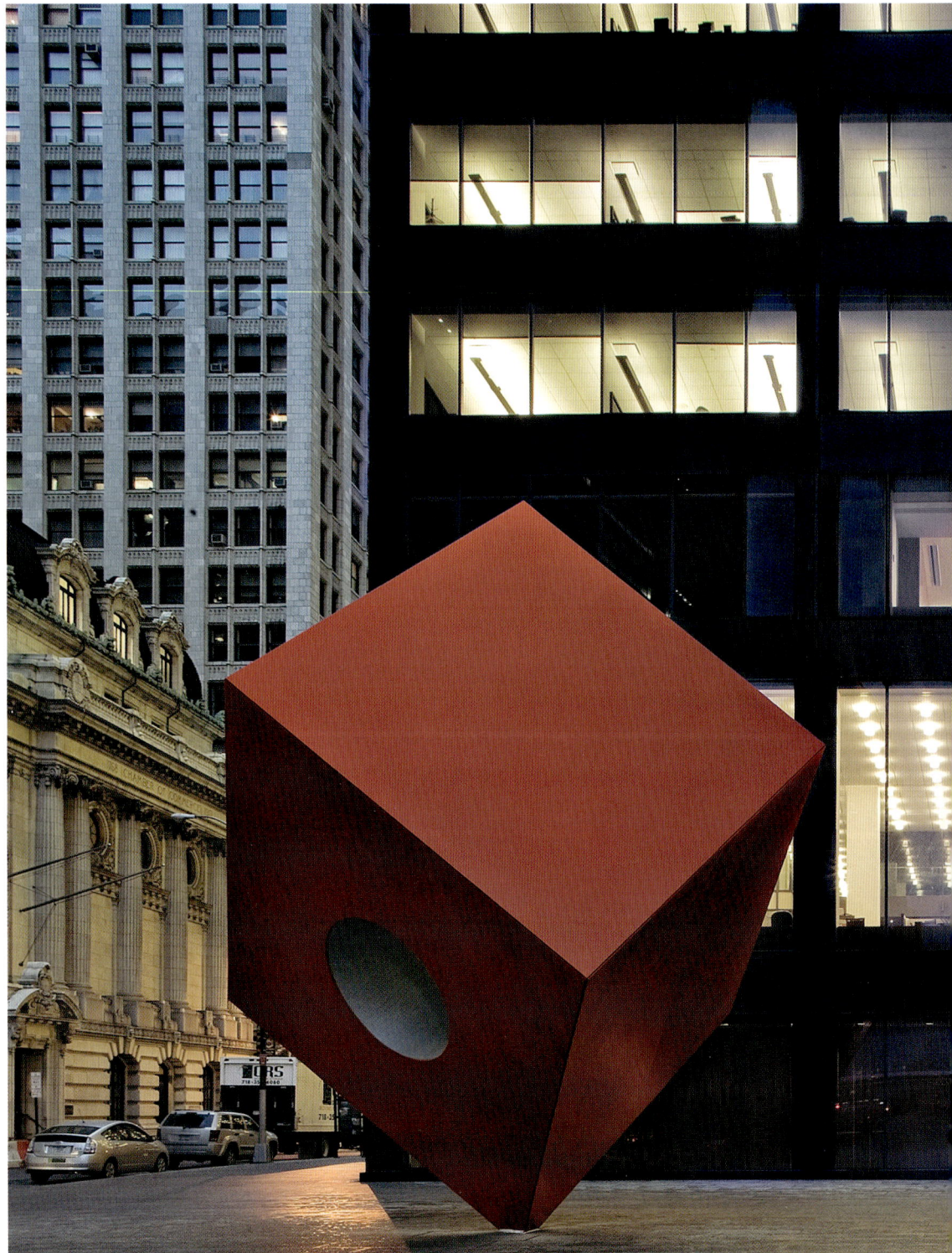

BROWN BROTHERS HARRIMAN

RIGHT: The CBS Building
under construction on the Avenue
of the Americas between 52nd
and 53rd Streets, circumscribed
by a construction fence in CBS's
characteristically elegant typeface.

BELOW LEFT: From above, the edge of
the CBS Building becomes a striking
abstraction.

BELOW RIGHT: Plan of the CBS
Building. Using reinforced concrete columns
on the outside wall brought solidity to the
Modernist tower and an opportunity for
the masonry piers to serve both a structural
and an aesthetic purpose.

OPPOSITE: The CBS Building by Eero
Saarinen, completed in 1965, was the first
reinforced-concrete tower to be built in the
city. With its black granite façade and gray-
tinted windows, it became known as "Black
Rock." Saarinen said he wanted it to be "the
simplest skyscraper in New York."

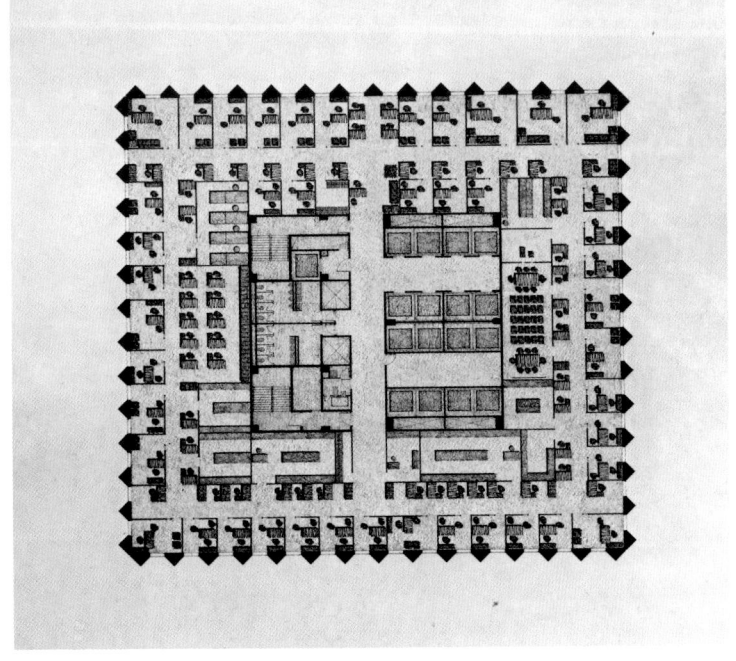

Proposal for the Solomon R. Guggenheim Museum, early rendering, Frank Lloyd Wright, 1944.

The critic Lewis Mumford was quick to see the differences between the Seagram Building and Lever House, not to mention the various lesser buildings that were sprouting up in midtown Manhattan. Mumford, no fan of austere glass buildings, described Seagram as "not just another business building but a singular monument . . . its aloof, aristocratic qualities are not likely to be often repeated in a city where—to resort to that classic confession of the realty financier—'money does not look ahead more than five years.'" Mumford concluded: "This seems to me the best skyscraper New York has seen since Hood's Daily News Building. . . . Lever House looks curiously transitory and ephemeral when one turns from one to the other. Somber, unsmiling, yet not grim, 375 [Park Avenue] is a muted masterpiece—but a masterpiece."[4]

The only other work of architecture in New York in the 1950s to equal the Seagram Building in significance could not have been more different: Frank Lloyd Wright's Guggenheim Museum, which was designed in the late 1940s but not completed until a few months after the architect's death in 1959. If the Seagram Building embodied the modern corporate elegance to which New York aspired, the Guggenheim represented something else altogether: brilliant artistic iconoclasm to some, troubling architectural arrogance to others. Wright's monumental form, in which pictures are hung on what are essentially balconies that spiral around a sky-lit atrium, seemed

neither to fit naturally into the streetscape of Fifth Avenue nor to accommodate easily all of the art that was displayed within it. But it also gave New York a modern interior space of awe-inspiring beauty and power, and both curators and museumgoers came to realize over the years that what it lacked in flexibility it made up in visual excitement and drama, and that its continuous gallery spiraling up and around was, for some kinds of art works, an ideal display space. Visitors could look across the atrium and see several floors of paintings at once, a vista that added a new and unique dimension to large, colorful works, like those of Kenneth Noland or Alexander Calder, to name but two.

It had not been easy to build. It took years to get the New York City Department of Buildings to approve Wright's plans and issue a

Solomon R. Guggenheim Museum by Frank Lloyd Wright, 1959.
RIGHT: *The glass dome above the Guggenheim's dramatic rotunda.*
BELOW: *The central atrium, one of the most striking interior spaces ever built in New York.*
OPPOSITE: *Among the most famous façades in New York, the Guggenheim's spiraling form clearly expresses the circulation ramp that guides visitors through the galleries.*

building permit, which did not come until May 1956, thirteen years after Solomon Guggenheim first hired Wright to build a museum for his collection of modern art in New York. Wright's first plans, completed in 1944, suggested a spiral that narrowed toward the top, like a ziggurat, in one version; another proposed straight sides, so the main section of the building looked roughly like a hexagon; and another drawing from that year suggested a spiral that widened as it ascended, roughly like the museum that was eventually built. It was something of an irony that Wright built the most famous building of his late career in New York, a city that he made almost a fetish of criticizing as too dense, too pressured, too lacking in the open space and open land that he claimed to favor. Wright liked to position himself as being anti-urban, but in fact he took a great deal of pleasure in being in New York, and skillfully used the city's role as the nation's media center to keep his name in front of the public. He used the occasion of the Guggenheim commission to take a long-term lease on suite 223 in the Plaza Hotel, which he kept until his death. The Plaza, designed by Henry Hardenbergh, was one of the only buildings in a traditional style that Wright consistently admired—indeed, it was one of the only buildings designed by an architect other than himself that he freely praised. The suite became his New York residence as well as his office, and Wright even claimed credit for stopping the hotel's management from embarking on an unsympathetic renovation of Hardenbergh's sumptuous, ornately paneled Oak Room, as un-Wrightian an interior as could be imagined.

When the Guggenheim opened, it was greeted with a mix of praise and outrage, and critics and the general public alike were divided about the building. Wright's new museum was "a war between architecture and painting in which both come out badly maimed," wrote John Canaday, the art critic of the *New York Times*.[5] But the paper's architecture critic, Ada Louise Huxtable, felt otherwise. She called the building "an impressive demonstration of modern construction in reinforced concrete at its most imaginative: the open space, the daring cantilevers, the unorthodox building shapes that add up to a spectacular new architecture of great visual excitement." Huxtable did worry, however, that "human and practical considerations were always subordinate to [Wright's] personal work of art."[6] And Lewis Mumford was similarly conflicted. "Those who respond to the interior do proper homage to Wright's genius," he wrote. "What other monumental interior in America produces such an overwhelming effect?" But Mumford went on to call the building "a Procrustean structure; the art in it must be stretched out or chopped off to fit the bed Wright prepared for it."[7]

Time has mellowed opinions on the Guggenheim considerably; despite its practical limitations, within a decade it had become one of New York's most beloved, most admired buildings, and attempts to alter or expand it over the years, even if they have gone forward, have generally been greeted with significant opposition. The same might be said of another museum a few blocks to its south, the new building erected by the Whitney Museum of American Art on Madison Avenue at the corner of 75th Street, designed by Marcel Breuer. A stern structure of dark granite in the shape of an inverted ziggurat, the building seemed, as it neared completion in 1965, to be utterly indifferent to its surroundings, a hostile object in the midst of the most genteel part of New York. Over time, however, the Whitney, too, would become not merely an accepted but a cherished part of the New York streetscape, and several attempts to expand it would be blocked in part on the grounds that they would compromise the integrity of Breuer's compelling design.

So, too, would there be battles to preserve certain other buildings from the 1960s that were viewed as eccentric more than ambitious, like Edward Durell Stone's Gallery of Modern Art at Columbus Circle, finished in 1965, and two buildings designed by Albert Ledner for the National Maritime Union, also finished in

ABOVE: *The Whitney Museum of American Art by Marcel Breuer, completed in 1966, was both an exhilarating and a brutal addition to Madison Avenue: an inverted ziggurat, paired with a sunken sculpture court and framed by sheer walls of concrete.*

OPPOSITE, TOP: *The lobby of the Whitney Museum.*

OPPOSITE, BOTTOM: *Section drawings of the Whitney Museum.*

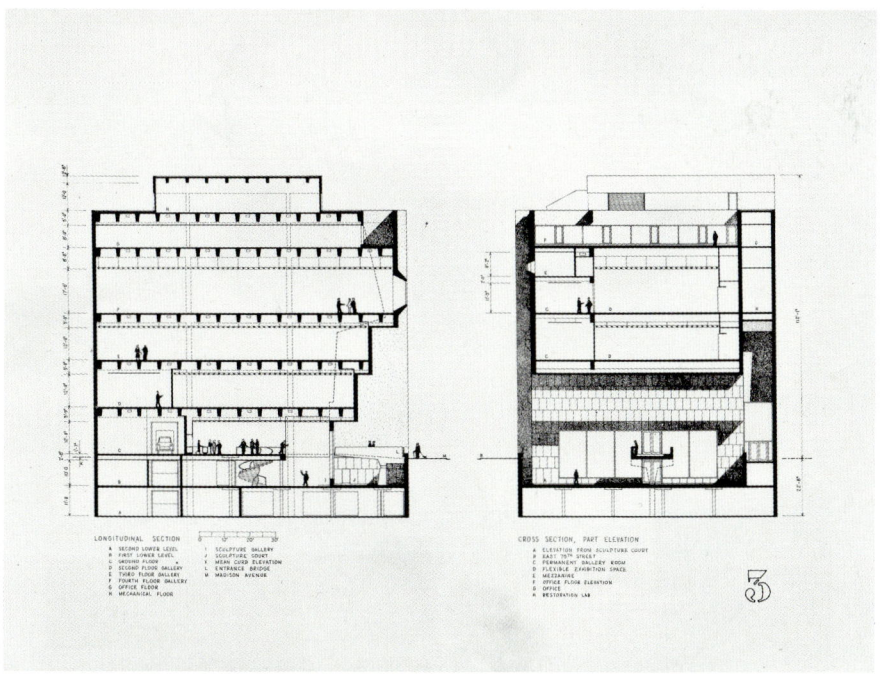

LONGITUDINAL SECTION

A SECOND LOWER LEVEL
B FIRST LOWER LEVEL
C GROUND FLOOR
D SECOND FLOOR GALLERY
E THIRD FLOOR GALLERY
F FOURTH FLOOR GALLERY
G OFFICE FLOOR
H MECHANICAL FLOOR

I SCULPTURE GALLERY
J SCULPTURE COURT
K MEAN CURB ELEVATION
L ENTRANCE BRIDGE
M MADISON AVENUE

CROSS SECTION, PART ELEVATION

A ELEVATION FROM SCULPTURE COURT
B EAST 75TH STREET
C PERMANENT GALLERY ROOM
D FLEXIBLE EXHIBITION SPACE
E MEZZANINE
F OFFICE FLOOR ELEVATION
G OFFICE
H RESTORATION LAB

LEFT: Gallery of Modern Art by Edward Durell Stone, 1965. Commissioned by the A&P heir Huntington Hartford to design a museum for his collection of representational art, Stone produced a memorable eclectic oddity that seemed neither modern nor traditional.

RIGHT: Fifth Avenue Synagogue by Percival Goodman, 1956.

the middle of the decade. The Stone building, designed for Huntington Hartford, heir to the A&P supermarket fortune, was a curious marble palazzo, at once delicate and awkward, its heavy mass balanced on dainty columns, its details alluding vaguely to the architecture of the Near East. If nothing else, its effete quality gave it distinction amid the glass boxes of Midtown, but decades later, attempts to preserve it failed, and it was reconstructed by the architect Brad Cloepfil as the Museum of Art and Design, with little of Stone's façade left. The Ledner buildings, compositions of round portholes meant to evoke ships, were romantic, if thin, attempts to make modern architecture pictorial, and over the years they, too, became familiar and more highly valued than they had been when new. (One of them ultimately became the Maritime Hotel.)

New Yorkers did not, however, show quite so much affection for the architecture of an even more ambitious cultural undertaking that would reach completion in the 1960s—Lincoln Center for the Performing Arts, a complex of six large buildings organized around a central plaza and sheathed in travertine. Lincoln Center was at once a vast urban-renewal project and the nation's first modern cultural center. Though it turned out to have a profound effect on the dynamics of both its Upper West Side neighborhood and the city's cultural environment in general, as a work of architecture it was, for the most part, conservative and dull, the opposite of Frank Lloyd Wright's and Marcel Breuer's different forms of adventurism. The complex was designed by an all-star roster of architects: Wallace K. Harrison, who had been involved in both the United Nations and Rockefeller Center, was tapped to design a new home for the Metropolitan Opera, which was to be the centerpiece; Philip Johnson, Mies van der Rohe's acolyte and his associate on the design of the Seagram Building, took on the New York State Theater, a hall for dance; Max Abramovitz, Harrison's partner, was in charge of a new concert hall for the New York Philharmonic; Eero Saarinen was asked to design the Vivian Beaumont Theater; Gordon Bunshaft was assigned a new branch of the New York Public Library for its collections on the performing arts; and Pietro Belluschi was given charge of the design for the Juilliard School of Music's new home.

It was hard to imagine a more eminent group of practitioners, at least in the United States. But, not unlike the international committee that had worked on the United Nations, the group struggled with the challenge of creating harmony among the individual egos around the table, and for all that the conceptual idea of Lincoln Center represented a bold leap for New York, the architecture that resulted seemed more as if it were a product of the cautiousness of the immediate postwar period. The main buildings by Harrison,

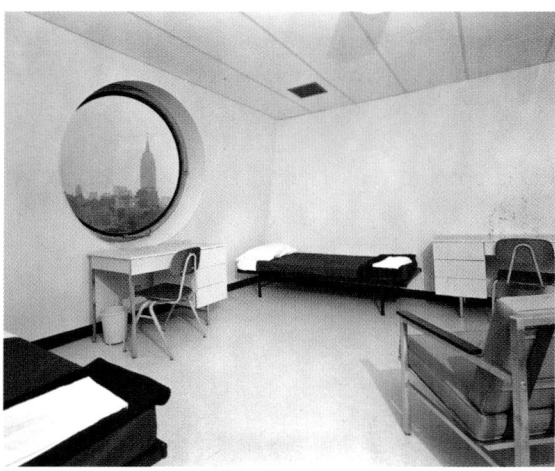

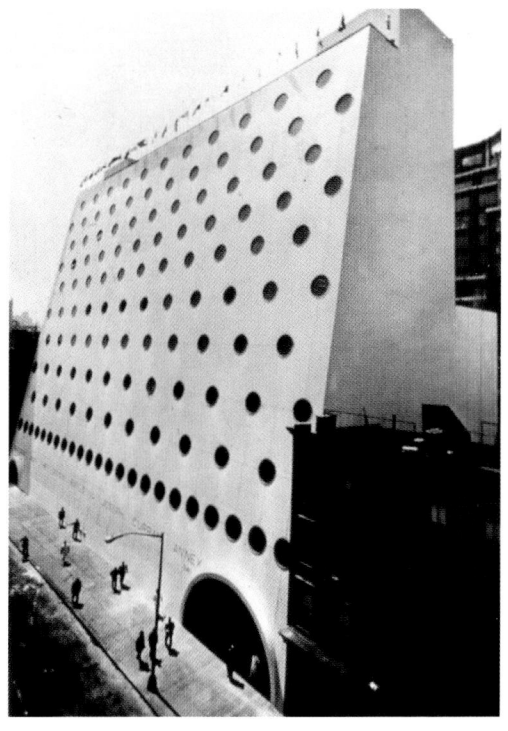

ABOVE: A bedroom in the National Maritime Union building by Albert Ledner, 1966. The building is now the Maritime Hotel.

RIGHT: The exterior of Albert Ledner's National Maritime Union. The porthole windows and sloping façade assured that this building would not be confused with Modernist boxes elsewhere in the city.

Arnold Newman

Portrait of Lincoln Center collaborators with a model of the complex. Left to right: Edward J. Mathews, Philip Johnson, Jo Mielziner, John D. Rockefeller III, Wallace K. Harrison, Eero Saarinen, Gordon Bunshaft, Max Abramovitz, and Pietro Belluschi.

Johnson, and Abramovitz were formal and vaguely classical, and were arranged around three sides of a large public plaza, loosely—very loosely—echoing Michelangelo's design for the Campidoglio on the Capitoline Hill in Rome. The arrangement did yield a superb, even noble, public space, largely designed by Johnson, with a circular fountain in the middle; Lincoln Center Plaza was quickly adopted by New Yorkers, who, especially in the early 1960s, were starved for decent public open spaces other than parks. The plaza at the Seagram Building was still relatively new when Lincoln Center was finished, and New Yorkers were just beginning to discover how much they liked the kind of public squares that might be found in a European city. They were not to get many of them, and none that would surpass Lincoln Center Plaza in scale and quality.

The success of the buildings around the plaza, however, was less clear. All three architects had produced initial schemes that were livelier than the ones that were built, although early versions of both Abramovitz's concert hall and Johnson's theater suggest that these architects' imaginations, left unchecked, did not necessarily yield buildings that would have been better in the long run. The first design for the concert hall had a huge box of glass projecting out from a solid stone mass, while the theater had a rounded façade at one point, and later acquired a somewhat prissy colonnade. Johnson's final version was considerably more dignified, at least on the exterior, with four pairs of columns creating a strong, subtle rhythm. When he began to design the Lincoln Center project, the Seagram Building was just being completed, but Johnson, paradoxically, had already begun to seek a distance from Mies van der Rohe, his primary mentor, and he was actively exploring a kind of modern classicism. Johnson was always the best architectural historian of Lincoln Center's many architects, the most intellectually inclined, and the only one whose inclination was to embrace precedent rather than to see it as an awkward compromise. His efforts yielded the best façade and the most sophisticated interior of the three major buildings, combining a serious understanding of classical precedent with more than a touch of garishness. Johnson's post-Miesian period produced a number of somewhat overblown works, and the theater at Lincoln Center is more restrained than many others. He gave the building a multistoried, grandiose interior space called the Promenade that he clearly wanted to be Lincoln Center's version of the public space in the Paris Opera, and if it struck many as glitzy and overdecorated, it nevertheless was one of the preeminent interiors of its age in the city. His designs for Lincoln Center underscored the extent to which Johnson saw himself not only as one of

New York's most prominent Modernists but also as the city's own *architecte du roi*.

Wallace K. Harrison was more truly the *architecte du roi*, however, as he was the favored architect not only of the Rockefeller family, New York's great philanthropists and builders, but also of the board of the Metropolitan Opera. Harrison had worked on Rockefeller Center in the 1930s, a project that was originally planned to include a new opera house, which he was to have designed; when the opera withdrew, Harrison remained its architect, preparing schemes for multiple sites over the years while working on Rockefeller Center, the United Nations, and numerous other projects.

Lincoln Center had its genesis in Robert Moses's slum-clearance efforts around Lincoln Square on the Upper West Side. Moses, the politically astute planning czar who had been overseeing most of the city's public works projects for decades, enlisted Harrison to interest the Metropolitan in considering his site, then filled with

OPPOSITE: The Promenade in Philip Johnson's New York State Theater (now David H. Koch Theater), a grand room that Johnson envisioned as the contemporary equivalent of the foyer at the Paris Opera: a place to see and be seen, and one of New York's favorite party spaces. The sculptures are by Elie Nadelman.

BELOW: Philharmonic Hall auditorium in its original form, designed by Max Abramovitz with acoustical engineering by Leo Beranek, 1962. The auditorium was subsequently reconstructed twice.

tenements and hardly a natural location for the city's most socially prominent cultural institution. Harrison saw the possibilities and convinced the Metropolitan to move to Lincoln Square in 1955; shortly thereafter, the idea arose of inviting other performing-arts organizations to join, in part to reduce the risk that the opera house would find itself alone in an unwelcoming neighborhood, as it had been since 1883, when its original home opened at Broadway and 39th Street. The idea of moving to Lincoln Square appealed to the New York Philharmonic, which had long played at Carnegie Hall, as a plan to replace Carnegie with an office tower, which was eventually abandoned, then seemed a serious possibility (see page 222). Thus Lincoln Center for the Performing Arts was born. It quickly expanded to include the other institutions, one of which, Lincoln Center Repertory Theater, was to be created specifically to occupy a new building.

Harrison, who had effectively been designing a new opera house for years, plunged enthusiastically into the one for the Lincoln Center site. His first schemes were modern, ranging from a design that bore some resemblance to the United Nations General Assembly Building to another that suggested the as yet unbuilt Sydney Opera House. These and numerous other Modernist essays did not align with the taste of the conservative management of the Metropolitan, and Harrison eventually came up with a version that had a front façade featuring five arches. Even that was not original to Lincoln

BELOW: Members of the Lincoln Center Artists Group pose around a model of Lincoln Center on its future site. Left to right: ballerina Alicia Markova, modern dancer Martha Graham, Juilliard president and composer William Schuman, soprano Lucine Amara, violinist Dorothy Pixley, Metropolitan Opera impresario Rudolf Bing, executive director of operations for the center Alfred Reginald Allen, Philharmonic managing director George E. Judd Jr., conductor and composer Leonard Bernstein, actress Julie Harris, and producer Robert Whitehead.

OPPOSITE: The groundbreaking ceremony for Lincoln Center was held On May 14, 1959. Among the attendees was President Dwight Eisenhower. He holds a shovel beneath a rendering of a proposal for the complex by Hugh Ferriss.

Center, as it was based on Harrison's own design for the Hopkins Center, a performing-arts building at Dartmouth College. The arched scheme, too, went through various iterations—Harrison ultimately produced forty-five versions of the Metropolitan Opera before the final design was achieved—and they represent a clear movement toward more conservative taste, as well as toward a tighter budget. By the time the final version was set, very few of the swooping, modern lines that had marked the early schemes were left. The *New York Times*'s architecture critic, Ada Louise Huxtable, judged the opera house "a sterile throwback . . . a curiously unresolved collision of past and present."[8]

There was considerably less hesitation about modernity in the other buildings of Lincoln Center, located just to the north of the plaza. Bunshaft's library had an entrance that was almost Miesian in its understatement; Saarinen's theater was an elegant composition that balanced a horizontal travertine mass over a glass base. Belluschi created a more active Modernist composition for the Juilliard School, in which the only conspicuously conservative

element was the sheathing in matching travertine. But the tension between the taste of New York's conservative establishment and that of its most prominent architects and designers cast a shadow, at least temporarily, over this portion of the complex as well. A large Henry Moore sculpture had been planned for the reflecting pool in front of Saarinen's theater, which was named in honor of Vivian Beaumont, a philanthropist and former actress, and a black metal sculpture by Alexander Calder, one of the artist's "stabiles," was to go near the entrance to the library. Lincoln Center's open space was technically under the jurisdiction of the New York City Department of Parks, and Newbold Morris, the Parks Commissioner, so disliked modern art that he initially refused to allow the sculptures to be installed. Even though neither piece represented the avant-garde of the age—by the mid-1960s both Moore and Calder were artists of the establishment, not the cutting edge—in

Model of the proposed auditorium of the Vivian Beaumont Theater, Eero Saarinen, 1965.

Morris's view, abstract art of any kind had no place in public space. His position was not shared by the rest of the city administration, however, and eventually the art was approved.

As widely successful as Lincoln Center's public plaza space was considered to be, it existed as a thing apart from the city, in effect an elevated platform removed from the surrounding streets. In the parlance of the day, it was a "superblock," which planners in the late 1950s often saw as a welcome alternative to the dense, crowded web of the existing city streets. A superblock was a chance to transcend the old by sweeping away the gridded pattern of streets and building a new kind of city on top of it—a city that would accommodate the automobile far more comfortably than the nineteenth-century layout of Manhattan could. Though Lincoln Center's plaza was welcoming to pedestrians, it sat atop parking garages and driveways for vehicle drop-offs, which raised it to a level some distance above the street. On its north and west sides, the complex presented not an inviting, open face to pedestrians, but a solid wall.

Lincoln Center may not have been typical of postwar New York architecture, but it came into existence in precisely the same way as almost every other urban-renewal project in those years: several blocks of old tenements and brownstones were condemned by public

ABOVE: Alexander Calder standing in front of the Library for the Performing Arts with a model of his stabile Le Guichet *(the ticket window), which would be installed in the same location.*

OVERLEAF: Eero Saarinen broke away from the classicism of the main buildings of the complex in his design for the Vivian Beaumont Theater, finished in 1965. Tucked beside it is Gordon Bunshaft's Lincoln Center Performing Arts Library and Museum. In the foreground is Henry Moore's sculpture Reclining Figure, *1965.*

*Juilliard School building, Pietro Belluschi,
1969. Belluschi retained the travertine of
the other Lincoln Center buildings but, like
Saarinen, departed from classicism, in this case
toward a more brutalist design.*

officials who took the view that troubled neighborhoods of the city
were unsalvageable; the land was taken over by a government agency;
and the buildings and streets that had been there were razed, to be
replaced, most of the time, by tall buildings set in open space. The
majority of the new buildings were high-rise housing complexes; a
few were institutional, like Fordham University, whose Manhattan
campus was built adjacent to Lincoln Center; and on rare occasions
the land was put to a cultural purpose, like Lincoln Center. It was
widely believed, at least during the 1950s, that whatever type of new
buildings were constructed, the wholesale removal of the existing
urban fabric would yield a cleaner, healthier, and safer city than trying
to fix up what was already there. And few people believed this with
more conviction than Robert Moses, who referred to the entire West
Side of Manhattan as "dismal and decayed." Moses began an ambitious series of "slum clearance" projects, a more honest term, surely,
than the euphemism "urban renewal."⁹

Besides Lincoln Center, few of these projects had much architectural significance, but the removal of old-fashioned streets and the smaller buildings that lined them had a major impact on the feel of neighborhoods, and hence on the culture of the city. In almost every case, planners and public officials attempted to justify the removal of the urban fabric by the desire to make a greater accommodation to vehicular traffic—narrow city streets, many planners thought, were choking the city, and the city would only continue to be viable if it could make itself, in effect, more like the suburbs. Thus New York, like many other cities, built highways through its dense core, often destroying existing neighborhoods in the process.

In the late 1950s, Moses proposed extending Fifth Avenue right through Washington Square Park to speed the flow of traffic downtown, a plan that might have passed without objection had the park been anywhere but in the heart of Greenwich Village, the historic neighborhood of townhouses and tree-lined blocks

Alice Tully Hall, Lincoln Center's chamber music hall, was set within the Juilliard building. It would later be redesigned by Diller Scofidio + Renfro.

Jane Jacobs at a press conference of the Committee to Save the West Village, 1961.

that had long been a home to many of the city's artists, writers, and civic activists, some of whom were already fighting Moses's plan to level some of its old townhouse blocks to make way for new high-rise buildings. A leader of the protesters was a Village resident named Jane Jacobs, who lived on Hudson Street and was a writer on the staff of *Architectural Forum.* Jacobs and her neighbors, many of whom were also mothers whose children played in the park, succeeded not only in stopping Moses's plan to bisect Washington Square Park but also in convincing the city to limit the demolition of old Village blocks to a fraction of the number Moses had originally intended to tear down. Jacobs had come to believe that the very premise on which most urban renewal was based—the destruction of the existing urban fabric—was fundamentally wrong, that the profession of city planning had no understanding of how cities really worked, and that most of the things architects and planners were doing to postwar cities were counterproductive. Streets were built for pedestrians, she argued, not for cars, and the success of an urban neighborhood depends largely on what kind of a pedestrian life it can engender, not in how convenient it may be for automobiles to pass through. Her own quarter of Greenwich Village was a disorganized, chaotic mess to planners who valued only order and clarity, but the reality was that it was a vibrant and economically healthy neighborhood with a welcome diversity and human scale, she said.

Jacobs put her ideas into a book called *The Death and Life of Great American Cities,* published in 1961, which argued that the low-rise brownstones and tenements of old urban neighborhoods, far from being a blight, were often far more conducive to successful

communities than the austere towers in open space that were replacing them. Jacobs's views came to be thought of as the antithesis of Robert Moses's, and her book played a key role in setting in motion a paradigm shift in attitudes toward planning and design. In the 1950s there were few critics of the bulldoze-and-rebuild approach to cities, and progressive liberals were often its leaders. Urban renewal was viewed as the design and construction component of social-welfare programs, as another of the ways in which a strong government could intervene to help the needy. By the mid-sixties, however, the tide was beginning to turn, due in significant part to Jacobs's writing. Many of Moses's later projects, including a particularly egregious proposal to cut a highway through lower Manhattan that would have decimated the old industrial neighborhood later known as SoHo, lost almost all citizen support and never went forward. (Jane Jacobs herself, committing an act of civil disobedience in protest against the Lower Manhattan Expressway, destroyed the records of the stenographer who was recording a public hearing about the project.)

Moses did manage to pull off one major architectural production in the mid-sixties, the New York World's Fair of 1964–65 in Flushing Meadows, Queens, the same site as the 1939 fair. He was given charge of the fair in part as a way of easing him out of his role as the city's urban-renewal czar, but in his new role he seemed no more inclined toward advanced thinking about planning and design than he had been in his slum-clearance projects. Indeed, Moses seemed to take pride in the fact that other than the layout, a virtual duplicate of the previous fair, the 1964–65 fair had almost no planning at all. And its architecture was a cacophonous

mix of different styles, sizes, and building types, ranging from a faux Belgian village to a Ferris wheel in the shape of a gargantuan automobile tire to a low, wide dome that was suspended from pipes set in the pattern of a spiral. There was no equivalent to the striking Trylon and Perisphere that had served as the architectural symbol of the 1939 fair and given it an aura of innovative design; the symbol of the later fair was as conventional as its motto of "Peace Through Understanding": the Unisphere, a vast globe made up of an open framework of steel. Moses, eager to see the fair make a profit, set high rental rates for individual pavilions, which had the result of encouraging large corporations to participate and reducing the number of American states and foreign nations. In some ways the fair felt like a sequence of corporate logos translated into buildings, and it was widely criticized as emphasizing commerce over the cultural values that many other world's fairs had at least aspired to.

There were some architectural high points, however. Philip Johnson and Richard Foster designed the New York State Pavilion as a monumentally scaled, open structure in the shape of an ellipse, with the world's largest suspended roof, made of translucent

OPPOSITE, TOP: Section drawing of the IBM Pavilion, designed by Eero Saarinen, 1964.

OPPOSITE, BOTTOM: Through the combined efforts of Eero Saarinen, who designed the egg-shaped theater structure, and Charles and Ray Eames, who created the exhibitions, the IBM Pavilion was the fair's most successful integration of a building and its contents.

plastic panels. It was complemented by a composition of three circular observation towers, the tallest of which reached 226 feet, and a circular theater. The pavilion managed to be at once fanciful and dignified, a difficult combination to pull off, but Johnson's eagerness to push the boundaries of prim taste, which caused some controversy over the interior of his New York State Theater, was well suited to the festive environment of a world's fair. Eero Saarinen conceived the design for the fair's other architectural success, the IBM Pavilion, which consisted of an enormous, egg-shaped structure perched atop a forest of tree-like columns. Visitors sat on bleachers that ascended from the ground through the columns into the egg, where they saw a film about the strange new world of computers by Charles and Ray Eames, Saarinen's longtime collaborators.

Most of the other memorable elements of the fair involved exhibitions, not buildings: the Johnson Wax Pavilion, which offered a film projected on a three-part screen called "To Be Alive";

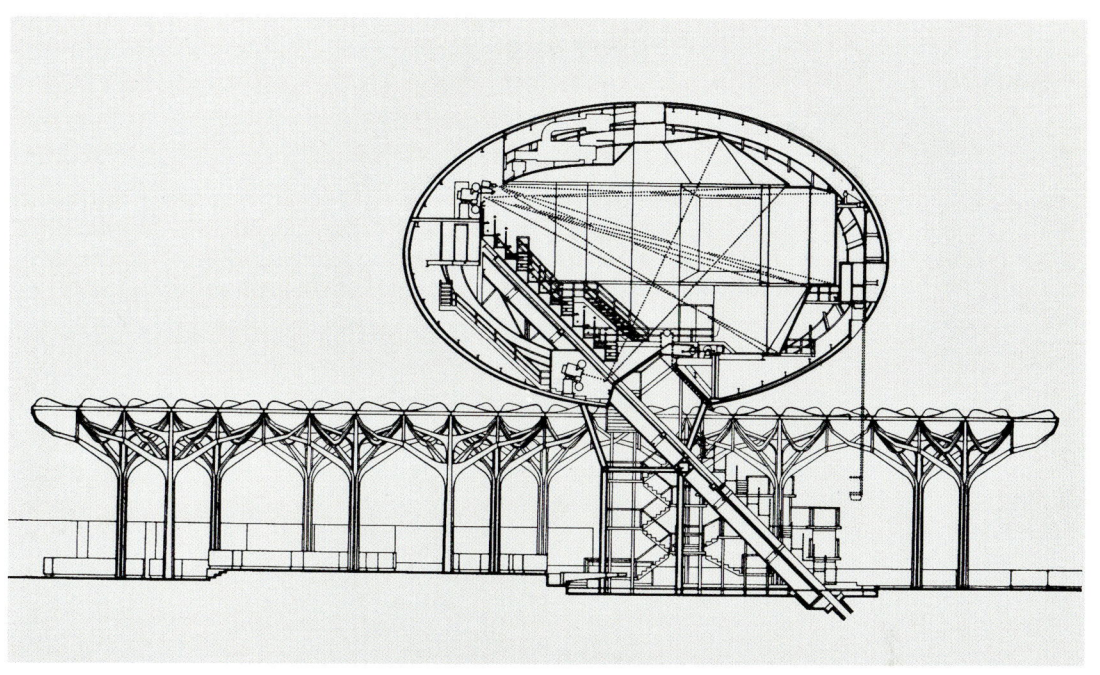

Pepsi-Cola's pavilion, where "It's a Small World" so delighted children that it eventually became a permanent part of Disneyland; and the Spanish Pavilion, known not for its architecture but for its elegant restaurant. In 1939, visitors to the General Motors Pavilion saw designer Norman Bel Geddes's spectacular vision of the future—a new world of expressways and high-rise buildings—but in 1964, neither General Motors nor anyone else presented as compelling and vivid a work of design. In some ways the most notable piece of design that most people saw for the first time at the fair was the Touch-Tone telephone.

Though the 1964–65 fair was neither the financial success that Moses had promised nor as architecturally and culturally noteworthy as the city might have hoped it would be, it did serve as a welcome distraction from pressing problems outside the fair's gates. Despite its increasingly prominent position as a world financial center and, thanks to the United Nations, a de facto world capital, New York was struggling. Many of the city's neighborhoods had been deteriorating for years as middle-class citizens moved to the suburbs and jobs often went with them. Whereas in 1945 few questioned whether there was any better place to do business than in Manhattan, by the late 1950s, the city seemed to many people to have become dirty, overbuilt, pressured, expensive, and even dangerous. In a celebrated series of columns in *The New Yorker* called "The Roaring Traffic's Boom," Lewis Mumford, the magazine's architecture critic, wrote that if the city "ceases to be a milieu in which people can exist in reasonable contentment instead of as prisoners perpetually plotting to escape a concentration camp, it will be unprofitable to discuss its architectural achievements. . . . For a whole generation, New York has become steadily more frustrating and tedious to move around in, more expensive to do business in, more unsatisfactory to raise children in, and more difficult to escape from for a holiday in the country."[10] Mumford's complaint was not only that there was too much traffic, but also that there were too many big buildings, too close together. He complained about the way Robert Moses had rebuilt the city to accommodate automobile traffic and also about the way real estate developers had tried to squeeze more and more skyscrapers into the already dense quarters of downtown and midtown Manhattan. Mumford, a longtime advocate of decentralization, was the anti-Moses *and* the anti-Jacobs, rolled into one.

Many of the city's largest corporations decamped to suburbia, where they built sprawling new headquarters, often amid landscaped gardens. Yet somehow the exodus to the suburbs seemed to do little to slow the tide of new construction in the city, where the towers continued to sprout, gradually through the fifties and at an

Manhattan House, designed by Skidmore, Owings & Merrill and Mayer & Whittlesey, 1950. The mother of all white brick apartment houses, the massive Manhattan House is actually a much more subtle pale gray brick. This full-block slab in a garden was an ambitious attempt to evolve a new design vocabulary for large-scale postwar luxury housing.

even greater pace in the sixties. Besides the work of Mies van der Rohe, Skidmore, Owings & Merrill, Eero Saarinen, and Harrison & Abramovitz, most of the new skyscrapers were banal glass boxes, many designed by Emery Roth & Sons, an architectural firm whose ambition seemed to decline with each succeeding generation. The aluminum building at 666 Fifth Avenue by Carson & Lundin was a rare exception to the plethora of glass; a favored witticism was that it was "the box that the Seagram Building came in."

The ensemble of ordinary buildings in a city often sets its tone far more than its individual pieces of architecture, and so the banal glass towers of the fifties and sixties came to define postwar New York, along with their residential counterpart, apartment blocks of white brick. If the mediocre office buildings of the age had the Seagram Building as a kind of aspirational model, the New York apartment houses of the time emulated Manhattan House, designed by Skidmore, Owings & Merrill and completed in 1950. But, just as the Seagram Building remained an island of distinction amid the many glass office towers that followed it, Manhattan House stood nearly alone among white brick (or, in its case, pale gray brick) postwar apartment houses.

DESIGN

Inside Manhattan House, the architect Gordon Bunshaft designed an apartment for himself and his wife that exemplified the trend for architects to take on the challenge of residential interiors. It was warmly austere, with classic furniture such as Mies van der Rohe's Barcelona chairs and a travertine floor and concealed lighting. Philip Johnson, John Bedenkapp, Armand Bartos, Edgar Kaufmann Jr., and Arthur Drexler, among other architects, designed notable modern apartments in the later fifties and early sixties, which, like Bunshaft's, attempted to combine a crisp Modernist sensibility with a degree of comfort and elegance. Around the same time, the furniture designer Ward Bennett created an apartment for himself in the storied, nineteenth-century Dakota that was at once minimalist and highly sensual, an experiment in proving that simplicity need not be either plain or cold.

Both the glass office towers and the white brick apartment houses were, in a sense, the architecture of *Mad Men*, the television drama that half a century later revived interest in the slim, sleek look of the 1960s, a look that was reflected in graphic design, furniture design, and interiors, as well as in the architecture of the

The architect Gordon Bunshaft and his wife, Nina, moved into Manhattan House when the building opened and Bunshaft designed his apartment's interior.

ABOVE: Living room of the Mrs. John D. Rockefeller III Guest House, designed by Philip Johnson, 1950. A Mies-inspired version of a courtyard-facing Roman villa, the guest house is an urban counterpoint to Johnson's celebrated Glass House in New Canaan, Connecticut, of 1949.

OPPOSITE, TOP: La Fonda armchair, designed by Charles and Ray Eames, 1961, for La Fonda del Sol restaurant, in the Time-Life Building.

OPPOSITE, BOTTOM: Good Design Exhibition, Museum of Modern Art, curated by Edgar Kaufmann Jr., 1953.

period. Gone was any hint of 1930s-style opulence, Art Moderne, streamlining, and other trends that had lingered through the 1940s. The thin, light quality of the glass architecture of the period called for thinner and lighter furniture, thinner and lighter products, and thinner and lighter graphic design, often punctuated by a certain flashiness and dazzle. Voluptuousness may have been in fashion in models and actresses, but not in furniture and objects. The cars of the 1950s, though not designed in New York, embodied the look of the era: they seemed to be made more of surfaces than of volumes, and the fins that sprouted out of them toward the end of the decade were a kind of exclamation point, a way of making the thinness flashy and more exciting.

Design was not only evolving in the late forties and early fifties but was also moving out of the rarefied precincts of a handful of sophisticated patrons' homes and architects' offices and inching into the mainstream. The Museum of Modern Art played a significant role in popularizing modern design, both by collecting and exhibiting modern furniture that was available in the marketplace and by presenting a series of exhibitions of what its curators considered well-designed consumer products. The museum's

Department of Industrial Design—its very existence an unusual statement for an art museum—was headed by Edgar Kaufmann Jr., whose father had commissioned Frank Lloyd Wright to build Fallingwater, his celebrated house in Bear Run, Pennsylvania, in 1937. A decade later, in 1947, Kaufmann was working at the Museum of Modern Art on an annual series of exhibitions called *Useful Objects*, which, he explained to the museum's director, René d'Harnoncourt, in a memorandum, "will be arbitrarily limited to 100 objects in order to emphasize our interest in the highest quality of design, and in the belief that participation in a limited show will be considered an honor tantamount to a prize award."[11] Kaufmann defined good design as "a thorough merging of form and function . . . revealing a practical, uncomplicated, sensible beauty."[12] He set a price ceiling of $100 on the objects included in the exhibition to underscore the pieces' accessibility to the general public, or at least to that portion of the public that could spend

up to $100 on a household object in 1947. Earlier iterations of the exhibition had grouped objects in price categories, starting as low as $5.00.

By 1953, the name of the show had been changed to *Good Design*, and that year it included, among other objects, a washing machine designed by Henry Dreyfuss; a dining table with a plywood and white linoleum top by Darrell Landrum; and chairs by Charles and Ray Eames. The criteria for selection, the catalogue stated, were "eye-appeal, function, construction and price, with emphasis on the first."[13] Kaufmann's price ceiling no longer held, but many of the two hundred objects in the exhibition were of modest cost. Inclusion in the show had become a valued stamp of approval for

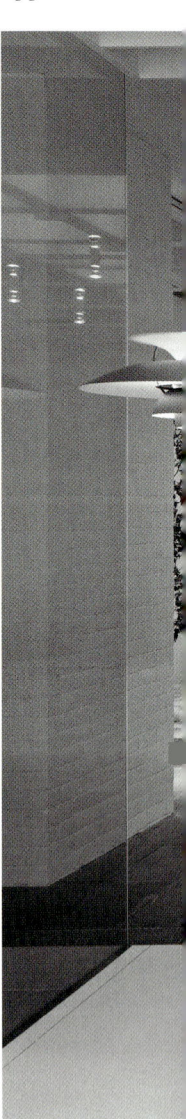

ABOVE: Kitchenwares department of D/R International, the second Design Research store in New York, designed by Ben Thompson and Paul Dietrich, 1963.

RIGHT: Georg Jensen showroom, designed by Warren Platner, 1968.

manufacturers and designers, who submitted eight thousand items in 1953 for the museum to consider. Besides furniture and lamps, there were floor coverings, fabrics, kitchen and cleaning equipment, and household appliances and accessories.

The museum was eager to promote the sale of its favored objects, and it did so both through cooperative arrangements with department stores and through its own retail store, which expanded its merchandise far beyond books and postcards. But there were other establishments, too, that spread the gospel of modern design in New York in the 1950s: the Swedish media conglomerate Bonniers brought an elegant Scandinavian sensibility to Madison Avenue, much as Georg Jensen had brought to Fifth Avenue. (If

there was any region of the world whose design aesthetic had a profound influence on New York's sensibility in the fifties and sixties, it was Scandinavia.) More wide-ranging than either Bonniers or Georg Jensen, however, was Design Research, or D/R, founded by the architect Benjamin Thompson in Cambridge, Massachusetts, in 1953. Thompson opened a D/R in New York in 1959, where the store sold modern furniture, fabrics, and household objects, all chosen by Thompson and his colleagues. D/R was initially so successful that Thompson moved it to larger and more prominent quarters in 1963.

The furniture company Knoll, founded in New York in 1938 by Hans Knoll, a German-born furniture maker, was perhaps the most prominent manufacturer in those years to embody the same broad, modern sensibility as D/R, which sold many of its products. Knoll became a significant force in design in the postwar era, producing furniture by, among others, the Danish-born designer Jens Risom; Eero Saarinen, whose "Tulip Chair" for Knoll became a classic; Marcel Breuer; Harry Bertoia; and Florence Schust Knoll, a Cranbrook Academy–educated designer who became Hans Knoll's wife and whose celebrated line of sofas and chairs with tufted upholstery and thin metal legs became a fixture in many modern offices. In the early 1960s Florence Knoll, by then Florence

Florence Knoll Bassett and Eero Saarinen.

LEFT: Executive office in CBS Headquarters, designed by Florence Knoll Bassett, ca. 1962.

BELOW: CBS president Frank Stanton's office, designed by Florence Knoll Bassett, 1964.

ABOVE: Knoll Showroom, designed by Florence Knoll Bassett, 1951.

OPPOSITE: Bertoia Side Chair, Harry Bertoia, 1952 (top left); Tulip Chair, Eero Saarinen, 1956 (top right); Pretzel Chair, George Nelson, 1952 (center left); Marshmallow Sofa, George Nelson, 1956 (center right); Coconut Chair, George Nelson, 1955 (bottom left); Risom Lounge Chair, Jens Risom, 1943 (bottom right).

Knoll Bassett, was given total charge of the interior design for Saarinen's new building for CBS, which on its completion in 1965 was probably as pure an example of the modern commercial design of its time as ever existed. Many of the early Knoll pieces were explorations of new manufacturing possibilities such as bent plywood or, in the case of Saarinen, plastic. And they often used minimal materials—such as the webbed seats on Risom's lounge chairs—that took the place of conventional upholstery.

Knoll's chief competitor, the Michigan-based Herman Miller Co., was equally influential in the rise of modern post-war design, largely because of the architect and writer George Nelson, who became the company's director of design in 1945

OPPOSITE: George Nelson's clocks were among the defining objects of the postwar design era. Top to bottom: Popsicle Stick Clock, 1950; Block Clock, 1947; Turbine Clock, 1958; Ball Clock, 1947.

ABOVE: A selection of George Nelson Pendant Lamps.

and brought Charles and Ray Eames, Harry Bertoia, Richard Schultz, and Isamu Noguchi into the fold. The company was best known for its Eames designs, but Nelson himself created a number of successful designs for benches, coffee tables, sofas, and chairs that Herman Miller produced. Nelson would also design a series of wall clocks such as the Ball Clock, the Sunburst Clock, and the Popsicle Stick Clock that have come to embody the aesthetic of the late fifties and early sixties as well as any piece of furniture.

When Thompson expanded Design Research, he took over a five-story, nineteenth-century townhouse on East 57th Street, opening up its interior to create a series of double-height spaces and mezzanines. He was far from the first architect to experiment with Modernist store design in New York. Morris Lapidus, who later achieved fame with his flamboyant Miami Beach hotels, designed numerous stores in New York; several of Lapidus's projects from the 1940s were notable for their use of curving glass,

BELOW: Front entrance to Bond's flagship store, Fifth Avenue, designed by Morris Lapidus, 1948.

OPPOSITE: Summit Hotel, designed by Morris Lapidus, 1961.

deeply recessed doors to enhance the size of the display windows, and large neon signs in striking Modernist fonts. The architects Morris Ketchum and Jose A. Fernandez were even more prolific than Lapidus in bringing modern design to the city streets, and to the scale of the pedestrian, with projects like Wallachs men's store on Fifth Avenue of 1955, designed by Ketchum, which had a large, open staircase in the middle and wide-open windows facing the street, or his Plymouth Shop on lower Broadway of 1948. A far grander work of modern design was Victor Lundy's

OPPOSITE: Wallachs Men's Store, Fifth Avenue, designed by Ketchum, Giná & Sharp, 1955.

ABOVE: Main staircase, Wallachs Men's Store.

LEFT: I. Miller, designed by Victor Lundy, 1961. The women's shoe emporium had an immense scale and yet was moody and intimate, almost sacred in appearance.

ABOVE: An interior conference center in the Institute of International Education, the great Finnish architect Alvar Aalto's only project in New York, 1964.

I. Miller shoe shop of 1961, at Fifth Avenue and 57th Street, an almost cathedral-like composition of wooden ribs, fabric, and mirrors that Olga Gueft, editor of *Interiors*, called "brilliantly original and a total integration of space, structure and mood."[14]

Less lofty in its physical form than the I. Miller shop, but perhaps more lofty in its aspirations, was an unusual interior space completed in 1964 by Alvar Aalto, the only work of the great Finnish architect in New York, for the Institute of International Education. A suite of conference rooms in a nondescript office building across from the United Nations, Aalto's interior, commissioned by Edgar Kaufmann Jr., was also based on wooden ribs, but in this case they were arranged in a reserved composition of birch rods, clustered to evoke trees. It was less spectacular than Lundy's shoe shop, but considerably more subtle.

ABOVE: Display pedestals in the Olivetti showroom and store, designed by Banfi, Belgiojoso, Peressutti & Rogers, 1954.

OPPOSITE: The store was known for its public typewriter on an outdoor pedestal.

Ten years earlier, in 1954, the Italian firm of Banfi, Belgiojoso, Peressutti & Rogers created one of Fifth Avenue's most memorable retail spaces, the showroom and store for the Olivetti Corporation, the Italian maker of office equipment, which was seeking to enhance its American presence. The architects gave Olivetti a high, elegant space with an open glass front, colorful Venetian-glass pendant lighting, a seventy-foot-long wall sculpture by Costantino Nivola, and display pedestals of dark green marble that rose in an unbroken curve from the green marble floor, as if portions of the floor had turned into tiny mountains. One of the pedestals was placed outside the front door with an Olivetti typewriter permanently mounted on it, inviting passersby to sample typing on it themselves. The poet Frank O'Hara, who worked nearby at the Museum of Modern Art, used the Olivetti display typewriter to type several of his poems. "Often this poet, strolling through the noisy splintered glare of a Manhattan noon, has paused at a sample Olivetti to type up thirty or forty lines of ruminations," O'Hara wrote on the jacket copy of his book *Lunch Poems*.[15]

Nineteen fifty-four was a good year for architect-designed retail spaces in New York, as it also marked the completion of a remarkable automobile showroom by Frank Lloyd Wright, intended for a Jaguar dealership but ultimately used to sell Porsches and, later, Mercedes-Benzes. Wright placed the cars on a curving ramp—shades of the soon-to-be-built Guggenheim Museum—although the result was far from the spectacular space it might have been, because all Wright had to work with was the low-ceilinged ground floor of an office building on Park Avenue.

The most important retail design of the entire period opened that year as well, and it was not, technically speaking, a shop, but a bank: Gordon Bunshaft's design for the Manufacturer's Trust

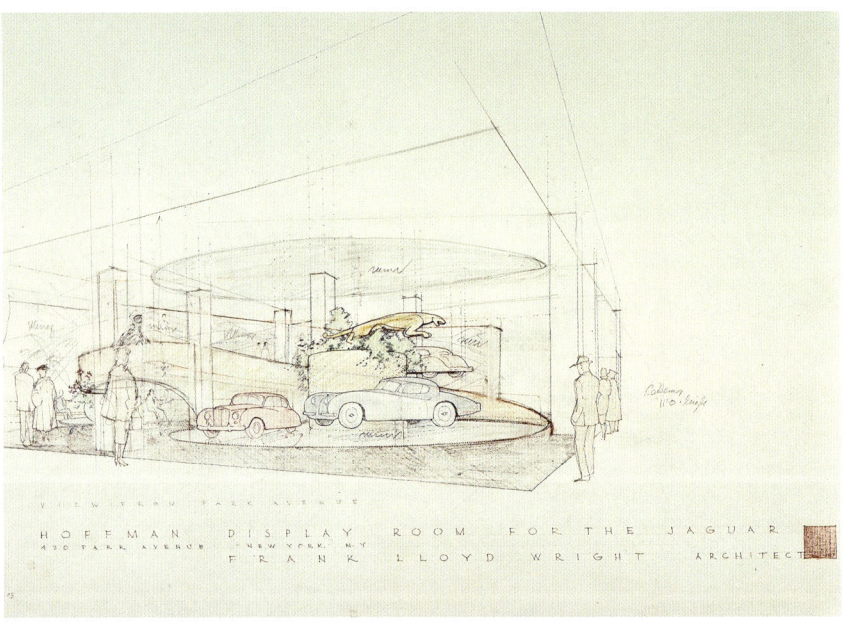

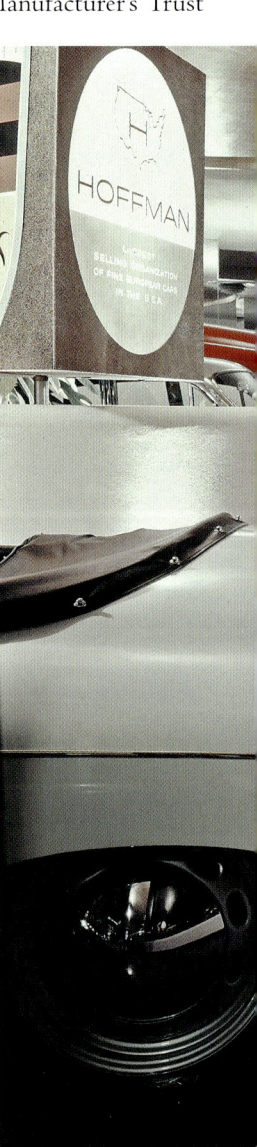

ABOVE: Concept drawing for the Maximilian Hoffman (later Mercedes-Benz) showroom, designed by Frank Lloyd Wright, 1954.

RIGHT: By placing the cars on a spiraling ramp, Wright gave the vehicles a sense of movement and the interior a dynamic energy.

Company at the corner of Fifth Avenue and West 43rd Street, an exceptionally elegant, four-story glass box. In an age when most banks were solid masonry buildings designed to give the impression of security, Bunshaft went in the opposite direction, deliberately making the bank resemble a retail establishment, and a most modern, open one at that. "We had the idea that it was time to get the banks out of mausoleums," Bunshaft's partner Louis Skidmore was quoted as saying.[16] But this bank was far more refined than the typical retail shop, with a sixty-foot-high glass curtain wall on the exterior and a decorative screen designed by Harry Bertoia on the main banking floor, which, in the manner of a Renaissance palace's *piano nobile*, was elevated one floor

ABOVE: Manufacturer's Trust Company, designed by Gordon Bunshaft of Skidmore, Owings & Merrill, 1954. The "crystal lantern," as Lewis Mumford would describe it, replaced solidity with transparency, signaling the end of the notion of the bank as a traditional structure of masonry.

RIGHT: Harry Bertoia's sculptural screen Golden Arbor, 1954, was designed for the interior of the Manufacturer's Trust Company. It is made of eight hundred intersecting panels of brass, copper, and nickel.

OPPOSITE: The Manufacturer's Trust Company vault, designed by Henry Dreyfuss, 1954, served both sculptural and functional purposes, identifying the building as a bank and suggesting that a glass bank could still be secure.

above the street. The elegant proportions and modest size of the building made glass architecture far more appealing than it was in tall skyscrapers. But the pièce de résistance of the interior was an enormous safe designed by Henry Dreyfuss. Set right behind the window on Fifth Avenue, in full view of passersby, it served at once as a reminder to the uncertain that this was a bank, as a sculptural element to the initiated, and as a source of comfort to patrons who might feel uneasy trusting their funds to bankers in a glass house.

Buildings like the Manufacturer's Trust, or the TWA Terminal at John F. Kennedy Airport, Eero Saarinen's breathtaking, fluid sculpture and paean to flight in concrete, not to mention Lever House and the Seagram Building, were almost invariably documented by Ezra Stoller, a gifted photographer whose cool, perfectly composed images in black and white became so closely identified with the famous architecture he photographed that his pictures have become, in some cases, almost as iconic as the buildings themselves. Stoller's architectural photographs, which rarely had people in them and showed buildings in cool, even light, emphasized the geometric and sculptural forms of modern architecture, and tended to present buildings as pure and perfect objects, largely disconnected from their contexts. Thus the Seagram Building was a sleek, soaring tower, the TWA Terminal a magnificent, swirling form of concrete, the United Nations a crisp slab against the sky.

Stoller was the preeminent photographer of modern architecture, although he did not play a central role in the city's broader community of photographers in the postwar years. But his contemporaries, photographers like Ruth Orkin, Andreas Feininger, Lisette Model, Helen Levitt, Evelyn Hofer, Diane Arbus, and Garry Winogrand, among many others—who the writer Jane Livingston has said constitute a "New York School" of photography—were as determined as Stoller to document the rise of modernity. Most of them did it in a different way, however, emphasizing the very things Stoller usually left out: people, movement, and the energy of the city itself. Stoller portrayed buildings as austere, ideal constructs, frozen in time; photographers like Winogrand emphasized spontaneity, frenzy, and surprise. Lisette Model, who was a mentor to Diane Arbus, caught people obliquely, creating subtle compositions that seemed to have insight into private lives. Helen Levitt often emphasized the poor, who seemed in her images at once alienated and deeply engaged with the city, which was almost always a powerful presence in her photographs. Model, Hofer, Levitt, and Arbus focused closely on people; Feininger stepped back to show a city

ABOVE: The swooping concrete form of Eero Saarinen's TWA Terminal at Idlewild (later John F. Kennedy International) Airport represented the cutting edge of both design and engineering at its completion in 1962.

OVERLEAF: TWA Terminal, interior. Saarinen wanted the sleek space to feel both dramatic and inviting, and to convey the excitement of the jet age. The interior surfaces are covered with circular, white ceramic tiles, giving the concrete forms a smooth continuity.

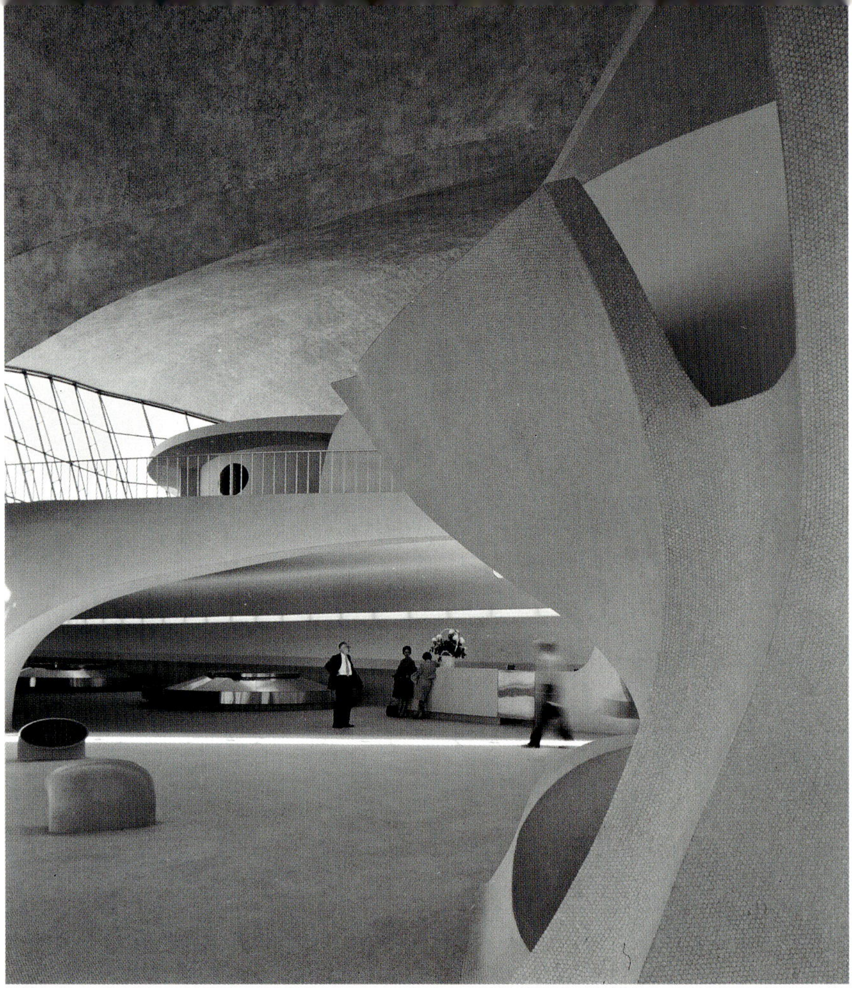

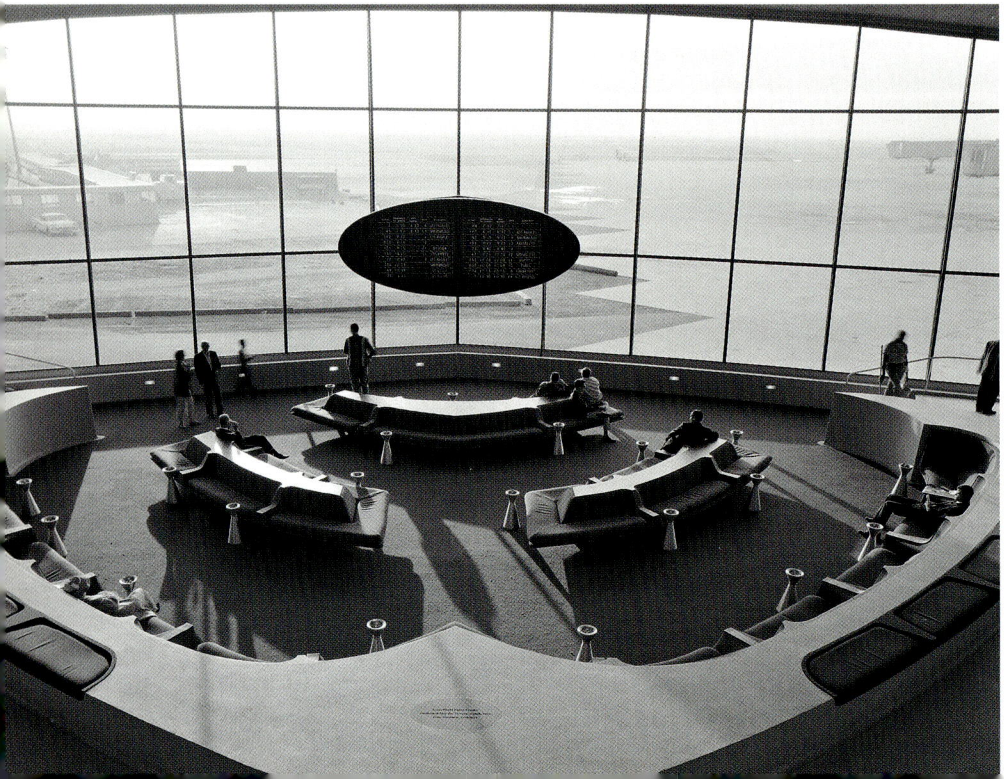

of huge crowds and dramatic vistas. In one of his most famous images, *Noon Rush Hour on Fifth Avenue*, from 1949, pedestrians fill every inch of Fifth Avenue, and you can feel their movement like a river on the sidewalk (see page 2). The photographers of the postwar New York School were not enamored with modernity as a technological achievement, which a previous generation—photographers like Alfred Stieglitz, Charles Sheeler, Margaret Bourke-White, and others—had documented. If it is possible to generalize about photographers who were in many ways quite different, it can be said that the major photographers in the postwar years took the twentieth-century city for granted as a backdrop and sought to probe the lives of its occupants, whether in the form of the sweeping images of Andreas Feininger, the quirky juxtapositions and strange characters that Arthur Fellig, the press photographer known as Weegee, took as his subjects, or the blunt, deadpan images of unusual people that later made Diane Arbus famous.

If many of the New York School of photographers represented a kind of "cinema verité" of still images, there was another group of celebrated photographers whose work was far more studied: the city's fashion photographers. Richard Avedon, Irving Penn, Lillian Bassman, and Henry Wolf were the most famous of them; George Platt Lynes, whose oeuvre was more varied and who after his untimely death became better known for his male nudes, was a prominent photographer of fashion as well. Here, there was no interest in portraying the reality of gritty, difficult lives or the intimate feelings of people who might otherwise have passed unnoticed amid the crowds. Avedon, who later achieved fame as a portrait photographer, and Penn photographed beautiful models in glamorous settings, every detail as precisely composed as in a still life. Their images were highly stylized but still minimalist, exquisitely crafted, sometimes with a hint of the surreal. Avedon's often captured movement and seemed to embody the flair of contemporary fashion. Penn's were deliberately more static. In their cool perfection, Penn's photographs resembled Ezra Stoller's images of modernist buildings more than those of photographers who photographed people.

The identity of these photographers was intimately connected to the magazines of the era, which themselves were evolving new attitudes toward graphic design. *Harper's Bazaar,* for many years the most daring, and later *Vogue* made the work of Penn and Avedon their centerpieces. Henry Wolf, while a noted photographer in his own right, oversaw graphic design at *Esquire* in the early 1950s, essentially remaking it into a sophisticated magazine with

Ezra Stoller, the photographer whose austere images of postwar modern buildings often defined contemporary architecture in the public's mind, here shot Eero Saarinen's TWA Terminal to evoke an abstract composition.

Weegee (Arthur Fellig), The Fountain,
*1950s. The setting is Washington Square Park
in Greenwich Village.*

Evelyn Hofer, The Bowery, New York, *1963.*

BAZ PER'S AR AR

34 NEW SCHEMES FOR THE SOUTH

LATE NEWS FOR LEGS: THE SHIMMERING STOCKINGS

GIFTS: THE THOUGHT IS THE THING

DECEMBER 1959
60 CENTS

VOGUE

SUMMER
PLANS:

The Black and
White Idea

The Linen Life

Transparent
Fashions

ADVANCE
RETAIL
TRADE
EDITION

Incorporating Vanity Fair
April 1, 1950
Price 50 Cents
in U. S. and Canada
$1.00 All Other Countries
COPYRIGHT 1950. THE CONDÉ NAST PUBLICATIONS INC.

OPPOSITE: Harper's Bazaar *cover by*
Richard Avedon, December 1959.

ABOVE: Vogue *cover by Irving Penn,*
June 1950.

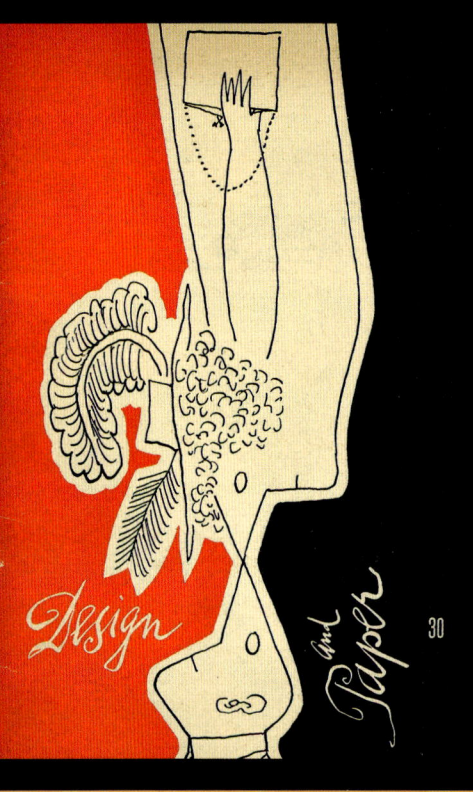

Design *and* Paper

30

Flair

February 1950

THE MONTHLY MAGAZINE   FIFTY CENTS

F O R T U N E

July 1963

500

Fortune's Directory of the Biggest Industrials

Japan's Hope—Business;   Taiwan's Muscle;   Red China's Economic Failure

MAY 1969
PRICE $1

Esquire

THE MAGAZINE FOR MEN

The final decline and total collapse of the American avant-garde.
See page 142

Campbell's
CONDENSED

TOMATO
SOUP

RIGHT AND BELOW RIGHT:
The Chase Bank logo, designed by Tom
Geismar in 1961, was the first instance
of an abstract, nonrepresentational logo
for a banking corporation. It is still in
use more than half a century later.

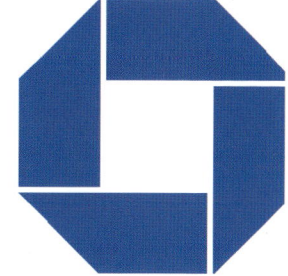

Mobil

*ABOVE: Mobil Corporation logo and proprietary
alphabet by Tom Geismar, 1964.*

*BELOW: The Museum of Modern Art sugar
packets by Ivan Chermayeff, 1960s.*

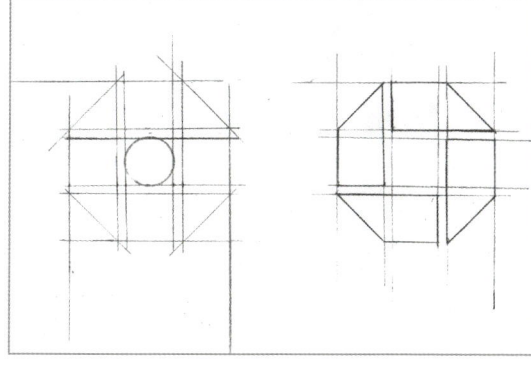

a modern, open feel, and later went to *Harper's Bazaar*, where he
brought a similar kind of graphic energy. Wolf, along with advertising executives like William Bernbach and George Lois and
graphic designers like Tom Geismar and Ivan Chermayeff, created
magazines, advertising, and logos beginning in the late 1950s that
were crisp, sharp, often abstract, and almost inevitably sophisticated and clever, reshaping magazine journalism, advertising, and
graphic design in the process.

OPPOSITE: Design and Paper *cover
by Saul Steinberg, 1950s (top left);* Flair
magazine cover, February 1950 (top right);
Fortune *cover by Chermayeff & Geismar
Associates, art director, Walter Allner, July
1963 (bottom left);* Esquire *cover by George
Lois, May 1969 (bottom right).*

BELOW: The E. V. Haughwout Building, designed by John Gaynor in 1857, which contained the world's first passenger elevator, is in many ways the Platonic cast-iron building. An exquisite example of the art of cast-iron façade design, it is one of the buildings that would have disappeared had the Lower Manhattan Expressway gone ahead.

OPPOSITE: The Haughwout Building's magnificently proportioned and elegantly detailed cast-iron façade was forged at Daniel Badger's foundry, Architectural Ironworks, located along the East River.

Not all of New York was gravitating toward the sleek, modern aesthetic of Henry Wolf and George Lois in the postwar years, of course. In the late 1950s and early 1960s, a number of artists who could no longer afford Greenwich Village—which, Jane Jacobs notwithstanding, was rapidly gentrifying and becoming less diverse than the neighborhood she celebrated in her book—took refuge farther downtown, in the old industrial buildings south of Houston Street, which soon became known as SoHo. Many of the buildings had exquisite cast-iron fronts—in fact, SoHo had the greatest concentration of nineteenth-century cast-iron buildings anywhere—but their landmark quality meant less to the artists than the fact that the neighborhood was viewed as off the beaten track, something of a no-man's land between the financial district of Wall Street and midtown Manhattan, and, even more important, that its buildings had large, open floor areas originally designed for manufacturing that could be ideal for painting. The industrial companies that had once filled the region were moving to larger, more spread-out facilities outside of Manhattan, and in some cases away from New York entirely, and many of the buildings lay empty. An unintended consequence of the city's plan to bulldoze much of the area for the Lower Manhattan Expressway was that the owners of the buildings in the area, facing an uncertain future for their properties, did not invest in them or, in some cases, even seek new tenants.

The first artists to live and work in the loft spaces in these buildings occupied them illegally. Artists had done this before in New York, but not until the rise of SoHo was there a concentration of them large enough to form an activist community. The artists of SoHo, at one point threatening an artists' strike, pressured the city to make loft living legal. In the early sixties, the city began to loosen its regulations to allow first artists, and

eventually almost anyone, to turn the manufacturing lofts into residential space. And where the artists lived, bars, restaurants, and shops gradually followed. But it wasn't until a few years later, when the controversial idea of cutting the Lower Manhattan Expressway through the area was officially declared dead, that the neighborhood was designated a historic district and its architectural treasures made safe from the threat of demolition. At that point, speculators began to turn SoHo into another place entirely, its shops and lofts more suited to the bank accounts of investment bankers than artists—a place that artists of the generation that followed SoHo's pioneers could not afford any more than their predecessors could afford Greenwich Village.

SoHo and its remarkable inventory of nineteenth-century cast-iron buildings came extraordinarily close to being lost. Many other landmarks in New York were not so lucky. The active pace of development in the city in the fifties and sixties, and the relatively limited consciousness New York had then of the value of historic buildings, meant that much of the city's finest architecture was demolished to make way for the new. Almost all of the postwar apartment buildings on Fifth Avenue occupied the sites of historic mansions, many by architects such as McKim, Mead & White, Trowbridge & Livingston, Ogden Codman, Horace Trumbauer, and Warren & Wetmore. On the West Side, the Charles Schwab mansion on Riverside Drive, one of the largest houses ever built in New York—it occupied a full block from Riverside Drive to West End Avenue—was torn down in 1948 to make way for a boxy red brick apartment house. In midtown Manhattan, numerous theaters were torn down to allow more office towers. The Roxy Theater, one of the most ornate movie palaces ever built, was a devastating loss when it was demolished in 1960 to make way for the new Time & Life Building. This followed the loss of several Broadway theaters in the 1950s, as well as the interior of the Center Theater—one of the gems of the original Rockefeller Center complex—which was gutted and replaced with more office space for the building in which it was housed.

Occasionally, demolitions made way for architecture of some quality. Uptown, Loew's 72nd Street Theater, a celebrated movie palace built in 1932 by Thomas Lamb and John Eberson, was only thirty years old when it was torn down. It was replaced by Emery Roth & Sons' Tower East, hardly its equal, but one of the city's better postwar apartment buildings. Gordon Bunshaft's Manhattan House took the place of the Third Avenue Transit Corporation's Second Empire–style car barn, designed by Henry Hardenbergh, architect of the Plaza Hotel and the Dakota apartments. But these were the exceptions, particularly in the postwar era. Most of the time, admired buildings were replaced with buildings whose only clear advantage over their predecessors was that they were bigger and more profitable.

New Yorkers grumbled about the loss of old buildings and worried that the architectural legacy of the postwar decades would be one of destruction more than creation. The feeling was summed up in a remarkable advertisement for the Plaza Hotel that ran in *The New Yorker* in 1965, just after it had become clear that the Plaza's grand and sumptuous neighbor, the Savoy Plaza Hotel by McKim, Mead & White, which had held sway over the southeast corner of Central Park since 1927, was going to be torn down to make way for another skyscraper, the General Motors Building. "It didn't happen all at once. They did it very gradually," the ad began. "'We can't alarm the people!' they said. So they removed a little house here. And a great hotel there. And then a few limestone banks and all the cast-iron store fronts they could find. . . . A few people grumbled. . . . But most people were complacent. Until they discovered that their city had been entirely replaced with glass. Soon after this, on one ghastly glittering morning, an observant executive walking

Cartoon by Alan Dunn, 1967.

"Landmarks Commission, I think!"

A RED TOWER REPLACING CARNEGIE HALL

The building boom that has been making over the old brownstone face of Manhattan with new façades of gleaming aluminum, green glass and copper-tinted steel will reach a new degree of flamboyance in the skyscraper to be erected on the site of Carnegie Hall. When the famous concert place is demolished in 1959, a new office building faced in panels of bright red porcelain will go up in its place. To liven up the effect even more, Architects Pomerance and Breines have offset the building's windows in diagonal instead of vertical rows to produce a strange-looking checkerboard pattern. Standing on stilts sunk in a broad plaza, the $22 million building will rise 44 floors above 57th Street.

All this was saddening news to the music lovers who have come to cherish old Victorian Carnegie Hall. Built as a business venture by Andrew Carnegie, a lover of Scotch bagpipe music, it opened in 1891 with a program partly conducted by Tchaikovsky. It became home for the New York Philharmonic and a magnet for the great musicians of the world. When it is demolished, U.S. music will lose one of its most acoustically perfect halls. But there was some good news for music lovers. As the office building goes up, Carnegie Hall's activities will move to Manhattan's new Lincoln Square cultural center and into a modern auditorium adjoining the new Metropolitan Opera House.

CARNEGIE HALL will offer two more full seasons of concerts and recitals before building is razed.

RED SKYSCRAPER will be reached from the street → level by a foot bridge spanning its sunken plaza.

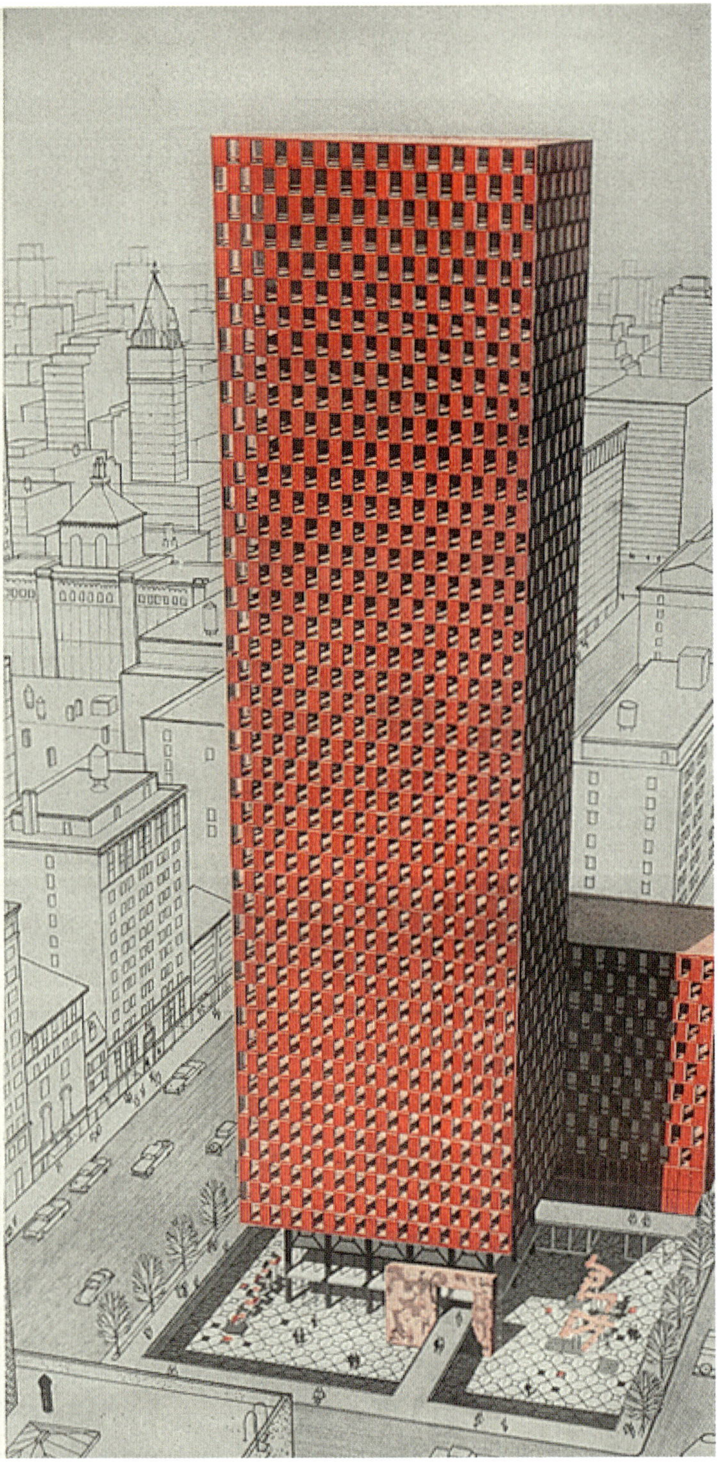

this, to work paused on Fifth Avenue at Fifty-ninth Street to clean his heavy dark goggles. Squinting, he looked around. And gasped! There was The Plaza where he had always remembered it. 'It can't be!' he said and rubbed his eyes. He looked again. 'It *is* there!' He called his wife. 'We'll go there tonight, before it's too late. Don't tell anyone!' he hissed." At the bottom of the page, in small type, the ad concluded: "This ad is fantasy, of course. But then again, so is life at The Plaza. Come live it."[17]

The year the ad appeared, the city had finally acceded to a rising tide of pressure from historic preservationists, who were alarmed by the ongoing toll the city's postwar growth was taking on older architecture and established the New York City Landmarks Preservation Commission, which was empowered to offer some degree of legal protection for those pieces of city architecture it deemed most valuable. It would take the experience of almost losing two of the city's most beloved landmarks and the actual loss of one of the most admired buildings in the city to turn the tide toward preservation. A plan in 1956 to replace Carnegie Hall with a forty-four-story office tower, its exceptionally garish, red, anodized-aluminum design merely adding insult to injury, was prevented only by the intervention of Alice and J. M. Kaplan, civic-minded philanthropists who were recruited by the violinist Isaac Stern and who ultimately persuaded the city to buy the concert hall and lease it back to a new nonprofit corporation that would operate it. But it took four years of political and financial maneuvering, and the building was not safe until 1960. No sooner had the threat of demolition been lifted from Carnegie Hall than another great New York landmark, the Dakota, among the grandest apartment buildings ever built in New York, was threatened by the decision of its owners to sell the building to the developer William Zeckendorf, who planned to replace it with a tall apartment tower. It, too, was a story worthy of *The Perils of Pauline*, with the fate of the building hanging in the balance until the last minute, when the tenants joined together and, with the help of another real estate developer, purchased the building and turned it into a cooperative. But these two dramatic rescues were not enough to prevent the demolition of many other buildings that were familiar, admired, and in almost every instance loved more than the ones that took their place.

And then two years later, in 1963, came the greatest failure of historic preservation in New York's history: the loss of Pennsylvania Station, Charles McKim's extraordinary monument to the power of railroads, the power of New York, and the idea of a noble entrance to a city. Penn Station was not only McKim's masterwork but also one of the greatest twentieth-century works of classicism ever built anywhere, and it was torn down not to make

OPPOSITE: The developer Louis J. Glickman's proposed skyscraper for the site of Carnegie Hall, designed by Pomerance & Breines, 1956. Life magazine, September 9, 1957.

ABOVE: *Charles McKim's vast Pennsylvania Station, a triumph of civic construction by a private railroad, filled two city blocks.*

BELOW: *The potential loss of Penn Station brought picket lines in front of the station in 1962. Philip Johnson and Jane Jacobs were among the protestors.*

OPPOSITE: *The glass-covered train shed in Penn Station contrasted with the solidity of the classical Concourse.*

TIMED BY
BENRUS

DOWN STAIRS FOR
INCOMING
TRAINS

~ LONG ISLAND TRAINS ~

Demolition of the Concourse.

way for a better work of architecture or even for a better train station, but for one of the city's dreariest new office towers and a new Madison Square Garden, which the architect Charles Luckman housed in a banal building that looked like a gargantuan drum. The station through which millions had entered and left New York was shoved underground, reduced to no more than an overgrown subway station, which led the architecture historian Vincent Scully to write, "[through] the rhythmic clarity of the generous big spaces of the station and the majestic firmness with which the great piers and columns and the coffered vault defined them . . . one entered the city like a god. Perhaps it was really too much. One scuttles in now like a rat."[18]

Pennsylvania Station was only fifty-two years old when demolition began in 1963. The *New York Times* editorialized: ". . . it is the shame of New York, of its financial and cultural communities, its politicians, philanthropists and planners, and of the public as well. . . . Any city gets what it admires, will pay for, and, ultimately, deserves. Even when we had Penn Station, we couldn't afford to keep it clean. We want and deserve tin-can architecture in a tin-horn culture. And we will probably be judged not by the monuments we build but by those we have destroyed."[19]

Less than two years after the wrecking ball first hit Penn Station, Mayor Robert F. Wagner signed the legislation establishing the New York City Landmarks Preservation Commission. It was a sign that New York did not want to be judged by the buildings it had destroyed, at least not entirely, and that it was prepared to do something to give the postwar years a better legacy. The law was not strong enough to prevent many future losses like the Singer Building, the Astor Hotel, and the Metropolitan Opera, all of which were demolished after the commission was established. But the law marked the clear beginning of a different age. And over the years it would be strengthened considerably, making New York a national leader in historic preservation.

The very different fate of New York's other great train station, Grand Central Terminal, is a testament to the progress that was being made. Grand Central's Beaux-Arts building, designed by Reed & Stem along with Warren & Wetmore and finished in 1913, was in some ways an improvement on Penn Station: if it was not quite as noble as a pure work of architecture, it came close, and its layout allowed for a much smoother, more efficient movement of passengers, vehicles, and trains than Penn Station's. In many ways Grand Central was a far more complete work of architecture, engineering, and urban design than Penn Station had been. But like Penn Station, it was viewed by the railroad that owned it as something of an albatross, and in the 1950s the New York Central Railroad encouraged numerous plans to add towers above the tracks, or even to replace the building altogether. The architect I. M. Pei produced one such plan in 1956 for an extraordinary tapered, round skyscraper, a striking design that looks more like towers produced in the twenty-first century than in the middle of the twentieth. Although it would have "replaced one landmark with another," in Robert A. M. Stern's words, it never had much likelihood of being realized.[20]

Various more practical, if more prosaic, plans came forth through the fifties, most of which situated the building to the north of the terminal, over the tracks that led trains into Grand Central. Their banality troubled even the developer behind the project, Erwin Wolfson, and in 1958 he asked Richard Roth, who then headed his father's firm, Emery Roth & Sons, if he might be

The demolition of Penn Station began on October 28, 1963, and took three years to complete. The outcry over the loss of the station encouraged the establishment of the New York City Landmarks Preservation Commission.

willing to take on as a collaborator another architect better known for his design excellence. Roth suggested Walter Gropius, one of the giants of modern architecture and the founder of the Bauhaus in Germany, who in turn suggested Pietro Belluschi, another Modernist of distinction. What they came up with, however, was a fifty-five-story tower of precast concrete in the shape of an elongated octagon that struck few people as representing any kind of design excellence. And instead of placing it on a north–south axis, as the Roth firm had done in its earlier, plainer glass schemes, the famous architects turned the building ninety degrees so it blocked the open vista up and down Park Avenue. The building may have been better looking than a plain box, but it was also an enormous mass looming over one of New York's greatest landmarks and blocking one of its most distinguished boulevards. Edgar Kaufmann Jr., in an essay entitled "The Biggest Office Building Yet," said that the building beside Grand Central "has failed to grasp the spirit of what is grand. . . . Its design shows

Grand Central Terminal, designed by Reed & Stem with Warren & Wetmore and completed in 1913, was a more fully resolved work of urban design and engineering than the even grander Pennsylvania Station.

none of the scale of urban grandness that is still exemplified in the station next door. The great architecture of New York at mid-twentieth century, it seems, has yet to be imagined."[21]

No other critic was any more positive. The building, Vincent Scully wrote, "smothers [the] scale" of Park Avenue. "In any terms other than brute expediency it should not have been there at all."[22] And the artist Claes Oldenburg mocked the building even more harshly with a drawing in which he imagined it as a vast, upside-down ice cream bar blocking Park Avenue, with traffic flowing through a bite out of its corner.

The Pan Am Building, as it was originally called, was never popular, but it was not the most troubling legacy of this period for Grand Central. Though a plan in 1961 to chop up the terminal's great south waiting room into three floors of bowling alleys does not appear to have ever been taken seriously, a plan to build a second huge tower directly over the terminal's main concourse was taken very seriously indeed. A developer working with the railroad hired Marcel Breuer, another distinguished early Modernist, who had

Pan Am (now MetLife) Building, designed by Emery Roth & Sons, Pietro Belluschi, and Walter Gropius, 1962.

been Gropius's student and who had designed the new Whitney Museum, to produce a tower even taller than the Pan Am Building. It was to be supported by trusses that would descend right into the terminal's main concourse, along with elevator shafts, effectively destroying Grand Central's architectural climax, the monumental interior space of the main concourse. Ada Louise Huxtable termed the project a "grotesquerie," and commented that although she considered Breuer a good architect, to say he had "done an excellent job with a dubious undertaking . . . is like saying it would be great if it weren't awful."[23]

Grand Central Terminal had been declared a city landmark after the Landmarks Preservation Commission was created, and under the provisions of the law, the commission had the right to block the proposal if it deemed it damaging to the landmark.

The commission denied permission, Breuer
revised his design, and it was rejected again.
At that point the developer and the railroad
sued the city, initiating a case that went all
the way to the Supreme Court, which, in a
6-to-3 vote, upheld the constitutionality of
the landmarks law, establishing for the first
time that historic preservation was a legitimate and legal form of government regula-
tion. Grand Central Terminal was the test
case, the centerpiece of an epic architectural
and legal struggle that emerged directly out
of the pressured, intense explosion of building in the postwar era, when New York
seemed only to want to get bigger, to build
more and more, whatever the cost.

The legacy in design and architecture of
the two decades following World War II is not
only one of excess, of course; the rise of the
historic preservation movement and the cre-
ation of the Landmarks Preservation Commission are testaments to
the fact that as more and more huge buildings went up, the forces
opposing unbridled growth were becoming stronger during these
decades. New York in 1965 was at once a more aggressive city than it
had been in 1945 and a more troubled one. It was increasingly a city
of glittering, shiny glass buildings symbolizing new and expanding
wealth, and a city of run-down, derelict neighborhoods of poverty
and crime.

"The city has never been so uncomfortable, so crowded, so
tense. Money has been plentiful and New York has responded,"
E. B. White wrote in a 1949 essay, "Here Is New York," that
would become a classic.[24] New York had always wanted to make
itself new, but it seemed more desperate than ever to do so in
the 1960s, as if in the hope that sleek glass buildings in the heart
of Manhattan could make up for crumbling tenements in other
parts of the city, not to mention the increasing tendency of
the middle class to abandon the city altogether. By 1965 New
York seemed to exemplify John Kenneth Galbraith's juxtaposition of "private affluence and public squalor." The city's office
towers were shiny and new, its parks were old and dirty. New
York would continue to be, as E. B. White put it, a "riddle in
steel and stone."

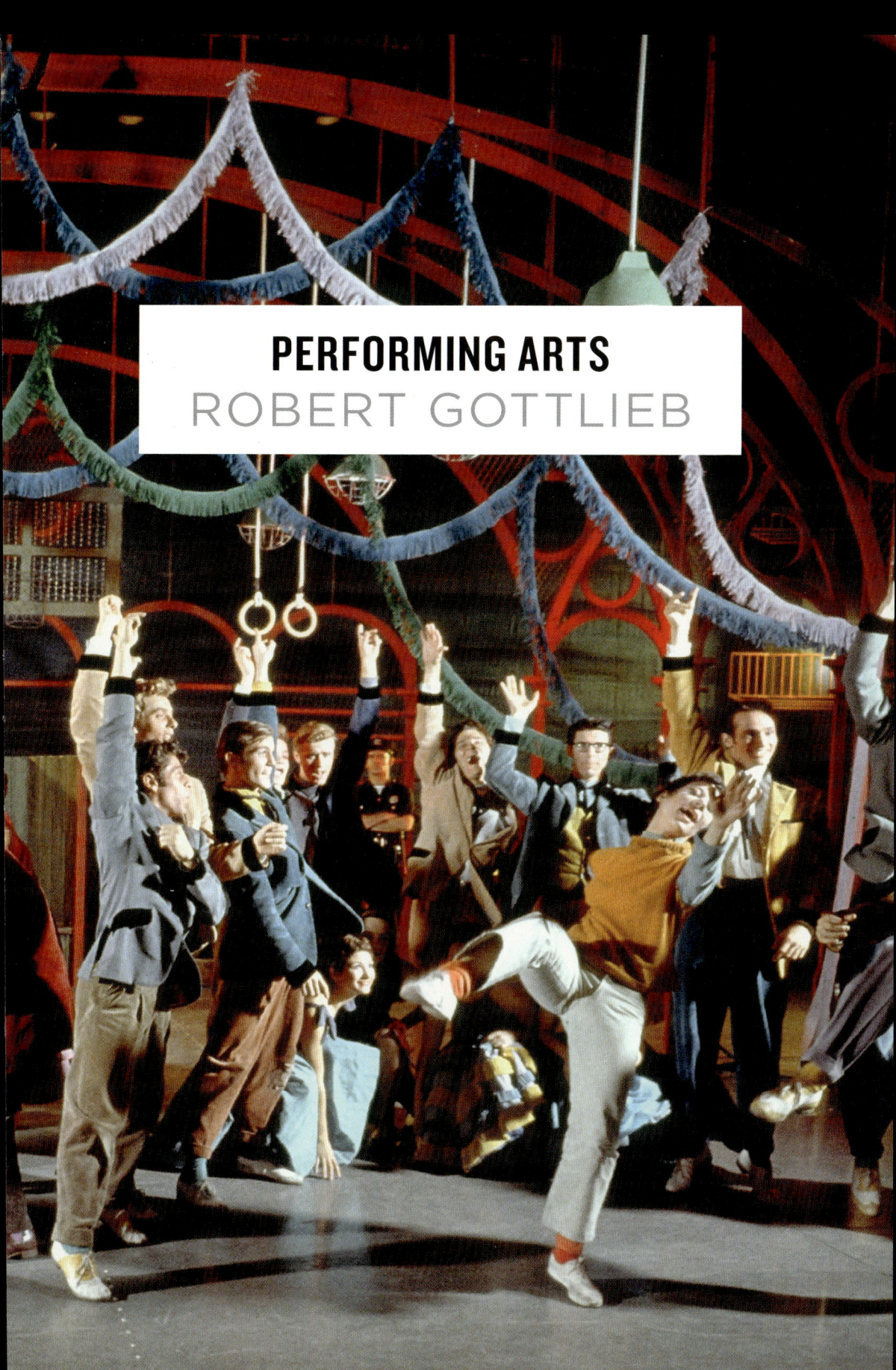

PERFORMING ARTS
ROBERT GOTTLIEB

OCTOBER 1951
THE Atlantic
DANCE to the PIPER
Agnes de Mille
50¢

DANCE

BALLET

By the mid-1960s, it was a given that New York City was the dance capital of the world, something that only twenty years earlier, no one could have predicted. Yes, America was the breeding ground of "modern dance," but before World War II ballet had been a sporadic phenomenon. For ballet, you went to Paris, to London, to Russia (not that anyone did). And occasionally ballet dropped in on us from abroad.

In 1910, a troupe called the Imperial Russian Ballet, starring Anna Pavlova and Mikhail Mordkin, toured the country, attracting considerable critical attention, and Pavlova went on appearing here for almost twenty years—her name practically synonymous with the idea of ballet. In 1916, with Europe in the grip of war, Diaghilev sent his Ballets Russes to America; a year later, the company was back, now under the leadership of Nijinsky, who was already losing his grip on reality. After Diaghilev's death (in 1929) and into the 1950s, various avatars of the Ballets Russes crisscrossed the country, popularizing "Russian ballet"—ballet had to be Russian to seem authentic—and making stars in America of such dancers as Alexandra Danilova, Alicia Markova, the "baby ballerinas" (Toumanova, Baronova, Riabouchinska), Anton Dolin, and Leonid Massine, whose popular choreography supplemented the *Giselle*s and the Diaghilev-Fokine repertory: *Les Sylphides, Schéhérazade, Le Spectre de la Rose, Petrouchka, The Dying Swan*, and the rest. The result: an awakening of interest in the art form, and the creation of ballet schools across the country, as touring dancers retired and stayed on in America to spread the word.

In England, Ninette de Valois founded the Sadler's Wells company, which after the war became the Royal Ballet. In occupied Paris, the Paris Opéra ballet kept going until the Liberation under the dubious leadership of Serge Lifar. In Russia itself, as the German invasion forged eastward, the dancers were moved to the city of Perm to continue their work. But America had no such institutions of its own—with two modest exceptions. On January 1, 1934, George Balanchine, imported from Europe by Lincoln Kirstein, opened the School of American Ballet, determined to produce dancers with the speed, athleticism, and attack that he felt represented this country (Astaire and Rogers were his ideals), and soon Kirstein was providing him with opportunities to create new ballets

PRECEDING PAGES: "Dance at the Gym" scene, West Side Story.

OPPOSITE: The cover of The Atlantic, *which was excerpting Agnes de Mille's brilliant memoir* Dance to the Piper. *Here she's seen in her breakthrough ballet,* Rodeo (1942), *which led to her choreographing Rodgers and Hammerstein's* Oklahoma!, *which changed Broadway history.*

RIGHT: Lincoln Kirstein, left, and George Balanchine, the founders of New York City Ballet and the School of American Ballet.

BELOW: Ballet Theatre (now American Ballet Theatre) on Broadway, 1946.

BOTTOM: The stage door at the New York City Center, where New York City Ballet performed from 1948 until it moved to Lincoln Center in 1964.

OPPOSITE: The movers and shakers of Ballet Theatre—"The Artistic Committee"—1947. Left to right: Jerome Robbins, Lucia Chase, Agnes de Mille, Oliver Smith, and Aaron Copland, in Miss Chase's apartment.

here, beginning with the magnificent *Serenade*, which he made for his new students in 1934. And in 1940, a rich woman named Lucia Chase founded Ballet Theatre (now American Ballet Theatre), dedicated to presenting a wide diversity of choreographic styles and a rich assortment of stars (including herself). Both the Kirstein-Balanchine and the Lucia Chase enterprises endured stormy weather through their early years, but eventually both triumphed, developing two rivalrous yet complementary organizations that essentially continue to dominate the world of American ballet today.

By the end of the war, in 1945, Ballet Theatre was in serious competition with the Ballets Russes—the impresario Sol Hurok presented them both at the Metropolitan Opera House. In the same spirit in which my parents took me to concerts by Vladimir Horowitz, Arthur Rubinstein, and Marian Anderson, my mother took me to a Markova-Dolin *Giselle* (my first ballet), and when I failed to respond to it, to an "all-boys" matinee program at Ballet Theatre of Eugene Loring's *Billy the Kid*, Agnes de Mille's *Rodeo*, and the smash hit *Fancy Free*, Jerome Robbins's first ballet, about three sailors on leave in New York. (It would become the musical *On the Town*.) As it happens, I didn't take to cowboys or sailors any more than I had to *Giselle*'s Wilis, but I had grasped that dance was important in our New York world—like opera and theater and art.

Apart from *Fancy Free*, the big winners in Ballet Theatre's early years were the powerful works of Antony Tudor: *Lilac Garden* and *Dark Elegies* from his English period and, more important, his 1942 triumph, *Pillar of Fire*, which established Nora Kaye as the leading dramatic ballerina of her time. Agnes de Mille produced her successful Lizzie Borden ballet, *Fall River Legend*; Balanchine created the dazzling *Theme and Variations* for Alicia Alonso and Igor Youskevitch; and the classical wing deployed its stars effectively. Whatever its financial difficulties, Ballet Theatre had quickly established itself as an important New York institution.

Meanwhile, the indefatigable Lincoln Kirstein, back from his service in the army, came up with a rarefied concept called Ballet Society for a subscription audience. In 1946, it presented one revolutionary Balanchine masterpiece, *The Four Temperaments*, at the

Jerome Robbins's Fancy Free *(1944), his first ballet and one of ABT's greatest hits. Left to right: Robbins, John Kriza, Harold Lang, Janet Reed, and Muriel Bentley. Set by Oliver Smith.*

ABOVE: Pillar of Fire (1942), Antony Tudor's hugely successful dramatic ballet. Left to right: Annabelle Lyon, Tudor, Lucia Chase, Nora Kaye, and Hugh Laing. It made instant stars of Kaye and Laing.

RIGHT: Cover of the laser video disc version of Michael Powell and Emeric Pressburger's wonderful movie The Red Shoes (1948), starring Moira Shearer, the beautiful Sadler's Wells ballerina, Robert Helpmann, and Léonide Massine. It ran in one small Manhattan movie house for over two years.

THE
RED SHOES

CLV/CAV
LASER VIDEODISC

3
Academy Award Nominations

Central High School of Needle Trades, and then in the spring of 1948, at the New York City Center, another one—*Orpheus*, to a commissioned score by Stravinsky, Balanchine's great collaborator, with décor by Noguchi. The manager of the City Center was so overwhelmed by Balanchine's accomplishments that he invited Kirstein to change the name of the company to the New York City Ballet and take up permanent residence in the theater. A teacher took me to one of these final performances of Ballet Society, and I was instantly converted—to ballet and to Balanchine.

While Ballet Theatre was attempting to define itself and City Ballet struggled to find an audience (Balanchine was considered elitist, and the City Center was rarely even half full), a series of shocks administered from abroad changed the game, broadening New Yorkers' idea of dance, making it fashionable, and setting new standards.

The spectacular French dancer Jean Babilée in Roland Petit's Le Jeune homme et la mort *(1946), libretto by Jean Cocteau. The visit to New York of Petit's Ballets de Paris in 1950 was a popular triumph.*

First, in 1949, came Sadler's Wells and Margot Fonteyn. Opening night at the Met—America's first full-length *Sleeping Beauty*—was a triumph of triumphs, a catalytic moment for the company and for New York. The way had been prepared by the two-year run of the movie *The Red Shoes*, which galvanized thousands of little girls to "take ballet," and whose star, Moira Shearer, was one of the Sadler's Wells ballerinas. But it was Fonteyn—on the cover of *Time*, of *Newsweek*—who gave ballet the star everyone could adore. As Kirstein put it, she had the art of *pleasing* more than other ballerina of the century.

The foreign invasion continued in 1950, when Roland Petit's Ballets de Paris was a sellout hit on Broadway, audiences wildly excited by the sexy and provocative Zizi Jeanmaire in his *Carmen* and the sexy and powerful Jean Babilée in *Le Jeune Homme et la mort*. The dancers were hot, the ballets were trendy, and the whole thing was *French*—this was soon after Dior's New Look had revolutionized fashion. Then came the Moiseyev folk dancers, the first postwar Russian invaders, their irresistible energy and virility thrilling audiences across America on their 1958 tour, their impact an echo of that of Sputnik, the year before.

Roland Petit and his wife, Renée (Zizi) Jeanmaire, in his internationally successful Carmen *(1949).*

RIGHT: The Moiseyev Dance Company, under the leadership of its founder, Igor Moiseyev, was the first major Russian dance company to appear in America after the war. It was presented at the Metropolitan Opera House in 1958 by impresario Sol Hurok and had fabulous success wherever it toured. You can see why!

BELOW: The great Bolshoi Ballet artist Galina Ulanova in Leonid Lavrovsky's Romeo and Juliet.

But it was the arrival of the Bolshoi Ballet in 1959 that made the biggest impact of all. Its season at the Met opened with Leonid Lavrovsky's full-evening *Romeo and Juliet* to Prokofiev's electrifying score and starring Russia's greatest dance artist, Galina Ulanova. She was forty-nine, and as youthful and innocent as ideal Juliets must be—until then, we had only seen filmed snippets of her transcendent art, balletomanes making pilgrimages to the scruffy Stanley movie theater, which was devoted to Soviet film. During the Bolshoi season, she also danced gloriously in *Giselle* and *Les*

Sylphides. And when the company moved to Madison Square Garden to satisfy the huge demand for tickets, she was a Dying Swan of overwhelming simplicity and pathos. Unlike her colleague the flamboyant Maya Plisetskaya, who was all bird, Ulanova was supremely human, and when she died, she was dead. Plisetskaya would rise, like the Phoenix, and die again—and again.

When the Kirov came to America from Leningrad for the first time two years later, their purer style made less of an immediate impression on New York than the Bolshoi had, but in the long run it was the Kirov style that changed everything. Because it was from the Kirov that the famous defectors defected: first, in 1961, Rudolf Nureyev, later Natalia Makarova (1970) and Mikhail Baryshnikov (1974). "Rudi'"s dramatic escape to the West, eluding his Soviet keepers in Paris's Le Bourget airport, electrified the world—ballet had become front-page news. But it was his breathtaking performances—the animal magnetism combined with the amazing athleticism—that changed ballet itself: He had set a standard that the world's other male stars now had to aspire to. Every one of his performances was an event—it was a repeat of the Nijinsky story—and when he joined Fonteyn (nineteen years his senior) in an ongoing partnership, they became international celebrities, making headlines for their off-stage activities as well as their art. Famously, on at least

one occasion the applause for their star turn in the *Corsaire* pas de deux lasted longer than the ballet itself.

New York—by then the acknowledged capital of the postwar world—was where dance artists now had to make or confirm their reputations. Nureyev danced everywhere, as later both Makarova and Baryshnikov would do, but the latter two would settle here. And the parade of companies from abroad continued—the Stuttgart Ballet, for instance, in the late sixties, with John Cranko's overwrought (and over-praised) dramatic vehicles. Britain's Royal—with the eternal Fonteyn, later with Fonteyn and Nureyev—turned up every other year or so.

And while the Europeans kept coming, New York's own companies kept growing. In 1949, only a year after City Ballet began, it had its first major hit. The impresario Sol Hurok sold to Balanchine at a bargain-basement price the gorgeous Chagall sets for *The Firebird*, and Balanchine re-imagined this famous Stravinsky/Fokine work for his leading ballerina (and wife at the time), Maria Tallchief. Suddenly the company was big box office, and its popularity was permanently confirmed five years later when he presented his magical *Nutcracker*, which is still performed by the company five or six weeks every fall and which led to a proliferation of *Nutcrackers* around the country—and introduced generation after generation of children to ballet.

Yearly, almost until his death in 1983, Balanchine created masterpiece after masterpiece of every kind; on the one hand there were story ballets

Balanchine's 1946 masterpiece The Four Temperaments, *the first and perhaps greatest of his abstract "black and white" ballets, to a commissioned score by Hindemith. It was originally created for Ballet Society, the forerunner of New York City Ballet, and was staged with ungainly and impractical costumes by Kurt Seligmann. When Balanchine added it to City Ballet's repertory in 1951, he stripped it to practice clothes, to the relief of the critics, the audience, and—most of all—the dancers.*

FEHL

ABOVE: *Balanchine's version of* Firebird *(1949) was City Ballet's first great hit, and made a star of its ballerina (and Balanchine's wife at the time), Maria Tallchief, shown here with Francisco Moncion.*

OVERLEAF: *Balanchine's* The Nutcracker, *created in 1954, went on to become the bread and butter of City Ballet (and countless other companies), packing theaters for weeks on end and introducing hundreds of thousands of children—and adults—to ballet.* LEFT: *The thrilling "snowflake" scene.* TOP RIGHT: *The "party scene" with William Dollar as Herr Drosselmeier.* BOTTOM RIGHT: *The final scene, with little Marie and her Nutcracker prince waving farewell to the Land of Sweets in a sleigh drawn by reindeer.*

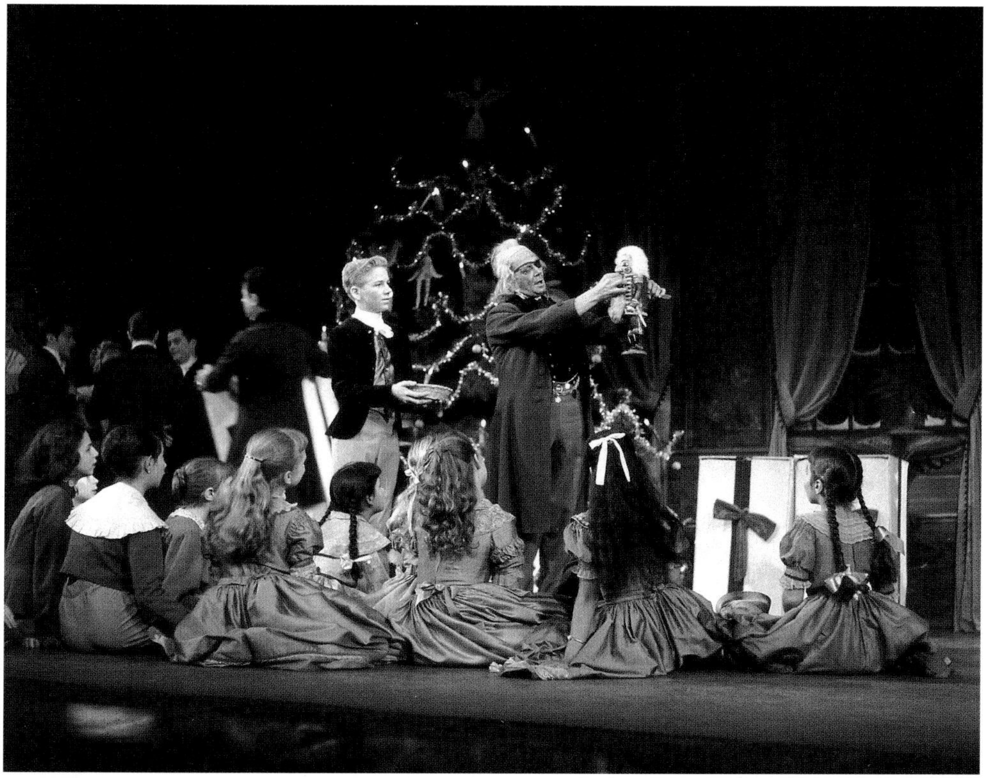

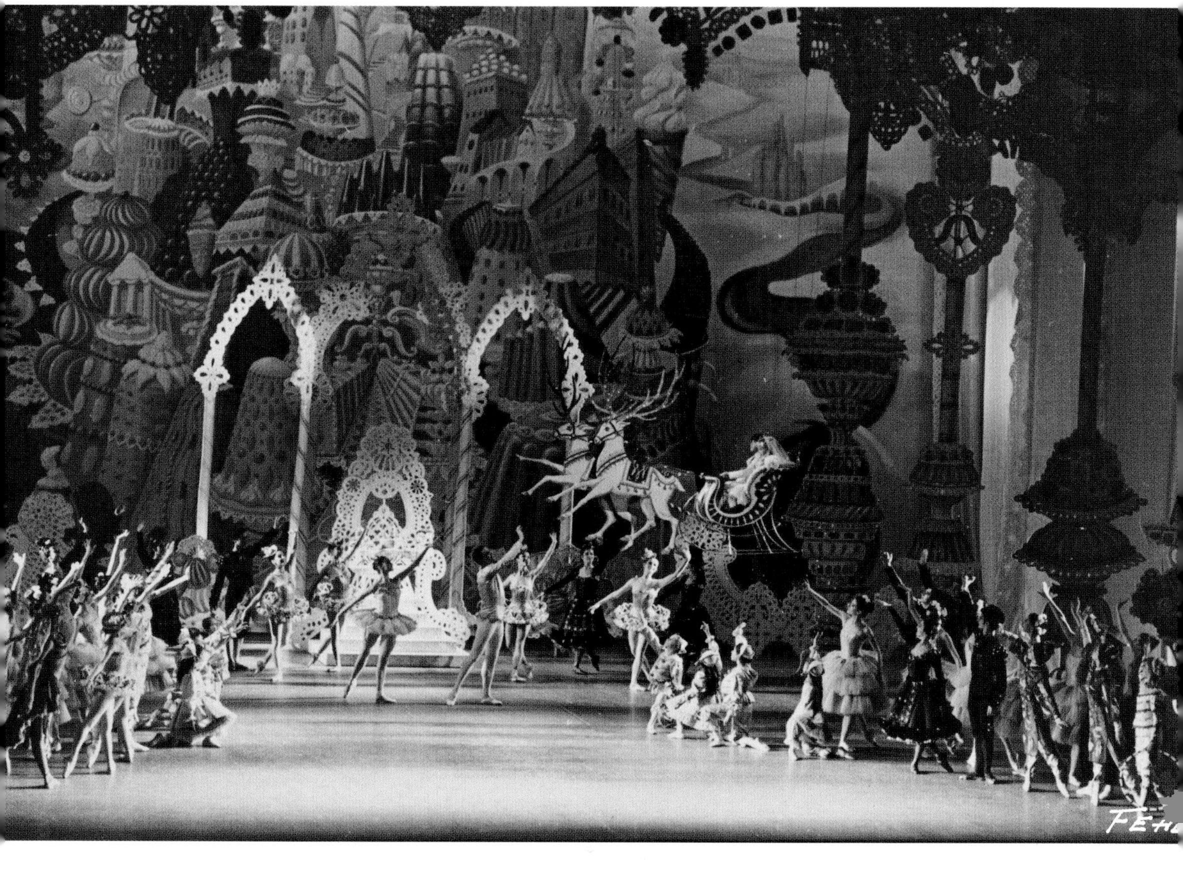

like *A Midsummer Night's Dream*, romantic ones like *Liebeslieder Walzer*, and riffs on classical dance like *Western Symphony* and *Stars and Stripes* that preserved and energized the classicism of his heritage, while on the other hand he advanced—revolutionized—the boundaries of ballet with such astonishing modern works as *The Four Temperaments* (1946), *Agon* (1957), and *Episodes* (1959). Through his genius, he had overcome the resistance of the Ballets Russes old-timers and the opposition of the *New York Times* critic John Martin and the idea that his ballets were merely cold and abstract to become the most significant choreographer and teacher of the century, perhaps of all time. Today, his repertory is performed everywhere, and his pedagogy dominates the American dance academy.

And while Balanchine was fulfilling his mission, his partner, Lincoln Kirstein, was working in other ways to forward dance in America. It was he who persuaded W. McNeil Lowry—director of the Ford Foundation's Arts and Humanities programs—to make an unprecedented $7.7 million grant to an assortment of dance institutions, of which $2 million went to City Ballet and almost $4 million to the School of American Ballet. The rest of the dance world was not pleased.

Meanwhile, Ballet Theatre (in 1957, it changed its name to American Ballet Theatre, or A.B.T.) was capturing the non-Balanchine audience with stars and star vehicles. Jerome Robbins had defected to City Ballet, where he would create such hits as *The Cage* and *Afternoon of a Faun* and, in 1969, returning to the company after an astounding series of megahits on Broadway, *Dances at a Gathering*. A.B.T. had a stream of

less illustrious choreographers but a parade of stars, from the home-grown, like Cynthia Gregory and the brilliant but neurotic Gelsey Kirkland, to the imported, such as Alicia Alonso and Erik Bruhn, to the émigrés Makarova and Baryshnikov, the biggest star of all. (Later, he would defect to City Ballet for the opportunity of working with Balanchine—and then re-defect, to become A.B.T.'s artistic director.)

Shortly after Lincoln Center came along, in 1964, the two major companies found themselves in direct competition, City Ballet at the State Theater, A.B.T. at the new Metropolitan Opera House across the Plaza, with frantic critics and fans sometimes darting from one house to the other in the course of a single evening. A highly personal bond was developing between performers and audience—dancers were known by their first names: Eddie (Villella) and Patty (McBride), Suzanne (Farrell) and Peter (Martins), Rudi (Nureyev) and Margot (Fonteyn), and of course the sublime Misha (Baryshnikov). No one in Diaghilev's audience had shouted out "Vaslav" or "Tamara" for Nijinsky and Karsavina. This was something new, and a confirmation of the feelings New Yorkers now had for ballet.

The city's third successful company, though on a much smaller scale than the Big Two, was the Joffrey Ballet, founded in 1956 by Robert Joffrey, though not a presence in New York until its first City Center season in 1966.

The company was more modern, more jazzy, than either of its big rivals, Joffrey himself an innovative choreographer (he had a big hit in 1967 with his semi-psychedelic *Astarte*, to a commissioned rock

OPPOSITE: *Tanaquil LeClercq in Balanchine's* La Valse *(1951), her signature role. Tragically, she was struck down by polio in 1956 and spent the rest of her life in a wheelchair. Her glorious "New Look" costume is by the consummate designer Karinska.*

score—it hit the cover of *Time*). The Joffrey would go on to give us Twyla Tharp's first cross-genre ballet, *Deuce Coupe*; a series of important Frederick Ashton and Ballets Russes revivals; Kurt Jooss's *The Green Table*; and—alas—an endless parade of second-rate pieces by Joffrey's partner and co-director, Gerald Arpino, which doomed the company to mediocrity. For a while, though, the Joffrey was a welcome and popular element of the New York dance scene. In 1964, its major funder, the batty Rebekah Harkness, withdrew her support and started her own ill-fated company, on which she spent a lot of money before it, and she, self-destructed.

1964 was also the year that Lincoln Center's State Theater (now vulgarly renamed the David H. Koch Theater) opened, built greatly to Balanchine's specifications, its primary function to provide a permanent grand venue for the New York City Ballet, although it shared the theater until recently with the New York City Opera. (While the building was being prepared, Balanchine, inspecting the site, stopped final construction because the orchestra pit wasn't large enough.) At first, its somewhat glitzy décor, anchored by two huge Elie Nadelman sculptures, offended City Ballet loyalists used to the shabbier and more human-scaled City Center, which had been home for sixteen years, but we got used to it, and the huge space on the mezzanine floor became a happy place for Balanchine's public to gather. More important, it gave him room for ambitious projects like *Jewels* (1967) and the Stravinsky Festival (1972), and somehow the move made City Ballet's ascendancy to the Big Time official—as happened in England when Sadler's Wells moved to the opera house at Covent Garden and became the Royal.

And then, two years later, the new Met opened and A.B.T. found a new home. The Met would in some ways be good for the company—adding to its allure for people in the money—although the necessity of filling such a huge theater every spring greatly limited the company's repertory: The old warhorses had to be kept relentlessly on parade, and alas, there are only so many nineteenth-century full-evening ballets that are viable. But even second-level story ballets worked for audiences when populated by bona fide stars. A.B.T., after its shaky start, survived and prevailed as an institution, and with its wide repertory, its sometimes valid, sometimes dubious star system, and its glamorous theater significantly added to the sense New Yorkers had of ballet as Occasion. It was a key element in the transformation of ballet in the city from the sad stepsister among the arts to a thriving cultural phenomenon.

LEFT: Balanchine surrounded by the four ballerinas of his 1967 full-evening, three-part masterpiece Jewels. *Clockwise from top right: Patricia McBride ("Rubies"), Violette Verdy and Mimi Paul ("Emeralds"), and Suzanne Farrell ("Diamonds"). Costumes, again, by Karinska.*

ABOVE: Balanchine and Stravinsky during rehearsals in 1963, presumably for Movements for Piano and Orchestra, *which premiered that year.*

Ballet, of course, was only part of the story of dance in New York in the postwar years. Early in the century, Isadora Duncan had hauled modern dance east from California on her way to conquering Europe and to self-destruction. Then came Ruth St. Denis and Ted Shawn, and through them to the quintessence of the form: Martha Graham. It was Martha, born in 1894, who became the iconic figure of the movement, by the 1930s a national treasure or joke, depending on how you saw it. (This was not unlike the way Eleanor Roosevelt was considered at this time.) Her first New York concert was in 1926, and by 1931 she had produced her first masterpiece, the rigorous, spiritual *Primitive Mysteries.* Her company was all female until 1938, when she accepted Erick Hawkins into it—she would marry him ten years later—and the presence of a male figure or figures enlarged the scope of her dramas. In 1940, *Letter to the World* (Emily Dickinson); in 1943, *Deaths and Entrances* (the Brontës); in 1944—by now the young Merce Cunningham had joined the company—her best-loved work, *Appalachian Spring,* with its starkly beautiful Noguchi set (they would collaborate on about twenty ballets) and its resonant Aaron Copland score.

She was now a commanding figure, and in the years directly following the war she produced a number of compelling dramas: *Dark Meadow, Cave of the Heart* (Medea), *Errand into the Maze* (Ariadne and the Minotaur), *Night Journey* (Oedipus and Jocasta). This was the start of her Greek period; Graham by now was reaching for the mythic and eternal. Her dancing, her personality both on- and offstage, were so powerful that she herself was becoming mythic. But by the early 1960s, her major work was behind her, leaving us with the joyous (and abstract) *Diversion of Angels,* the radiant Saint Joan ballet *Seraphic Dialogue,* and in 1958 the climax of her classical adventures, the full-evening *Clytemnestra,* in which, needless to say, she dominated as the tragic, driven queen. Her annual or semi-annual seasons, usually two or three weeks long, were a spectacular element of the New York dance scene. Alas, by the late sixties, as physical erosion forced her to stop dancing, she deteriorated into alcoholism and rage, dismissed her natural heirs, and produced a series of unworthy works that for a while we tried to pretend were worthy. But in the decades immediately following the war, she was, and deserved to be, the dominant force in the world of modern dance.

She was certainly not alone, though. Of her immediate contemporaries the most important was Doris Humphrey, who had worked side by side—but not hand in glove—with her in the Denishawn

company, until each of them decided to leave behind Miss Ruth's orientalisms and strike out into new territory, Graham with her technique based on contraction and release, Humphrey with her pattern of fall and recovery. Humphrey was less dramatic, more austere than her rival, more cerebral. She never reached Graham's level of popularity—she was never a celebrity—but her works were intensely admired: *Soaring, Air for the G String, Life of the Bee, The Shakers.* Today, what little remains of her work looks somewhat quaint, but in her day her influence was enormous—first, during her extended, successful partnership with the equally serious (except when he was funny) Charles Weidman, another escapee from Denishawn, and then for seven years as artistic director of the José Limón dance company (he had been her student).

Humphrey had to stop dancing early, in 1945, but her work as a choreographer went on, and even more important, so did her work as a teacher. She was for many years at the famous Bennington

OPPOSITE: Martha Graham's Clytemnestra *(1958), her largest-scale undertaking, with Helen McGehee, left, as Electra, Bertram Ross as Orestes, and Graham herself as Clytemnestra.*

BELOW: Doris Humphrey and Charles Weidman in Humphrey's Square Dances *(1939).*

OVERLEAF: The Alwin Nikolais company in Tensile Involvement *(1953).*

School of the Dance and later was a central presence at Juilliard's dance division, which she helped found in 1951, and where she taught—a revered figure—until her death seven years later.

Another of the Bennington group was Hanya Holm, who came to America in 1931 as an acolyte of the renowned German Expressionist Mary Wigman. Holm settled here, becoming equally important as a choreographer and an educator, but her late popularity came, surprisingly, when she produced the dances for such musicals as *Kiss Me Kate* and *My Fair Lady*. From the ultra-serious Wigman

Jose Limón's The Moor's Pavane *(1949), with its original cast: Limón as Othello, Lucas Hoving as Iago, Pauline Koner as Emilia, and Betty Jones as Desdemona.*

Rudolf Nureyev as Othello in Limón's
The Moor's Pavane.

to Cole Porter was a considerable leap, but Holm made it easily and triumphantly. Her most illustrious direct descendant was the imaginative and stimulating Alwin Nikolais, who studied with her and danced for her before establishing his Nikolais Dance Theatre at the Henry Street Settlement House. There, for a period in the fifties and sixties, his magical experiments with lighting, costume, and complex stage effects—luminescent paint, for one—drew avid dance lovers to the Lower East Side.

But apart from Graham, the largest presence in modern dance in the immediate postwar years was José Limón. He was born in Mexico in 1908, and by 1929 he was in America, performing with the Humphrey-Weidman company. During the next dozen years he appeared on Broadway, danced with imposing ex-Graham dancer May O'Donnell, and after a stretch in the armed forces during the war, founded the José Limón Dance Company in 1946. (It had its first New York season only a year later.) Limón was a powerful stage presence, strong, dramatic, and virile, and his company flourished, at first under Humphrey's direction, and then his own. In 1949 he premiered what would become his signature work, *The Moor's Pavane,* a meditation on the Othello story to music by Purcell and magnificent Renaissance costumes by his wife, Pauline Lawrence. It is one of the few modern dances to have been taken up by ballet companies (A.B.T., for one), providing a vehicle for Rudolf Nureyev, among others, and it retains its power today.

Program cover of Katherine Dunham's dance revue Bal Nègre, *which opened in New York on November 7, 1946.*

The Limón company is a triumph of survival, still performing in America and abroad, though its repertory has expanded beyond the works of its founder. Among its more successful revivals are *The Emperor Jones* and *Missa Brevis*, both of which testify to Limón's seriousness of purpose and artistic intelligence.

There were countless modern dance groups and dancers on view in New York through the postwar period; among the famous women were Pearl Lang, a major Graham dancer and prolific choreographer; Pearl Primus, who married dance to African ethnography; Valerie Bettis (*A Streetcar Named Desire*); and the astonishing Katherine Dunham, who spearheaded the phenomenon of black dance in America and around the world as choreographer, dancer, teacher, cultural ambassador, sociologist, writer, and social activist.

The dominant new choreographers of the period, however, were two white men, both of whom emerged from Martha Graham's company: Merce Cunningham and Paul Taylor. Leaving Martha after six years, Cunningham, a brilliant, speedy dancer, joined with his partner, the avant-garde composer John Cage, to create a revolutionary dance aesthetic, generally divorced from music—pure movement, highly disciplined, with a touch of ballet (Cunningham

Katherine Dunham performing in her Afrique, *1940s.*

Ellen Cornfield in Merce Cunningham's Minutiae *(1954), with music by John Cage and décor by Robert Rauschenberg.*

had studied at Balanchine's School of American Ballet). His work grew more and more abstract, the "drama" residing in the structure and detail of each piece, and in the subtlety and clarity of the movement. Along the way, he added the element of chance, often linked to the I Ching, to the process by which he created his pieces. If he generally eschewed choreographing to music, he was closely allied with the major visual artists of his day, in particular Robert Rauschenberg (who at times acted as his stage manager), Jasper Johns, Roy Lichtenstein, Frank Stella, and Andy Warhol. Among the two hundred or more works he created, some of the most highly regarded are *Suite for Five, Rainforest, Sounddance, Ocean, Biped, Winterbranch,* and *Summerspace* (which was also danced by New York City Ballet, on pointe).

From his early crucial season at Black Mountain College in North Carolina in 1953 (he had left Graham in 1945) to the year of his death, 2009, his invention never dried up and his influence grew. He chose to have his company disband after his death, but his artistic heirs are today teaching and staging Cunningham works here and in Europe. By the end of the postwar period, he was a central presence in the New York dance world, and he remains so. If any single choreographer succeeded Balanchine as having the greatest impact on dance in his moment, it's Cunningham.

Paul Taylor is a very different story. He, too, was a superb dancer—big, muscular, explosive, masculine, yet on occasion goofy. Graham presented him mostly as a stud, but she was supportive of his choreographic efforts, affectionately referring to him as "the naughty boy" of dance. (In one of his earliest pieces, he simply stood still; in another, he just walked back and forth to the recorded sound of a telephone operator announcing the time; a famous review of this concert consisted of four inches of blank space. Years later he would wryly claim to be the godfather of the Judson Dance Theater, famous for its embrace of everyday movement).

After seven years he left Graham, though not before 1959, when—for a Graham-Balanchine collaboration—he created an extraordinary solo for Balanchine's *Episodes*. (Balanchine offered him a job at City Ballet—*Apollo*, etc.—but he wasn't interested.) In 1962, he and his young company had a popular breakthrough: *Aureole*, to Handel—one of his earliest works set to Baroque

ABOVE: Left to right: John Cage, Merce Cunningham, and Robert Rauschenberg, 1964.

BELOW: Carolyn Brown in Cunningham's Walkaround Time (1968), with décor by Jasper Johns, featuring seven inflatable pillows painted with images from Marcel Duchamp's The Bride Stripped Bare by her Bachelors, Even (The Large Glass).

music. More than 135 works later as of 2014, and at the age of eighty-three, he is still producing vigorous new dances, at least two a year. The range of his effects is enormous, from the cheerful, smashing finale of his signature work, *Esplanade*, to the plangent autumnal *Sunset*, to the devastatingly bleak *Last Look*, to *Company B*, set to the Andrews Sisters, the skull beneath the skin visible through his rompy look at World War II. Taylor can be sly, lyrical, outrageous, joyous, despairing—like Walt Whitman, whom he evoked in his late work *Beloved Renegade*, Paul Taylor contains multitudes.

Of all the modern dance troupes, the most popular in recent years, both in America and around the world, has been the Alvin Ailey Dance Company. Ailey, who died in 1989, combined religious impulse, jazz, Africanisms, and Broadway smarts, and under his successor, Judith Jamison, his company flourished. (Its new artistic director is Robert Battle.) Ailey, who had studied and performed with the talented Lester Horton in California, came to New York and danced in various companies and in Broadway musicals until starting up his own company in 1958. His first hit was *Blues Suite*, but his greatest success came in 1960 with *Revelations*, probably the single most performed—and loved—dance work of our time, its combination of spirituality, drama, and joy irresistible. In any Ailey season—the company plays for five weeks at the City Center every fall—*Revelations* will appear on more than three-quarters of the programs, the audience beginning to clap at the first sound of the score. It's a revival meeting all by itself.

By 1965, the world of modern dance was changing. A few years earlier, a concert at the Judson Memorial Church by a group of young choreographers and dancers had started the revolution that would come to be known as post-modern dance, work based on everyday movement—walking, running, etc.—rather than the more formal structures and techniques of ballet or modern. Among the leading practitioners of this movement were Trisha Brown, Lucinda Childs, Robert Dunn, David Gordon, Meredith Monk, Steve Paxton, and Yvonne Rainer, a number of whom are still performing or have recently retired. And then on April 29, 1965, the feisty young Twyla Tharp, who had worked with Graham, Cunningham, and Taylor, presented her first creation: *Tank Dive*. Over the next half century, she, more than any other choreographer, would hasten the process of merging modern with ballet, and infiltrating film and musical theater. She, too, is very much with us today.

But it was not only ballet and modern dances and dancers that made New York City the dance capital of the world. Balanchine's School of American Ballet had become the premiere ballet academy in the country. The Dance Division of the New York Public Library's Performing Arts branch, largely the brainchild of Lincoln Kirstein, moved to Lincoln Center and established itself as the most important dance archive in the world. America's two greatest dance writers—the poet Edwin Denby and Arlene Croce,

who founded the essential magazine *Ballet Review* and would go on to become *The New Yorker*'s superlative dance critic—were important elements of New York's artistic and intellectual life. And then there was a performance group in a category all its own: Radio City Music Hall's Rockettes—thirty-six tall young women who four or five times a day thrill the Hall's vast audience, every performance climaxed by the lineup of all the girls strutting and high-kicking away. Talk about synchronized dancing!

THEATRE ARTS

ANC

february

1958

50 cents

THEATER

The story of the theater in New York in the years after the war is really fourfold: the swarm of plays and acting companies from abroad; the emergence of a new group of talented American playwrights; the proliferation and success of what became known as Off Broadway; and significant developments in the Broadway musical.

THE BRITISH INVASION

In 1946, Britain's Old Vic theater arrived in New York with a starry company led by two of the nation's most eminent actors—Laurence Olivier and Ralph Richardson. The repertory was dazzling: both parts of *Henry IV*, with Olivier as Hotspur in Part 1 and Justice Shallow in Part 2, and Richardson as Falstaff in both; *Uncle Vanya*, with Richardson as Vanya and Olivier as Dr. Astrov; and the astounding double bill of *Oedipus Rex* and Sheridan's *The Critic*, with tour-de-force back-to-back performances of Olivier as Oedipus and Mr. Puff. This visit was a huge triumph with critics and the public—comparable to the success, three years later, of Britain's Sadler's Wells ballet. And Olivier would be back in 1951 with his wife, Vivien Leigh, in Shakespeare's *Antony and Cleopatra* and Shaw's *Caesar and Cleopatra*: She was charming in the latter, but underwhelming in the former.

England's other leading classicist, John Gielgud, who had played on Broadway in the 1930s, had a series of successes in New York during this period: *Much Ado about Nothing*, opposite Margaret Leighton; his definitive *The Importance of Being Earnest*; and his one-man Shakespeare recital, *Ages of Man*. (Gielgud also successfully directed many plays in New York, including the highly esteemed *Medea* starring Judith Anderson, with Gielgud as Jason.) And following this first invasion of the British stars came Michael Redgrave, Paul Scofield, Rex Harrison, and eventually Richard Burton. Perhaps the biggest English star of all was Julie Andrews—first in *The Boy Friend*, then, of course, in *My Fair Lady* (opposite

Harrison), finally in *Camelot*, with Burton. Then on to film glory in *Mary Poppins* and *The Sound of Music.*

This stream of major British performers was not only a challenge to American actors, who lacked their technical training, but a way for Broadway audiences to experience the great plays. There were American productions of the classics, too, often starring the capable Maurice Evans, and some directed by Margaret Webster, including her famous 1944 *Othello* starring Paul Robeson as the Moor and José Ferrer as Iago. (I was taken to see it the night of my graduation from junior high school, disappointed because it wasn't a musical.) But no one was fooled—these home efforts were well meaning but second best.

A parade of British playwrights was also doing well on Broadway, from the conventional Terence Rattigan (*The Deep Blue Sea, Separate Tables, The Winslow Boy, The Sleeping Prince*) to Christopher Fry—his *The Lady's Not for Burning*, starring and directed by Gielgud, and with Pamela Brown, struck some as precious and pretentious, others as elegant and poetic—and T. S. Eliot, whose surprise hit, *The Cocktail Party*, starring Alec Guinness and Irene Worth, was talked about everywhere, ran for a year, and won the Tony for best play. It

John Gielgud performing his brilliant Shakespeare one-man show, Ages of Man.

The famous 1946 Broadway season of Britain's Old Vic theater. LEFT: Ralph Richardson as Falstaff hauling away the corpse of Olivier's Hotspur in Shakespeare's Henry IV, Part 1. ABOVE: Olivier as Puff in Sheridan's spoof comedy, The Critic.

involved an unhappily married London couple and a woman who goes off to Africa to die, eaten by ants, as a missionary—in other words, a drawing room comedy with martyrdom. But it was by the most famous poet in the world.

George Bernard Shaw was still a potent name on Broadway: both *Man and Superman* and *Heartbreak House* with Maurice Evans, *Pygmalion*

ABOVE: The play's success also landed Eliot on the cover of Time *magazine (March 6, 1950).*

RIGHT: T. S. Eliot had a big (surprise) hit on Broadway in 1950 with his play The Cocktail Party. *It ran for a year and won the Tony for best play. Left to right: Cathleen Nesbitt, Alec Guinness, Eileen Peel, Ernest Clark, and Robert Flemyng.*

with Gertrude Lawrence and Raymond Massey, *The Millionairess* with Katharine Hepburn, *Saint Joan* with Siobhan McKenna, and the all-star concert version of the "Don Juan in Hell" scene from *Man and Superman*, with Charles Laughton, Charles Boyer, Cedric Hardwicke, and Agnes Moorhead. In 1946, Katharine Cornell brought *Candida* back to Broadway—her fifth production of it since 1924—this

time with the young Marlon Brando as Marchbanks. Throughout this period, Shaw was generally accepted as the greatest English playwright after Shakespeare. *Sic transit* . . . And there was always Noël Coward, in just about any capacity the theater could offer. None of his postwar plays had the success of the earlier ones—up to and including the wartime *Blithe Spirit*—but his cabaret acts, his television and film appearances, his songs, his fiction, his presence as the essence of sophistication kept him in the forefront of the entertainment world. And there were revivals, too, like the production of *Private Lives* that Tallulah Bankhead used as a vehicle for her outrageous camping, which played on Broadway for a year and then around and around the country, and which Coward hated. By the end of the sixties, the play was back on Broadway, this time with Brian Bedford and Tammy Grimes.

*Shaw again. **ABOVE**: Maurice Evans, who appeared in* Man and Superman, The Devil's Disciple, The Apple Cart, *and* Heartbreak House, *contemplating a bust of the Master.* **RIGHT***: Raymond Massey and Gertrude Lawrence in* Pygmalion. **OPPOSITE***: Katharine Hepburn in* The Millionairess.

Three Broadway Joans. TOP: *Siobhan McKenna in Shaw's* Saint Joan. CENTER: *Ingrid Bergman in Maxwell Anderson's* Joan of Lorraine. BOTTOM: *Julie Harris in Jean Anouilh's* The Lark.

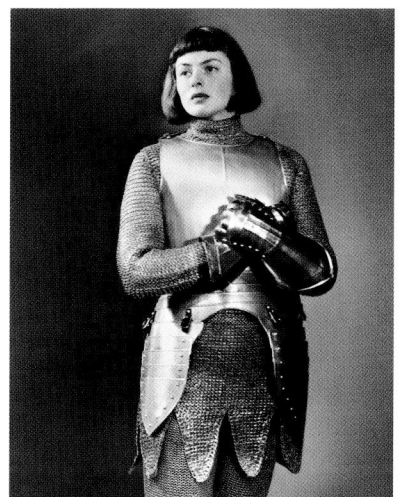

Noël Coward in his play Nude with Violin.

But the times were changing, and the next generation of British playwrights was something new and different. The herald of this new drama was John Osborne's savagely anti-establishment *Look Back in Anger* in 1956. Among his plays to come was *The Entertainer*, with Olivier at his very greatest as a broken-down vaudevillian, but Osborne's talent faded relatively early. The playwright who succeeded him here was Harold Pinter, beginning in 1962 with *The Caretaker*, starring Alan Bates, Donald Pleasence, and Robert Shaw, and followed within the decade by *The Birthday Party* and *The Home-coming*. Pinter's obscure, compressed style and mysterious intentions fascinated and baffled New York audiences, who after half a century (and a Nobel Prize) continue to value him in countless revivals. Shakespeare, of course, is always with us, but Shaw has dwindled away, as have the plays of Rattigan (despite occasional revivals), Fry, and Eliot. The English playwrights of the period who survive are that odd couple, Harold Pinter and Noël Coward.

ABOVE: Donald Cook on top of Tallulah Bankhead in Coward's classic comedy Private Lives.

OPPOSITE: Laurence Olivier's great performance in John Osborne's The Entertainer.

The British invasion was still at its height in the early sixties when that other British invasion—into pop music—was taking place, led by the Beatles, the Stones, and the Who. But Britain didn't have things all to itself. There was an unprecedented surge of theater arriving from the Continent—from France, really. The playwrights included Jean Anouilh (*Time Remembered*, with Richard Burton, Helen Hayes, and Susan Strasberg; *The Lark*, with Julie Harris as Joan of Arc; *Waltz of the Toreadors*, with Ralph Richardson), and Jean Giraudoux (*The Madwoman of Chaillot*, an anti-establishment romantic satire with Martita Hunt winning the Tony, and *Tiger at the Gates*, with Michael Redgrave). Sartre was represented by *No Exit* and *Red Gloves* (with Charles Boyer).

It was during these years that Jean Genet exploded off Broadway with the ferocious vision of *The Maids*, *The Blacks*, and *The Balcony*,

Kenneth Haigh and Alan Bates in Osborne's revolutionary Look Back in Anger.

and that Eugène Ionesco, the leading exemplar of the Theater of the Absurd, was presented in a series of startling productions: *The Bald Soprano, The Lesson, The Chairs,* and—most important—*Rhinoceros,* which in 1961 provided Zero Mostel with a triumphant Broadway vehicle. There were individual German successes, too: Peter Weiss's *Marat/Sade*; Rolf Hochhuth's *The Deputy*; Swiss playwright Friedrich Dürrenmatt's *The Visit* (with the Lunts). The most significant, if not the most successful, import from abroad was the 1956 Broadway production of Samuel Beckett's *Waiting for Godot,* starring Bert Lahr and E. G. Marshall. *Endgame, Krapp's Last Tape,* and *Happy Days* would follow, off Broadway. Beckett's bleak, tragicomic take on life distressed or offended some of the audience back in the fifties and sixties, but no one doubted his genius or his influence.

Nothing like this influx of serious theater from England and Europe to New York had happened before, and it would never

happen again. At the time, it seemed natural—with the city now "the capital of the world," everything and everyone came here, so why not the cream of world theater? A quick look at what's available on Broadway today reminds us of how special a time it was back then, and how foolish we were to take it all for granted.

LEFT: Jean Giraudoux's The Madwoman of Chaillot. *Left to right: Estelle Winwood, Martita Hunt, and Nydia Westman.*

BELOW: Eugène Ionesco's Rhinoceros, *with Zero Mostel and Eli Wallach.*

*BELOW: Bert Lahr and E. G. Marshall in
Samuel Beckett's* Waiting for Godot.

PRECEDING PAGES: Tennessee Williams's
The Glass Menagerie. *Left to right:*
Anthony Ross, the sublime Laurette Taylor,
Eddie Dowling, and Julie Haydon.

BELOW: Opening-night party for A Streetcar
Named Desire. *Left to right: playwright*
Tennessee Williams, producer Irene Mayer
Selznick, and director Elia Kazan.

OPPOSITE: A Streetcar Named Desire,
with Marlon Brando and Jessica Tandy. Brando
blew her (and everyone else) off the stage.

Broadway before the war had been booming. There was a string of well-made, commercially successful comedies and dramas by writers such as Robert Sherwood, S. N. Behrman, Philip Barry, George Kaufman and Moss Hart, Sidney Howard, and others. More ambitious writers like Maxwell Anderson and Elmer Rice were still at work, and Lillian Hellman had made a noisy splash with *The Children's Hour*, *The Little Foxes*, and *Watch on the Rhine*. And Clifford Odets, a key member of the radical Group Theatre, had triumphed with *Waiting for Lefty*, *Awake and Sing!*, and *Golden Boy* before going to Hollywood and watching his talents diminish. (Of his postwar theater work, only *The Big Knife* and *The Country Girl* were of any consequence.)

The new American theater announced itself in 1945, with the New York premiere of *The Glass Menagerie*, the first substantial play by Tennessee Williams, motored by one of the greatest performances ever seen on our stage: Laurette Taylor in the role of the maddening, affecting mother, Amanda Wingfield. Taylor had made a miraculous comeback from years of alcoholism, and she was transcendent—so real, so true, that you couldn't believe this was *acting*. I was fourteen when I saw her, and it was an overwhelming experience; the theatrics of Helen Hayes, Katharine Cornell,

Lynn Fontanne, Ethel Barrymore, and the other First Ladies of the American Stage faded away. And when Williams's next play, *A Streetcar Named Desire*, followed two years later, it was confirmed that a tremendous talent was at hand. The performance of the young Marlon Brando was as electrifying as Laurette Taylor's had been—here was acting genius to match that of the British theatrical knights, and of a new kind: brutally realistic, explosive, dangerous. In the countless productions of *Streetcar* since then, it has

been seen as Blanche DuBois's play—a diva vehicle. Back then, it was Stanley Kowalski's; the perfectly capable Jessica Tandy didn't stand a chance against him.

Williams's run of successes was astounding. Between 1948 and 1963 he produced *Summer and Smoke*, *The Rose Tattoo* (Maureen Stapleton), *Camino Real* (a failed experiment), *Cat on a Hot Tin Roof* (Barbara Bel Geddes as Maggie the Cat), *Orpheus Descending*, *Suddenly Last Summer*, *Sweet Bird of Youth* (Geraldine Page), *The Night of the Iguana*

Three Tennessee Williams heroines.
OPPOSITE: *Geraldine Page in* Sweet
Bird of Youth *(with Paul Newman).*
LEFT: *Barbara Bel Geddes as Maggie the
Cat in* Cat on a Hot Tin Roof
(with Ben Gazzara and Burl Ives).
BELOW: *Maureen Stapleton in* The Rose
Tattoo *(with Phyllis Love and Don Murray).*

Arthur Miller's Death of a Salesman. *Left to right: Mildred Dunnock, Arthur Kennedy, Cameron Mitchell, and Lee J. Cobb. The set was by Jo Mielziner, who also designed* A Streetcar Named Desire, South Pacific, Guys and Dolls, *and* Gypsy, *among many others.*

(Bette Davis and Margaret Leighton), *The Milk Train Doesn't Stop Here Anymore.* His later work was not enthusiastically received, but this group of plays—constantly revived—would become as central to American theatrical history as Eugene O'Neill's had been in the twenties and early thirties.

If Williams had a rival—and they were inevitably compared and contrasted—it was the more moralistic, less magical Arthur Miller.

In 1947, *All My Sons*, loosely based on Ibsen's *An Enemy of the People*, was a substantial success, but it was *Death of a Salesman*, two years later, that made his reputation as an important American playwright. He was earnest, he was liberal, and he married Marilyn Monroe. *The Crucible* was another hailed work, the Salem witch trials used as an attack on McCarthyism. *A View from the Bridge*, *Incident at Vichy*, and *The Price* were all modestly successful, but the play that made the loudest noise

BOTTOM: Salesman's author, Arthur Miller, left, and director, Elia Kazan. Their long relationship was severely tested by political disagreement, sexual rivalry, and diverging career arcs.

THE GREATEST PLAY OF OUR GENERATION!

PULITZER PRIZE

N. Y. CRITICS' AWARD

death of a Salesman

RIGHT: *Barbara Loden, wife of Elia Kazan, and Jason Robards Jr. in Arthur Miller's* After the Fall, *based on his marriage to Marilyn Monroe.*

BELOW: *Arthur Miller's* The Crucible.

was *After the Fall*, a savage look at his marriage to Monroe. Like Williams, he fell into disfavor—*The Price*, in 1968, was his last success in the theater.

Another playwright who for a while looked as if he might be of lasting significance was William Inge, whose first Broadway play, *Come Back, Little Sheba*, made a splash in 1950, and whose second, *Picnic*, was a big hit (and won the Pulitzer Prize). *Bus Stop* was also a success—it starred the wonderful Kim Stanley, probably the most talented of her generation of actresses, in the role of Cherie (Marilyn Monroe in the movie). *The Dark at the Top of the*

ABOVE: William Inge's Picnic, *starring Ralph Meeker and Janice Rule and directed by Joshua Logan.*

LEFT: Kim Stanley as Cherie (with Albert Salmi) in Inge's Bus Stop. *Marilyn Monroe was at her best in the movie version.*

LEFT: Edward Albee.

BELOW: Albee's marital free-for-all, Who's Afraid of Virginia Woolf? *Left to right: Arthur Hill, George Grizzard, Melinda Dillon, and Uta Hagen.*

OPPOSITE: Eugene O'Neill's searing autobiographical Long Day's Journey into Night. *Standing: Bradford Dillman and Jason Robards Jr.; seated: Florence Eldridge and Fredric March. Many critics believe it's America's greatest play.*

Stairs was yet another success—each of these last three plays, all set in the Midwest, ran for more than a year—but that was it, apart from the script of *Splendor in the Grass,* which won him an Oscar. His career petered out, and he committed suicide at the age of sixty.

The last of the important playwrights who came to prominence in this period was Edward Albee, whose *The Zoo Story* made a tremendous impact when, in 1960, it was paired off Broadway with Beckett's *Krapp's Last Tape.* The play that confirmed his reputation as a major dramatist was that fierce marital battlefield *Who's Afraid of Virginia Woolf?*—a critical and commercial sensation. Albee's career has had its ups and downs, but he has kept going well into his eighties—outlasting by decades the slightly older generation that preceded him.

But the most important American play of the immediate post-war period, and considered by many to be America's greatest play, was written before the war yet not produced until 1956—Eugene O'Neill's brutal family drama *A Long Day's Journey into Night,* starring Fredric March and his wife, Florence Eldridge. This anguished play, based on the marriage of O'Neill's parents, had overwhelming force, and it won O'Neill his fourth Pulitzer Prize. Another magnificent play of his, *The Iceman Cometh,* was also produced years after it was written, as were two other plays he had written in the early forties and stowed away: *A Moon for the Misbegotten* and *A Touch of the Poet,* all staged between 1946 and 1958. This final flourish of a writer of immense talents confirmed his reputation and justified (if it needed justification) his Nobel Prize—the only one ever awarded to an American playwright.

The most commanding figure in the postwar Broadway theater, however, was neither a playwright nor an actor but a director: Elia Kazan. He had come up through the Group Theatre in the thirties, directed some successful plays, most importantly Thornton Wilder's *The Skin of Our Teeth* (and, surprisingly, a hit musical—Kurt Weill's *One Touch of Venus,* with Mary Martin), and was one of the founders of the Actors Studio in 1947. But his fame and influence really took hold with a series of major productions by America's new playwrights that began with Miller's *All My Sons* and soared with *A Streetcar Named Desire* and *Death of a Salesman.* Among his other important productions: *Cat on a Hot Tin Roof, Sweet Bird of Youth, The Dark at the Top of the Stairs,* Archibald MacLeish's *J.B.,* and Miller's *After the Fall*—all this while maintaining an equally triumphant career in Hollywood (Oscars for *On the Waterfront* and *Gentleman's Agreement*).

Actors from Brando to James Dean to Warren Beatty agreed that he was the most inspiring director they ever worked with, and "The Method," the approach to acting worked out at the Actors Studio,

greatly by him, has dominated American acting ever since. When he grew tired of directing he began to write, and his novel *The Arrangement* became the number-one best seller of 1967. Kazan revealed himself in his superb autobiography, *A Life*, as a deeply conflicted, angry, driven, and generous man. "The work of Elia Kazan," wrote the highbrow theater critic Eric Bentley, "means more to the American theater than that of any current writer."

Kazan's colleague at the Group Theatre and the Studio, and a formidable critic himself, was Harold Clurman, who directed forty or so plays, including Odets's *Awake and Sing!* and *Golden Boy*. After the war, he went on to such successes as Carson McCullers's *The Member of the Wedding* (with Julie Harris and Ethel Waters), *Bus Stop*, and Lillian Hellman's *The Autumn Garden*—as well as Rodgers and Hammerstein's *Pipe Dream*. He remains a revered figure in the American theater. As does the other major figure from the Group Theatre, Lee Strasberg, who became the most famous and influential teacher (and guru) American theater has ever had: As head of the Actors Studio, he dominated the thinking of a generation of actors, from Marlon Brando to (famously) Marilyn Monroe.

OPPOSITE: An Evening with Mike Nichols and Elaine May. *Masters of satirical improvisation, they were the funniest, wittiest, most charming comics of their day.*

ABOVE: Mike Nichols's production of one of Neil Simon's biggest hits, Barefoot in the Park. *Left to right: Mildred Natwick, Elizabeth Ashley, Kurt Kasznar, and Robert Redford.*

Paul Douglas and Judy Holliday in Garson Kanin's huge hit comedy, Born Yesterday.

Two other brilliant, and even more commercially successful, directors were important in the postwar period—one, Josh Logan, a veteran going back to two Rodgers and Hart musicals and other hits of the thirties; the other, Mike Nichols, the cleverest new guy in town. Logan, despite a bipolar condition, directed three of the greatest hits of the time—Irving Berlin's *Annie Get Your Gun*, with Ethel Merman, in 1946; *Mister Roberts*, with Henry Fonda, in 1948; and Rodgers and Hammerstein's *South Pacific*, with Mary Martin and Ezio Pinza, in 1949. The first two ran almost three years each; the last, almost five. This was Broadway commercial theater at its most potent.

Nichols, after a triumphant half year on Broadway with his partner, Elaine May, in their two-person show, began his directing career in 1963 with Neil Simon's *Barefoot in the Park*, starring Robert Redford and Elizabeth Ashley, which ran for more than 1,500 performances. Simon went on to become the most successful commercial playwright of our time—forty years of hits—while Nichols went on to direct other Simon plays like *The Odd Couple*

THEATRE arts

The play "MISTER ROBERTS" by Thomas Heggen and Joshua Logan

MARCH 1950

50c

Two unique comediennes, almost dementedly unalike. LEFT: *Beatrice Lillie (Lady Peel) had only to step onto the stage and you were laughing. She was from the theatrical world of Noël Coward and Gertrude Lawrence, and appeared mostly in revues; her most famous song, "There Are Fairies at the Bottom of My Garden."* Her Evening with Beatrice Lillie *played on Broadway for eight months.* ABOVE: *Mae West—tough, bawdy, outrageous—was a giant movie star in the 1930s, famous for lines like "Come up and see me sometime" (to Cary Grant) and (to her maid), "Beulah, peel me a grape." In 1949 she brought back to Broadway her own play* Diamond Lil, *which had wowed them twenty-one years earlier, and was celebrated on the cover of* Theatre Arts *magazine.*

and *Plaza Suite,* and many other notable shows (including the recent triumph *Spamalot*), as well as becoming one of Hollywood's leading directors—his first two films: *Who's Afraid of Virginia Woolf?* and *The Graduate.* It's a career that curiously echoes Kazan's.

And let's not forget another formidable figure of the period: Garson Kanin (married to the actress Ruth Gordon), who, apart from his notable work in the movies and in books, directed Susan Strasberg in *The Diary of Anne Frank,* Barbra Streisand in *Funny Girl,* and not only directed but wrote one of the most successful comedies in Broadway history, *Born Yesterday,* which made a star out of Judy Holliday and ran for almost four years.

And finally, a tip of the hat to two uncategorizable comic geniuses of the twentieth century: Beatrice Lillie, colleague of Noël Coward and Gertrude Lawrence, and to many the funniest woman who ever lived in her glorious *Evening with Beatrice Lillie,* and the sublime Mae West, reinventing herself yet again in a Broadway revival of her own play *Diamond Lil.*

Although Broadway was turning out hit after hit, the way New Yorkers were going to the theater was changing. There had always been small theater groups bringing new or obscure work to the public—the most visible, the Provincetown Players, who evolved into the Provincetown Playhouse, best known for promoting the early work of Eugene O'Neill, including *The Emperor*

Jones (1920) and *Desire Under the Elms* (1924). But Off Broadway as we know it was a phenomenon of the postwar years. There was the Phoenix Theatre, which for many years presented distinguished casts in distinguished revivals (*Mary Stuart*, for instance, with Irene Worth and Eva Le Gallienne, and the Siobhan McKenna *Saint Joan*, which then moved to Broadway), as well as new plays such as Arthur Kopit's *Oh Dad, Poor Dad, Mamma's Hung You in the Closet and I'm Feelin' So Sad*, directed by Jerome Robbins, and the Ionesco double bill of *The Chairs* and *The Lesson*. Probably the Phoenix's most successful commercial venture was the Mary Rodgers–Marshall Barer musical *Once Upon a Mattress*, which made Carol Burnett a star.

At the other end of the spectrum was The Living Theatre, the creation, in 1947, of the avant-garde couple Judith Malina and Julian Beck, whose work was deeply influenced by Antonin Artaud. Their provocative productions of *The Connection*, the theater's first bold presentation of the drug world, and *The Brig*, a furious assault on the brutality of military prisons, were both sensations, but the Becks also gave us original and powerful versions of Pirandello. By the mid-sixties they were in Europe, at the forefront of the radical activist movements in politics and art. After Beck's death, Malina carried on alone in New York until 2013, when, at eighty-six, she finally retired to the Actors Home—promising to be back.

And then there was Ellen Stewart's La MaMa Experimental Theatre Club, also known as Café La MaMa. In 1961, Ms. Stewart rented a basement in a tenement building on the Lower East Side. The fledgling theater faced severe adversity both financial and bureaucratic, and moved from venue to venue one step ahead of the city inspectors, but it survived. As a theater devoted to new playwrights,

OPPOSITE: Life in a United States Marine Corps military prison, as portrayed in The Living Theatre's *anti-military play* The Brig, *by Kenneth H. Brown.*

BELOW: Ellen Stewart (center) of Café La MaMa, later known as La MaMa Experimental Theatre Club, surrounded by her "babies" at a production meeting in La MaMa's first permanent home.

and putting on a play a week, it served a crucial function for beginning dramatists (among them, Lanford Wilson, Sam Shepard, and Harvey Fierstein) and directors (Tom O'Horgan)—and it serves the same purpose today.

There were many Off Broadway theaters of a wide variety of sizes, among them the Cherry Lane and the Theatre de Lys. The economics of Broadway might have been growing prohibitively expensive for producers and audiences, but Off Broadway was affordable. It became an essential training ground for new playwrights, directors, and actors, serving as stock companies once did. And it produced a number of immense successes, among them the famous revival of the Weill-Brecht *Threepenny Opera* (1954), with Lotte Lenya, which ran for more than six years, and the whimsical little musical *The Fantasticks* (1960), the longest running show in American history—more than 17,000 performances spread over forty-two years. Nothing tops cute.

By far the most important Off Broadway phenomenon was the Public Theater, begun by Joseph Papp in 1954 as the Shakespeare Workshop, which traveled Shakespeare productions throughout the boroughs—a modest beginning that led to one of New York's most treasured attractions, the annual free Shakespeare in the Park seasons. The Public now has five separate theaters on its premises and has been a crucial launching pad for countless shows, beginning with the one that Papp chose in 1967 to open his huge new facility on Lafayette Street, *Hair: The American Tribal Love-Rock Musical*, which moved to Broadway and ran for four years. It was the first of the fifty-four Public Theater productions that have made that move, including *That Championship Season* and *The Normal Heart*. Four of them were Pulitzer

Prize winners, including the show that became the longest-running musical in Broadway history (until it was overtaken by *Cats*): *A Chorus Line*. New York theater would have been very different without Joe Papp's Public.

Everything that took place in the two decades after the end of World War II—the foreign invasion, the new playwrights and directors, the Actors Studio, Off Broadway, the confidence of a city newly awakened to its responsibilities and opportunities—made for what now looks like a golden age. In the following fifty years there would still be hits, stars, artistic excitement, but the tide had turned. It would be movies, and then television, that dominated the world of entertainment;

The 1967 opening of its grand new facility on Lafayette Street with the world premiere of the rock musical Hair *marked the end of an era and the beginning of a new one for the Public Theater.*

instead of stage actors moving to Hollywood, we now have television actors moving on to Hollywood, and then occasionally dropping in on the stage—to prove that they're real actors, or to revive flagging careers. That happened in the old days, too, but with a difference: When in the early fifties Jennifer Jones turned up on Broadway in *Portrait of a Lady* or Olivia de Havilland condescended to Juliet, they were practically laughed off the stage. Today, movie stars with no stage experience are still turning up on Broadway in classic roles, but their celebrity is enough to earn them standing ovations. This doesn't really affect the cultural climate, though; the theater isn't dead, but it's no longer center stage.

MUSICALS

The American musical has also gone through tremendous changes over the past half century, and once again, the postwar period was a golden era. In the twenties and thirties, snappy new shows and opulent operettas dominated the scene—on the one hand, the Gershwins and the Astaires, Cole Porter and Ethel Merman, Rodgers and Hart; on the other, Sigmund Romberg's *The Student Prince, The New Moon,* and *The Desert Song* and Rudolf Friml's *Rose-Marie* and *The Vagabond King*. What's lasted from these musicals is the great treasury of popular songs that live on independently of them, from "The Man I Love" to "Night and Day"; the shows are dead. And from the operettas we have the kitschy but irresistible Jeanette MacDonald–Nelson Eddy movies.

Where's Charley?, *Frank Loesser's 1948 musical adaptation of the classic farce* Charley's Aunt, *featured choreography by Balanchine and starred Ray Bolger as the imaginary "Aunt" from Brazil, "where the nuts come from."*

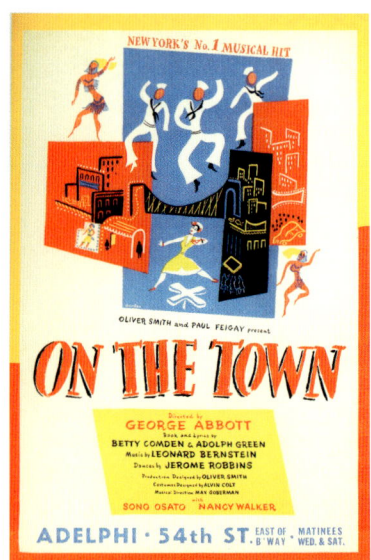

The one exception, apart from the Gershwin opera *Porgy and Bess*, is the 1927 *Show Boat*, which many believe to be not only the first musical to truly integrate songs and book but also the greatest of all musicals, with its incomparable songs by Jerome Kern and Oscar Hammerstein and its powerful story involving show business, miscegenation, the maturing of America. Its many revivals testify to its enduring strengths, and the 1936 film version, with Irene Dunne, Paul Robeson (singing "Ol' Man River"), and Helen Morgan (singing "Bill"), does it full justice.

Show Boat was a glorious combination of operetta and musical play. What really jump-started the maturing of musical comedy itself was Rodgers and Hart's *On Your Toes* (1936), due to the choreography of George Balanchine and his brilliant ballet "Slaughter on Tenth Avenue." This was a show not just *with* dance but *about* dance, and Balanchine went on to do three more musicals with Rodgers and Hart, as well as a number of others, including the wonderful all-black

OPPOSITE, BOTTOM: *The creators of the ebullient musical* On the Town. *Left to right: Leonard Bernstein, music; Jerome Robbins, choreography, based on his ballet* Fancy Free; *and Betty Comden and Adolph Green, libretto and lyrics (they also starred).*

ABOVE: *Mary Martin as Peter Pan teaching the Darling children to fly in the famous* Peter Pan *production of 1954 that attracted a record audience of fifty-five million people when it was first broadcast on television the following year.*

OVERLEAF: *Jerome Robbins's glorious "Bathing Beauty Ballet" (unofficially, the "Keystone Kops" ballet) from* High Button Shoes.

WEST SIDE STORY

TOP: *The creators of* West Side Story. *Left to right: lyricist Stephen Sondheim, playwright Arthur Laurents, director Harold Prince, producer Robert E. Griffith, composer Leonard Bernstein, and choreographer Jerome Robbins.*

Cabin in the Sky, Song of Norway (with Alexandra Danilova), and, in 1948, Frank Loesser's *Where's Charley?*, starring Ray Bolger (who, pre-Oz, had been the hoofing star of *On Your Toes*).

Broadway, however, was only a holding game for Balanchine; once New York City Ballet was in business, he was finished with the Great White Way. The person who really changed the perception of dance's place in the musical was Agnes de Mille, whose work for *Oklahoma!* was hailed as a revelation, and who went on to

The Sharks and the Jets get out their knives *in* West Side Story.

choreograph and direct a cluster of other hit shows: *Bloomer Girl, Carousel, Brigadoon,* and *Gentlemen Prefer Blondes.* After her, dance was a central element of almost all musicals.

Indeed, there were two young men whose achievement would surpass hers. One was Jerome Robbins, her ex-colleague from Ballet Theatre, who in 1944 helped transform his hit ballet *Fancy Free* into the hit musical *On the Town* (music by Leonard Bernstein, libretto and lyrics by Comden and Green). Soon

LEFT: Gypsy Rose Lee (the real-life Gypsy) visits with Sandra Church (the young Gypsy in Gypsy) and Ethel Merman (Mama Rose). With music by Jule Styne, lyrics by the young Stephen Sondheim, and directed by Jerome Robbins, Gypsy is widely considered one of the greatest of all musicals.

ABOVE: Ethel Merman, Jack Klugman, and Sandra Church in Gypsy.

RIGHT: Zero Mostel and Maria Karnilova in bed, in the gigantic hit Fiddler on the Roof. Jerome Robbins in charge again.

he was choreographing other major Broadway shows, including *High Button Shoes*, with its madcap "Keystone Kops" number;
Irving Berlin's (and Ethel Merman's) *Call Me Madam*; Rodgers and
Hammerstein's *The King and I*, with the celebrated "The Small
House of Uncle Thomas" scene and the polka to "Shall We
Dance" for Gertrude Lawrence and Yul Brynner. And his greatest successes lay ahead: *West Side Story, Gypsy, Fiddler on the Roof* (the
first Broadway musical to play 3,000 performances). He was now
completely in charge, as director as well as choreographer. By the
time he went back to ballet in 1969, retiring from the musical
theater (except for the anthology show *Jerome Robbins' Broadway*, in
1989), he had established himself as a show business genius and
had made the choreographer/director the central force in musical theater. There were still great stars—Merman in *Gypsy*, for
instance, or Zero Mostel in *Fiddler*—and there were still strong
scores and books (*Gypsy* again), but these shows were nevertheless
seen as Jerry Robbins creations.

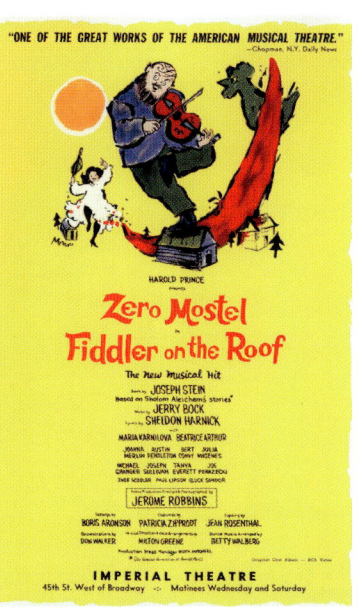

BELOW: Eddie Foy in The Pajama Game. *The high point was Bob Fosse's dance number "Steam Heat."*

Bob Fosse was the other young choreographer/director whose work became a major force on Broadway, beginning with his first choreographed show, *The Pajama Game* ("Steam Heat"), and its successor, *Damn Yankees* (each played for more than 1,000 performances), and going on to *Redhead*, *Sweet Charity*, and the whimsical *Pippin*, which ran for almost five years and is back on Broadway as I write. And in 1975 came what would be his greatest success: Kander and Ebb's *Chicago*, which ran for years in its original production (its 1996 revival has already run for seventeen years—more than 7,000 performances—making it the longest-running American musical in Broadway history). Fosse died at the age of sixty in 1987, and the revival's staging and choreography were done by his protégée Ann Reinking, modeled on the original. But the performer he is most linked with is Gwen Verdon, whom he made into a star—and married.

For all their extraordinary success, Robbins and Fosse were by no means the only major choreographer/directors who transformed the Broadway musical into a genre greatly dominated by dance. Gower Champion won Tony after Tony for such shows as *Bye Bye Birdie*, *Carnival!*, and two of the greatest hits in history:

DON'T EAT CANDY AT YOUR MACHINE

TURN OFF LI

You ar
DON

Hello, Dolly! in 1964, and in 1980, *42nd Street,* which ran for eight years. Alas, he died on the day of its triumphant opening. Another great talent, Michael Bennett, died even more tragically, at the age of forty-four, from AIDS. His first success was with *Follies,* his last was with *Dreamgirls,* and in between, in 1975, he created *A Chorus Line,* which moved from the Public Theater to Broadway, where it played more than 6,000 performances and won the Pulitzer Prize for drama. Previously, only four musicals had won Pulitzers, beginning with the Gershwins' brilliant political satire *Of Thee I Sing* in 1932, followed by Rodgers and Hammerstein's *South Pacific* in 1950, *Fiorello!* in 1960, and *How to Succeed in Business Without Really Trying* in 1962.

Another Fosse triumph—Damn Yankees, starring his muse, Gwen Verdon, as Lola ("Whatever Lola wants, Lola gets").

But if Broadway in these years was dominated by anyone, it was the song-writing and producing team of Richard Rodgers and Oscar Hammerstein, who in 1943 had created *Oklahoma!* and given Agnes de Mille her chance. The show was the greatest success of its time—it was so hard to get tickets that their scarcity became a joke, a subject for cartoons in *The New Yorker.* *Oklahoma!* had a great score, superb staging by Rouben Mamoulian, and a star in the robust Alfred Drake ("Oh, What a Beautiful Mornin'"). Its nostalgia for the values of the frontier past, its rousing optimism, had special meaning for wartime America. And *Oklahoma!*

OPPOSITE: John Raitt and Jan Clayton in Rodgers and Hammerstein's Carousel, *their follow-up to* Oklahoma!

ABOVE: Richard Rodgers and Oscar Hammerstein II.

BELOW: Gertrude Lawrence and Yul Brynner in The King and I.

OVERLEAF: Jerome Robbins's "The Small House of Uncle Thomas" ballet from The King and I.

was only the beginning for Rodgers and Hammerstein: *Carousel*, *South Pacific*, *The King and I*, and *The Sound of Music* were the main events to follow—all legendary shows, always with us, both in revivals and in the movies made from them. R & H's success carried over to their production company when they brought to the stage another of the greatest hits of the period—*Annie Get Your Gun*, which gave birth to half a dozen hit songs, including the iconic "There's No Business Like Show Business," which goes on making theater people feel good about themselves. This was Irving Berlin's biggest Broadway hit. Just as *Kiss Me, Kate* (also with Alfred Drake) was Cole

Rodgers and Hammerstein's South Pacific.
BELOW: *"There Is Nothing Like a Dame."*
TOP RIGHT: *Mary Martin and Ezio Pinza.*
BOTTOM RIGHT: *Mary Martin "wash[ing]*
that man right out of her hair."

Ethel Merman's greatest hit, Irving Berlin's Annie Get Your Gun. *ABOVE:* Merman with Harry Bellaver as Chief Sitting Bull. *RIGHT:* Annie's "Wild West Show," with Ray Middleton and Merman front and center. Yep, "There's No Business Like Show Business."

Porter's biggest hit, *Guys and Dolls* was Frank Loesser's, and *My Fair Lady* was Lerner and Loewe's.

The latter three shows appear on most lists of the all-time-greatest musicals, along with *Show Boat* and *Oklahoma!* (*My Fair Lady*, with Julie Andrews, Rex Harrison, and Shaw's *Pygmalion*, was, in fact, a phenomenon on the order of *Oklahoma!*—everyone wanted to see it and no one could get in.) And these were the years that also gave us *Brigadoon*, *Finian's Rainbow*, *Wonderful Town* (Rosalind Russell), *Bells Are Ringing* (Judy Holliday), *Gentlemen Prefer Blondes* (Carol Channing), *A Funny Thing Happened on the Way to the Forum* (Zero Mostel), *How to Succeed in Business Without Really Trying* (Robert Morse), *Funny Girl* (Barbra Streisand), *The*

Mary Martin singing "Do-Re-Mi" with the von Trapp children in Rodgers and Hammerstein's tremendous hit The Sound of Music. *On to Hollywood and Julie Andrews!*

Music Man (Robert Preston), and *Hello, Dolly!* (Channing again, followed by everyone from Betty Grable and Ginger Rogers to Pearl Bailey). There was even room for a reversion to operetta with huge hits like *Kismet* and *Man of La Mancha.* ("The Impossible Dream," from the latter, may be the model for the over-the-top anthemic inspirational numbers that led inexorably to *Les Miz*'s "I Had a Dream." Although we can't in all honesty absolve *Funny Girl*'s "People" and *The Sound of Music*'s "Climb Every Mountain.")

Almost every one of these musicals produced songs that went straight into the mainstream of popular music and have stayed there. At first they fed the repertories of the leading pop singers of the day: Sinatra, Crosby, Perry Como, Doris Day, Jo Stafford, Rosemary Clooney, Tony Bennett, Nat King Cole, and their coevals all jumped on the best of the new show songs and both issued them as singles and laced their LPs with them. Because these songs were so strong musically, they then became the

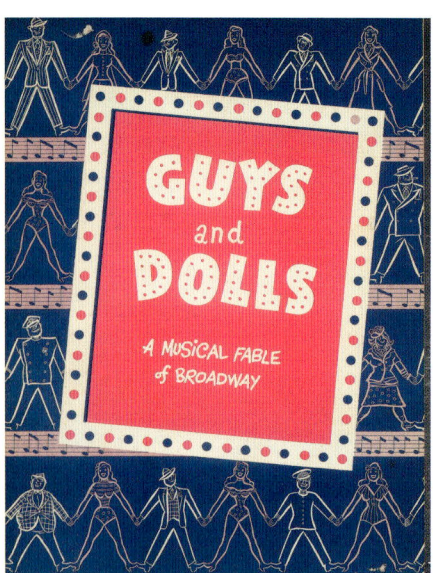

RIGHT: *The immortal underground crap-game scene in Frank Loesser's* Guys and Dolls, *based on the stories of Damon Runyon. Robert Alda as Skye Masterson is shooting the dice.*

One of Broadway's greatest successes was My Fair Lady, based on George Bernard Shaw's Pygmalion. Book and lyrics by Alan Jay Lerner, music by Frederick Loewe, sets by Oliver Smith, costumes by Cecil Beaton, and directed by Moss Hart. The songs include "I Could Have Danced All Night," "On the Street Where You Live," and the all-time showstopper, "The Rain in Spain." OPPOSITE: Julie Andrews, Rex Harrison, Alan Jay Lerner, and Frederick Loewe. Moss Hart is seated behind Lerner and Loewe.

FAR LEFT: The "Ascot Gavotte" scene, with, front and center, Cathleen Nesbitt, as Mrs. Higgins; John Michael King, as Freddy Eynsford-Hill; Julie Andrews, as Eliza Doolittle; Rex Harrison, as Professor Henry Higgins; and Robert Coote, as Colonel Pickering.

ABOVE: Julie Andrews and Rex Harrison in front of the Covent Garden opera house, before she becomes My Fair Lady. The show ran on Broadway for six and a half years.

Dorothy Lamour as Dolly.

Pearl Bailey as Dolly.

Ginger Rogers as Dolly.

Betty Grable as Dolly.

Carol Channing—the original Dolly of Hello, Dolly!

ABOVE: Barbra Streisand in her career-making role as Fanny Brice in Funny Girl. *Among her numbers: "People" (of course), "The Music That Makes Me Dance," "I'm the Greatest Star" (yes, Barbra), and "Don't Rain on My Parade." No one has ever dared to.*

OVERLEAF: A Funny Thing Happened on the Way to the Forum, *music and lyrics by Stephen Sondheim, produced by Hal Prince, directed by George Abbott, and starring Zero Mostel (far left), but behind the scenes, Jerome Robbins.*

property of jazz musicians. And to a large extent they constitute the repertory of today's cabaret performers and even, increasingly, classical singers. No wonder: The men who wrote the finer Broadway musicals, from Berlin and Kern and the Gershwins to Porter and Rodgers and Bernstein were superior composers who worked either alone, like Berlin and Porter and Loesser, or with equally talented lyricists, like Hart and Hammerstein. There's no one remotely as talented working on the musical stage today. The only current writer whose work is taken equally seriously is Stephen Sondheim, who was recognized first as a lyricist—*West Side Story* for Leonard Bernstein, *Gypsy* for Jule Styne—before he began composing as well. His remarkable string of influential musicals—often staged by Harold Prince (who has received eight Tony Awards for direction) and five designed by the great Boris Aronson (who also designed *Cabaret* and *Fiddler*)—includes *A Funny Thing Happened on the Way to the Forum, Company, Follies* (another sentimental bath for theater people), *Sweeney Todd, Sunday in the Park with George,* and *Into the Woods.* But Sondheim is a phenomenon of the post-postwar generation, and his frequently dark work has little in common with jubilant musicals like *Guys and Dolls* and *My Fair Lady.*

The Great American Songbook as it developed on Broadway (and Hollywood) gave us roughly half a century of enduring work before it shut down—just the way nineteenth-century lieder, silent film, and the Victorian novel shut down. The solid, satisfying book musical likewise died the death.

A number of things have happened in the following half century to take its place, some deplorable, but some terrific: rock 'n' roll musicals, most successfully *Grease*; exhilarating black nostalgia musicals, from *Ain't Misbehavin'* (Fats Waller) to *Bring in 'da Noise, Bring in 'da Funk*, starring the tap phenomenon Savion Glover; white nostalgia musicals featuring the music of past musicals—*42nd Street*, Tommy Tune's *My One and Only* (Gershwin); shows to the hits of major pop music stars (Abba's *Mamma Mia!*; The Four Seasons' *Jersey Boys*; Twyla Tharp's Billy Joel show, *Movin' Out*; Carole King's *Beautiful*); rock-spiritual works like *Jesus Christ, Superstar*; Andrew Lloyd Webber's faux-operatic spectacles, from *Cats* to *Phantom of the Opera*; the ultimate show-biz musical, *A Chorus Line*; the ultimate revue, *Oh! Calcutta!*; a string of Disney exploitations of Disney movies—including the original and stirring *The Lion King*, now in its seventeenth year, and the highest-grossing show in Broadway history; up-from-Off-Broadway hits like *Rent* and *Avenue Q*. And, yes, the very rare show with an old-fashioned kind of book: *The Producers, Billy Elliot, The Book of Mormon*. Plus revivals, revivals, revivals, to feed the audience's nostalgia for Broadway's heyday. And let's not forget *Forbidden Broadway*, which has been sticking it to musicals on and off since 1982.

Clearly, this hasn't been a sterile period, or a boring one; it would even be fair to say that it's been more varied and inventive than the "golden" period that more or less came to an end in 1965. But has it been as satisfying?

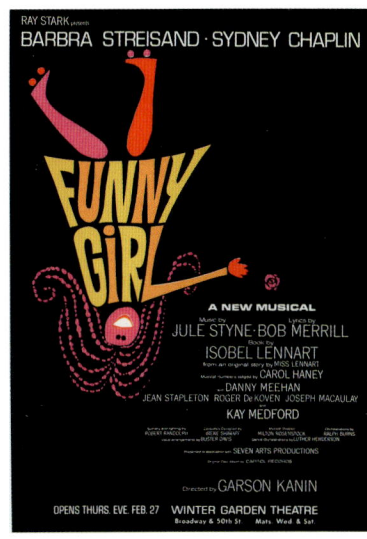

NIGHTLIFE

JAZZ

Until the repeal of Prohibition, in 1933, New Yorkers out on the town after hours found their way to the scores—the hundreds—of speakeasies, where you could get a drink and have a little fun. And maybe the illegality added to the fun. As the Hearst columnist Louis Sobol put it, "The Speakeasy Era was a sizzler for excitement, danger, larceny, romance, intrigue,—and murder. . . . Along drab side streets of New York, dark and guarded doors opened into a spreading world of soft lights, seductive scents, silken music, adroit entertainment, smoke and laughter—of perfection of food and services, of wines and liquors of first qualities—and, of course, the big thrill was that we were all doing something unlawful."

It wasn't until repeal that jazz descended in a thrilling wave down from Harlem and found a natural home on 52nd Street—known to one and all simply as The Street. (It ran from Fifth to Seventh Avenue.) The speakeasies were transformed as if by magic into legit clubs, and by the mid-thirties, countless jazz artists were playing there, from the great pianist Art Tatum (he'd been around in the speakeasy era, too) to Billie Holiday and Lee Wiley and Mabel Mercer. Swing was in—52nd Street was also known as Swing Street—and Count Basie in 1938 led the way for other Big Bands like Woody Herman's. But by the time the war ended, swing had more or less ended too, and early bop had followed it down from Harlem. A bop quartet led by Dizzy Gillespie and Oscar Pettiford turned up at the Onyx in 1944, and soon Charlie Parker, Fats Navarro, Kenny Clarke, and the rest of the bop stars were on The Street too. Until about 1950, 52nd Street was *the* place to go for jazz—unless you were up in Harlem at Minton's or the Savoy or the Apollo. And it was a place for feeling good. One club owner reminisced years later, "Patrons seldom went to one club. You just went to The Street. And then you wandered from club to club, depending on whom you wanted to hear. . . . Excitement spilled over into The Street itself. It was always like a festival night in Greenwich Village's Little Italy. Half of the action was on the sidewalk."

And then it fell into decline. The club owners started bringing in girlie acts—strippers. (In 1949, the Onyx was featuring Zorita, the stripper with a snake.) And west of Sixth, it was practically

OPPOSITE: *By 1952, jazz had become so respectable that there was nothing odd about holding a jazz concert at Carnegie Hall. It had been fourteen years since Benny Goodman—The King of Swing—broke the ice there with the most famous jazz concert of all time, known on records later as "Jazz at Carnegie Hall." (He also broke the color barrier: Among his colleagues there that night were Count Basie, Lionel Hampton, Lester Young, and Johnny Hodges.) This flyer announcing the 1952 concert features equally illustrious names, black and white. The only "repeaters" were some of Duke Ellington's crew, who had been on hand all those years before.*

The three greatest female vocalists of the jazz era all frequently played in New York venues—downtown, uptown, across town. We'll never see their like again. *BELOW:* The ineffable, tragic Billie Holiday, at the Downbeat on 52nd St. in 1947, though without her trademark white gardenia tucked behind her ear. *OPPOSITE, TOP:* The glorious Ella Fitzgerald at the Downbeat in 1947, as Dizzy Gillespie looks on, entranced. Ella began as a kid by winning a competition at the Apollo and ended up as Queen of Scat—actually, queen of everything. *OPPOSITE, BOTTOM:* The divine Sarah Vaughan, ca. 1951, renowned for her impressive musicianship and huge, almost operatic voice.

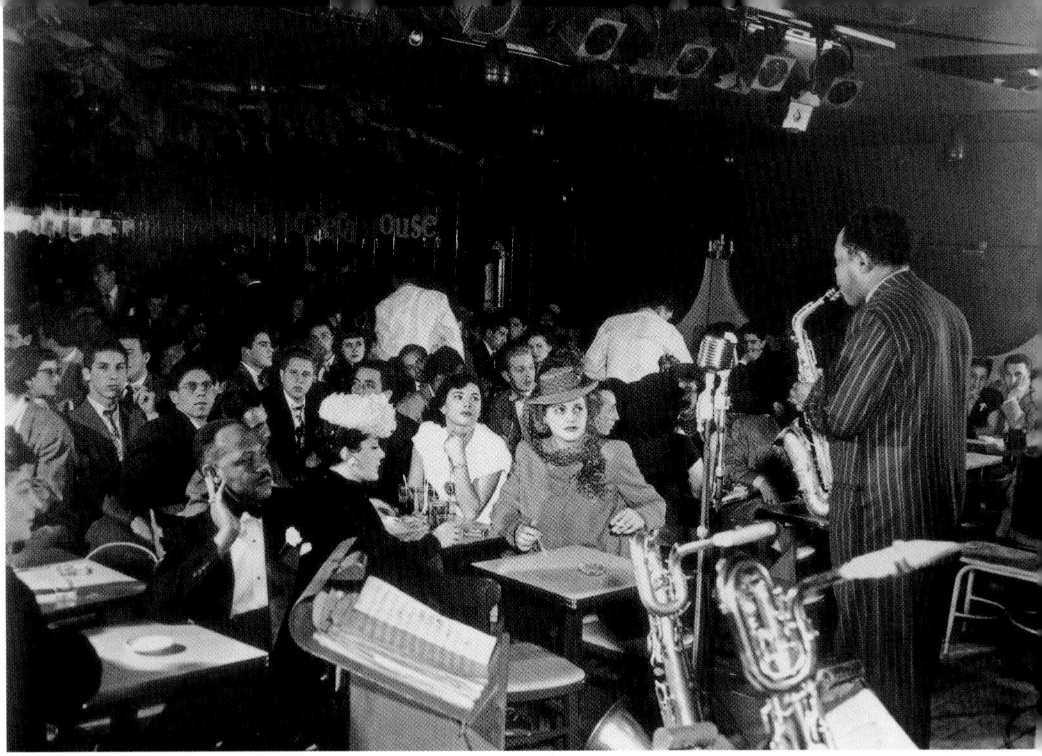

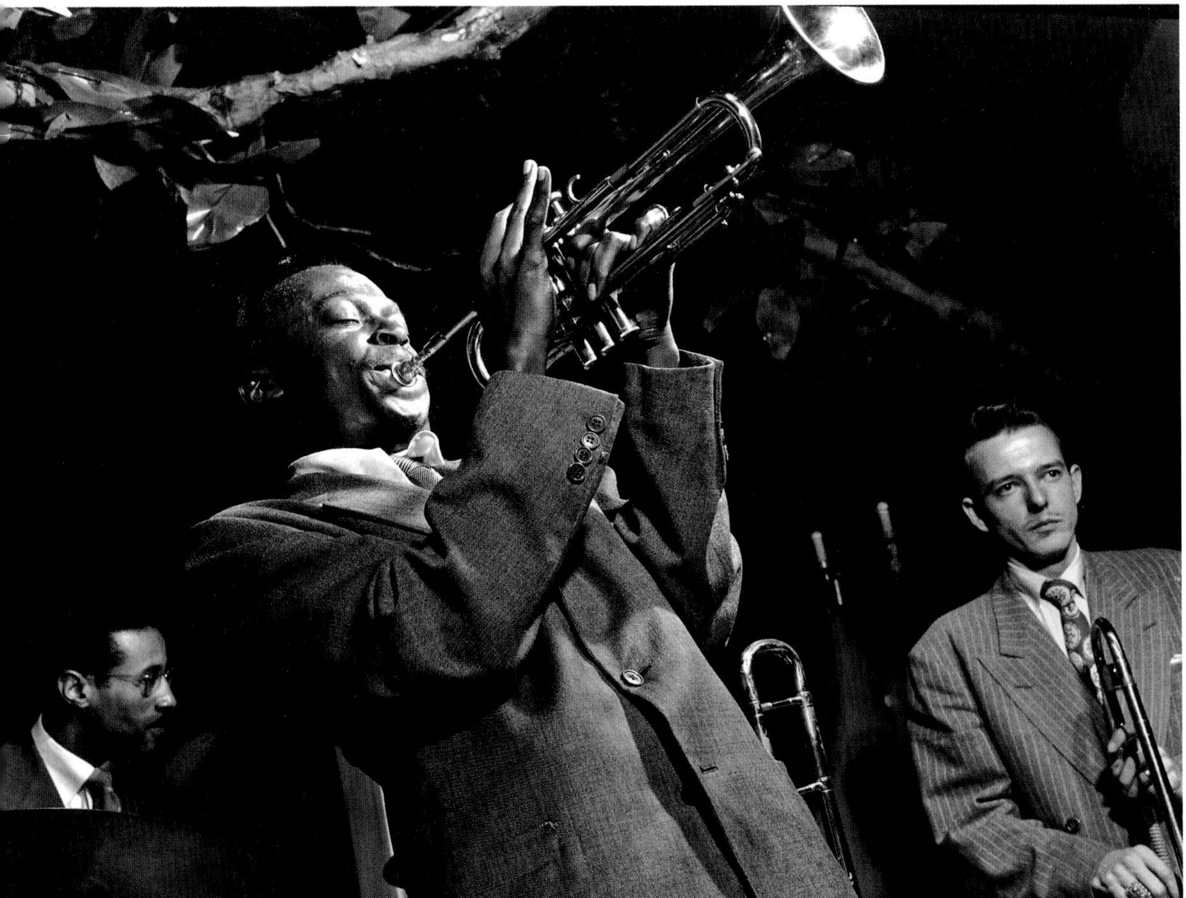

all Chinese restaurants: A columnist wrote, "52nd St. is being strangled by a G-string dipped in soya sauce." Nothing could stop the postwar Midtown building boom, and as the giant corporate buildings went up, jazz moved out. *The New Yorker* mourned: "Jazz is hard to find in midtown." Arnold Shaw, author of the definitive *52nd St.: The Street of Jazz*, wrote, "In a survey that I personally made in '54, I found six strip joints and only one jazz club operating between Fifth and Sixth Avenues." What still remained of Midtown jazz had moved to Broadway, in the vanguard the Royal Roost, which in 1948 morphed from a chicken restaurant (hence its name) into a highly successful bop jazz club, featuring all the usual suspects.

Only a year later came the famous Birdland, named after Charlie "Bird" Parker, by this point the most famous figure in modern jazz. It opened late in 1949, and according to one source, 1,400,000 customers paid its admission fee in its first five years. Everybody played there—and went there. It lasted only fifteen years, though—by 1965 it was gone. But the equally famous Roseland Ballroom wasn't. In the thirties, it featured Louis Armstrong, Count Basie, and other big swing orchestras—Tommy Dorsey, Glenn Miller, Harry James. It was always about dancing, and that continued to be the case when in 1956 it moved from 51st to 52nd Street, just west of Broadway,

Three jazz greats. OPPOSITE, TOP: *Charlie "Bird" Parker, a founder of bebop, performing at the Royal Roost, 1948.* OPPOSITE, BOTTOM: *Miles Davis at the Royal Roost, 1948.* BELOW: *The quintessential boppist, Dizzy Gillespie, at the Downbeat, ca. 1946–48.*

billed as "a magnificent metropolis of melody and merriment." It could hold up to 3,200 people standing, and it stayed true to its roots: "Cheek-to-cheek dancing," its owner said in the face of disco, "that's what this place is all about." Roseland is now gone, but in the end it was about other things as well, serving as a venue for all kinds of special events, from Radiohead concerts to a Hillary Clinton birthday party to Vampire Weekends.

Of course, jazz also lived in other parts of the city during the twenty years after the war. It certainly flourished in Harlem, even though by 1940 the famous Cotton Club—Duke Ellington, Lena Horne—was a thing of the past. There was the Apollo, best known for its amateur contest nights—it was at one of these that the seventeen-year-old Ella Fitzgerald

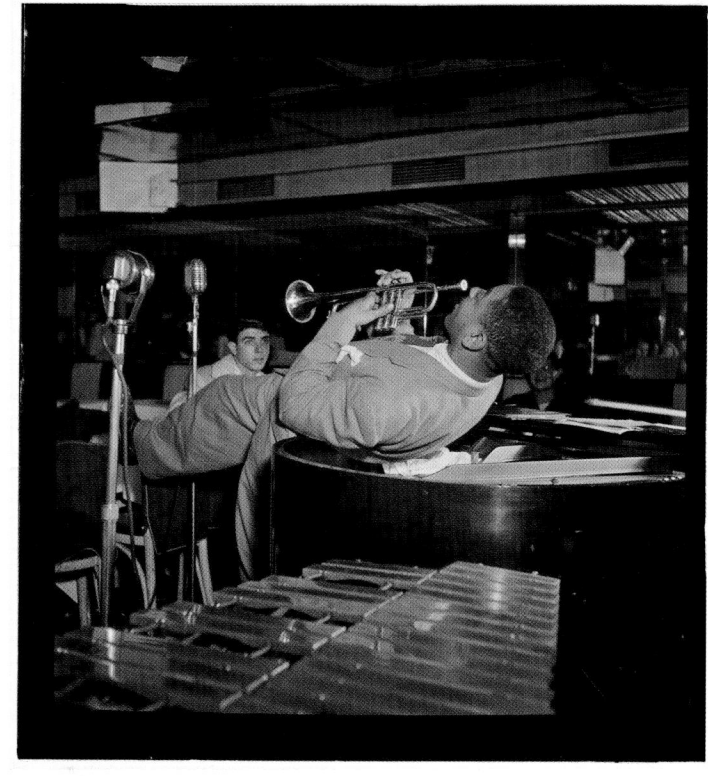

*LEFT: A typical amateur night
at the Apollo in the 1940s.*

*ABOVE: The Count of Swing meets the
Queen of Soul at the Apollo—where else?*

jump-started her legendary career. White performers played there as well as blacks—the wonderful jazz singer Anita O'Day, for one—and in the early sixties, James Brown played and recorded there. There was Minton's Playhouse, with its famous cutting sessions, the place where bebop really got going. And there was the huge Savoy Ballroom, where the Chick Webb band featuring Ella played for years—it was 10,000 square feet in size, and could accommodate 4,000 customers. It lasted until 1958, and has been immortalized by that swing classic "Stompin' at the Savoy"—"Savoy, the home of sweet romance. / Savoy, it wins you at a glance. / Savoy, gives happy feet a chance / to dance."

And jazz lived on downtown, too—for instance, at the Five Spot Café, on Cooper Square in the Bowery, which opened in 1956 and for long stretches featured such musicians as Cecil Taylor, Thelonius Monk (with John Coltrane), and Ornette Coleman, who made his New York debut there. If you were serious about jazz, you went to the Five Spot. And eventually, after exhausting itself with folk, comedy, poetry, and cabaret singers, in 1957 the Village Vanguard switched to jazz—which it still provides, almost sixty years later!

BELOW: A gathering outside Minton's—the birthplace of bop—in 1947. Left to right: Thelonius Monk, Howard McGhee, Roy Eldridge, and Teddy Hill.

OPPOSITE: Dancers at the Savoy Ballroom in the 1940s (top) and 1950s (bottom).

OVERLEAF: Composer-musician David Amram at the Five Spot Café, 1957.

CABARET

The Blue Angel, the Bon Soir, Le Ruban Bleu, the Malmaison, the Café Carlyle, the Living Room, the Red Carpet, the Tender Trap, the Versailles, the Village Vanguard, Café Society Downtown, Café Society Uptown, Upstairs at the Downstairs, Downstairs at the Upstairs, the Den in the Duane, the Drake Room, the Maisonette (at the St. Regis), the Peacock Alley (at the Waldorf), the Persian Room (at the Plaza), Spivy's . . . These are only some of the glamorous names of the clubs where intimate cabaret acts provided New Yorkers with endless pleasure and amusement. That so many of these names are French suggests the degree to which this kind of entertainment reflected the pleasures Americans had experienced in comparable Parisian *boîtes* both before and after the war. And, indeed, one of the most successful performers

of the era was the great Edith Piaf, who made numerous appearances in New York at the aptly named Versailles.

The smaller rooms might seat as few as sixty customers, jammed into a smoke-filled space with few amenities. No one cared, as long as the entertainment was entertaining. One of the most famous comedy acts in cabaret history opened at Max Gordon's Vanguard in 1939— five scared kids calling themselves the Revuers. Two of those kids were Betty Comden and Adolph Green, who went on to write countless hit musicals and movies, from *On the Town* to *Singing' in the Rain*. Their colleague and pal, Judy Holliday (born Tuvim), went on to glory in *Born Yesterday, Bells Are Ringing* (a musical written for her by Betty and Adolph), and a string of hit movies, starting with *Adam's Rib*. The literate, sophisticated material the Revuers produced to the delight of Vanguard audiences can be inferred from one of the condensed classics they came up with, *Les Misérables*: "Jean Valjean, no evildoer, / Stole some bread 'cause he was poo-er. / A detective chased him through a sewer. THE END!" The story of the Revuers is significant because it foreshadows the role cabaret would go on to play in the entertainment world, as young, talented, unknown performers, paid almost nothing, were spotted, applauded, and snatched up by Broadway, television, and Hollywood.

Max Gordon not only ran the Vanguard, but was also part owner of Le Ruban Bleu, which was the idea of Herbert Jacoby, an émigré

OPPOSITE: Edith Piaf, France's "Little Sparrow" ("La Vie en rose," "Je ne regrette rien"), at her favorite New York venue, Versailles.

ABOVE: The Revuers, at Max Gordon's Village Vanguard. Left to right: Adolph Green, John Frank, Betty Comden, Alvin Hammer, and Judy Holliday (still Judy Tuvim).

Woody Allen starting out, at Herbert Jacoby's Blue Angel, 1960.

from Paris, who opened the club in the late thirties. Eventually, Jacoby ceded control of it to Julius Monk and went on to open the famous Blue Angel—far more chic and formal—at whose "red-carpeted entrance," as James Gavin tells us in *Intimate Nights*, the bible of the Golden Age of New York Cabaret, "dozens of performers began their careers, including Barbra Streisand, Mike Nichols and Elaine May, Carol Burnett, Johnny Mathis, Tom Lehrer, Phyllis Diller, Shelley Berman, Pearl Bailey, Harry Belafonte, and Woody Allen." (Burnett's breakthrough number was "I Made a Fool of Myself over John Foster Dulles.") And then there were Yul Brynner (who "sat on the piano and sang Russian folk songs, while playing the guitar") and, in 1945, the twenty-year-old Bobby Short. Prices were high at the Blue Angel, the place itself was cramped, and the atmosphere—the bar room had all-black décor—was somewhat glum (like Jacoby himself), but none of that kept it from being *the* classy nightspot. One of the more conspicuous repeating customers, a friend of Jacoby's, was Senator John Kennedy, who both brought pickups to the club and pursued (and caught) various women involved with the shows.

Performers at the Angel tended to be less happy with the venue than the customers were, the performance area was so constricted. As singer Dorothy Loudon put it—she worked there frequently in the late fifties and early sixties—"It was like trying to do an act on top of a cocktail napkin." Loudon was yet another cabaret artist who graduated to Broadway, eventually to her Tony Award–winning performance as the wicked Miss Hannigan in *Annie*.

The famous clubs veered from the ultra-sophisticated Blue Angel to the ultra-leftist Café Society Downtown (on Sheridan Square) and its more soigné sibling, Café Society Uptown (on 58th, off Park). Their proprietor was Barney Josephson, who trail-blazed racially integrated performances and audiences beginning in 1938, when his first show featured Billie Holiday.

Pearl Bailey being toasted by Gloria Vanderbilt and Truman Capote at the Blue Angel in celebration of her twentieth anniversary in show business, 1955.

New Yorkers clubbing at Barney Josephson's Café Society Uptown.

(His motto: "The wrong place for the Right people.") One of his most successful projects was transforming Lena Horne, then a relatively invisible band singer with the Charlie Barnet orchestra, into the superb soloist she became—he even took her to Bergdorf's to have her properly "gowned." No good deed goes unpunished: As America went into its postwar, Joseph McCarthy, anti-Communist paranoia, Josephson and his clubs were destroyed by the right-wing Hearst columnists Walter Winchell, Westbrook Pegler, and Dorothy Kilgallen, and by 1950, he was forced to sell his Café Societies. Perhaps his most important legacy: in 1939, he introduced Holiday to her most famous song, "Strange Fruit."

It was the brilliant Julius Monk who at his Downtown started a wildly successful new trend, the full-scale (if only four-person) revue, rather than a series of individual acts. He began in 1956 with *Four Below*, one of the four being Dody Goodman. Then came *Take Five, Pieces of Eight*, etc.—all hits that played for months. Eventually, he moved to a new club at the Plaza, where his last hurrah was called PLaza 9-. But time had marched on, and by the early sixties, the flamboyant Monk was a defeated man. A sad decline for the showman who, in the early forties, had brought Imogen Coca and Maxine Sullivan to the Ruban and given a leg up to the young but upcoming Liberace.

The list of notable performers who either started or furthered their careers in these and other clubs is just about endless: apart from those Gavin identified, there were Bette Midler, Kaye Ballard, Eartha Kitt, Tammy Grimes, Mae Barnes, Peggy Lee, Blossom Dearie, Julie Wilson, Mary Louise Wilson, Lily Tomlin, Madeline Kahn . . . Sometimes they jumped straight from a club to, say, the *Ed Sullivan Show* and instant fame. Sometimes it took longer. And of course sometimes it didn't happen at all . . . but that's show business.

The most famous singer of them all was the revered Mabel Mercer, born black and poor in England, who—wherever she performed, in big rooms or small—was so distinctive, her phrasing so sensitive, her elocution so precise (some said lah-di-dah),

Performers at Julius Monk's last club, PLaza 9- camping it up, early 1960s.

A quartet of superb chanteuses. RIGHT: Mabel Mercer, at Tony's West Side, 1946. BELOW LEFT: Lena Horne, at the Paramount Theater, 1947. BELOW RIGHT: The ever-glamorous Julie Wilson. OPPOSITE: The one and only Eartha Kitt, at the Blue Angel, 1952.

Announcing Lenny Bruce down in Greenwich Village, where he felt at home.

that generations of singers, most famously Sinatra, claimed her as their inspiration and greatest influence, despite her modest voice, which in her later years severely eroded. No one (except Cole Porter) seemed to mind. One of her greatest services to musicians was her genius for ferreting out obscure songs by old masters and new, significantly expanding the repertory. A great deal of pretentious stuff has been written about Mabel Mercer (even the estimable James Gavin could write, "Mercer possessed an almost magical ability to lighten the heart and to elevate the lovestruck spirit"), and her diction was often über-pretentious, but she herself was far from pretentious: She was direct, unde-manding, hard-working, and, not unlike Ella Fitzgerald, a rock of integrity.

And then there was Lenny Bruce. He made his New York debut in 1959, trailing his national reputation as beyond outrageous, at the Den in the Duane (seating capacity, eighty) and was a smash. The following year he was talked into appearing at the fashionable and formal Blue Angel, which he hated and whose regulars walked out in droves while his own fans turned his weeks there into a financial bonanza. He was a lot happier when he moved downtown to the Village Vanguard, where the audience was far more receptive than the Angel's to such material as his monologue as Father Flotsky, who quit the priesthood because he found confessions so boring: "One out of fifty is sexually stimulating, but the rest—whew! It's the same trite crap over and over, week after week." It was on the very stage where Betty and Adolph and Judy had made their mark twenty-one years earlier, but Betty and Adolph and Judy could never have imagined Father Flotsky. New York was a different place, the world was a different place, and cabaret had gone just about as far as it could—and did—go.

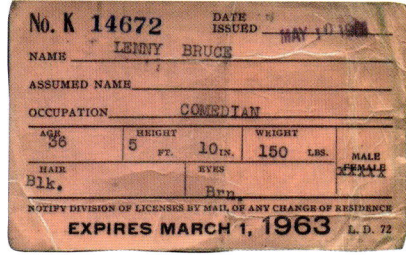

Lenny Bruce's official identification card, front and back, allowing him to work in New York clubs.

NIGHTCLUBS

There was another kind of club important in New York during the years from the mid-thirties to the mid-sixties: the big, booming nightclubs.

Perhaps best known was the Latin Quarter, opened by Lou Walters (father of Barbara) in 1942 on the corner of Broadway and 47th Street. As its name suggests, it was one of the many night spots that were all Latin American and a mile wide—its South-of-the-Border rivals included not only the famous Copacabana but such places as the Casa Mañana, Club Gaucho, Riobamba, La Conga, El Chico, El Barracho, et al. The Latin Quarter itself, according to Gavin, boasted twenty-seven chorus girls, two dance orchestras, and from five to a dozen acts, often including such top-of-the-line stars as Frank Sinatra, Sophie Tucker, and Mae West.

The Copa, backed by the mobster Frank Costello, opened in 1940, and we're told that the famous Copa Girls were often dolled up in pink hair, numberless sequins, mink panties and bras, and fruited turbans. (The menu was chiefly Chinese.) The parade of stars included some who also appeared at the Latin Quarter, but expanded to include Belafonte and, in the mid-sixties, Sammy Davis, Jr. (breaking the house record), Sam Cooke, and the Supremes.

Comparable big, star-studded venues were the Persian Room at the Plaza, the Cotillion Room at the Pierre, the Versailles, and the Empire Room at the Waldorf. Of all of them, the one I most regret not having been to was the huge International Casino, where, Gavin assures us, "girls atop miniature airplanes

Lou Walters's Latin Quarter. Everybody played
there, from the Andrews Sisters and Carmen
Miranda to Frank Sinatra and Mae West.
LEFT: The chorus girls strut their stuff.
ABOVE: The performers get ready in their
dressing room.

descended from the ceiling, a train charged onstage as planes rolled out onto runways alongside the wings, and two staircases dropped from the roof bearing tap-dancing chorines in one-piece costumes that might have gotten them thrown off the beach." Those were the days.

Finally, where did upper-crust night-life New Yorkers go to dine? If they were sports types, to Toots Shor's. If they were theater types, to Sardi's, or maybe Lindy's, for the cheesecake (immortalized in *Guys and Dolls*). To the 21 Club, of course, or just 21, and before that—during its days as a speakeasy, Jack

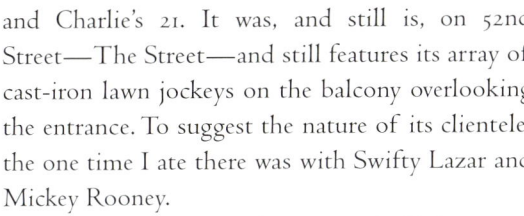

and Charlie's 21. It was, and still is, on 52nd Street—The Street—and still features its array of cast-iron lawn jockeys on the balcony overlooking the entrance. To suggest the nature of its clientele, the one time I ate there was with Swifty Lazar and Mickey Rooney.

Far swankier was the famous Stork Club, opened in 1929 by ex-bootlegger Sherman Billingsley and eventually the hottest of hot spots. Its clientele included Walter Winchell, who helped make it famous, the Kennedys, Marilyn Monroe, Grace Kelly and Prince Rainier (the story of their engagement broke there), and Billingsley's very special friend, Ethel Merman, who brought in the theater crowd. Billingsley was famous for his generosity to his customers, but can it be true that one waiter's sole job was to light La Merman's cigarettes?

Perhaps most chic of all was El Morocco, with its famous zebra-striped banquettes. Here café society mixed with politicians, financiers, highest-level movie stars (Clark Gable, James

LEFT: The Copacabana, the Latin Quarter's great rival, where everything was hot and Latin except the food, which was Chinese.

ABOVE: Toots Shor (standing) greets dinner guests at his restaurant, 1948. Left to right: Yankees Johnny Lindell and Joe DiMaggio, National League president and later Baseball Commissioner Ford Frick, Detroit Tiger Hank Greenberg, and Tigers' manager Steve O'Neill.

The opening-night party—at Broadway's most famous restaurant, Sardi's—for A Raisin in the Sun, *1959*. At right, playwright Lorraine Hansberry, chatting with Harry Belafonte; center, Sidney Poitier; far right, Godfrey Cambridge.

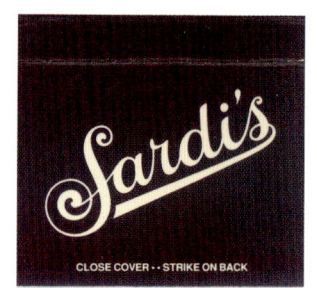

Stewart), and the just plain rich. Here's where you'd head after slumming at some less exalted place—if you were one of the above. Its fame was cemented by the rich, talented society photographer Jerome Zerbe, who spent years taking pictures there and placing them in strategic venues. If you come upon any photo of a restaurant interior with zebra stripes, you know where you are, and you know who probably took the picture. You also wish you were there.

Of course, while theater, dance, cabaret, jazz, and nightclubs were evolving in these postwar years, contributing to a highly specific sociology and atmosphere, other areas of life were burgeoning as well. Design grew infinitely more sophisticated than it had been, and advertising benefited from that growth. (Given our speedy emergence from Depression hardship and wartime restraint, the economy flourished, spending was way up, and advertising became more important than ever as it accompanied and stimulated the boom.) But the advertising industry itself, like the publishing industry, was invisible. The great new phenomenon—the thing that changed America the way cars had changed it half a century earlier—was television, and for the most part the business of television took place in New York. Yet you would hardly have noticed that unless you were one of the (mostly) out-of-towners who lined up at a few theaters to see favorite shows being broadcast. For the most part, television in those days was considered (and was) pure commerce, and didn't impinge on the city's cultural life, just as, in the thirties and forties, no one knew or cared where radio was coming from. There was no umbilical connection in the minds of New Yorkers between their city and radio and television, the way Broadway stood for theater or the way Hollywood stood for the movies. The United Nations, yes—that was essential New York, and highly visible; *I Love Lucy*, Milton Berle, Edward R. Murrow, no. New Yorkers might watch them, but they weren't ours.

Still other aspects of New York life chugged along as before (and after). The opera remained the opera, apart from new names—Callas, Tebaldi, etc.; even the move in the mid-sixties from the old Met to Lincoln Center didn't change things. And classical music kept its central place in New York cultural life: The major event was the saving of Carnegie Hall from developers. Again, new names emerged and old ones faded, but the world of music remained the same. Central Park, the Bronx Zoo, Radio City Music Hall—all quintessential New York, but none specific to the great flourishing of the city in the twenty years following the war.

OPPOSITE, TOP: Writers Ernest Hemingway, left, and John O'Hara, right, flank Stork Club owner Sherman Billingsley.

OPPOSITE, BOTTOM: A bevy of Kennedy women at the Stork: Jackie, Pat, Ethel, Jean, and Eunice.

BELOW: At the ultra-chic El Morocco, with its famous zebra-striped banquettes, world-renowned figure-skater-turned-film-star Sonja Henie and Liberace.

OVERLEAF: The Stork Club's menu. At the Stork, apparently, everybody was always happy!

STORK CLUB

3 EAST 53RD ST. N.Y.C.

ALBERT DORNE

NOTES

VISUAL ARTS

1 Steven Naifeh and Gregory White Smith, *Jackson Pollock: An American Saga* (New York: Clarkson N. Potter, 1989), p. 495.

2 Ibid.

3 Ibid., p. 435.

4 Ibid., p. 443.

5 Ibid., p. 445.

6 Ibid., p. 444.

7 Ibid., p. 450.

8 Jacqueline Bogard Weld, *Peggy: The Wayward Guggenheim* (New York: E. P. Dutton, 1986), p. 330.

9 Ibid., p. 329.

10 Ibid., pp. 314–15.

11 Ibid., p. 330.

12 Ibid.

13 Ibid., p. 55.

14 Ibid., p. 288.

15 Ibid., p. 330.

16 Matthew Spender, *From a High Place: A Life of Arshile Gorky* (New York: Alfred A. Knopf, 1999), p. 285.

17 Ibid.

18 Hayden Herrera, *Arshile Gorky: His Life and Work* (London: Bloomsbury Publishing, 2003), p. 479.

19 Spender, *From a High Place*, p. 288.

20 Ibid., p. 289.

21 Ibid.

22 Ibid., p. 102.

23 Ibid., pp. 98 and 97, respectively.

24 Ibid., p. 100.

25 Ibid., p. 66.

26 Ibid., p. 98.

27 Ibid., p. 284.

28 Nouritza Matossian, *Black Angel: The Life of Arshile Gorky* (New York: Overlook Press, 2000), p. 355; Herrera, *Arshile Gorky*, p. 498.

29 W. H. Auden, "The Exiled Writers," an interview by Benjamin Appel, *Saturday Review of Literature* 22, no. 5 (October 19, 1940).

30 Dore Ashton, "The City and the Visual Arts," in Leonard Wallock, ed., *New York: Cultural Capital of the World 1940–1965* (New York: Rizzoli, 1988), p. 124.

31 Spender, *From a High Place*, p. 196.

32 John Russell, *Matisse: Father and Son* (New York: Harry N. Abrams, 1999), p. 83.

33 Ibid., p. 256.

34 *Art in America* 92, no. 11 (November 2004), p. 158.

35 Russell T. Clement, *Les Fauves: A Sourcebook* (New York: Greenwood Publishing Group, 1994), p. 125.

36 Thomas B. Hess, *Barnett Newman* (New York: Museum of Modern Art, 1971), p. 23.

37 Clement Greenberg, "The Present Prospects of American Painting and Sculpture," in *Clement Greenberg: The Collected Essays and Criticism*, ed. John O'Brian, vol. 2, *Arrogant Purpose, 1945–1949* (Chicago and London: University of Chicago Press, 1986), pp. 160–70.

38 Rebecca Roberts, ed., *MoMA: Highlights since 1980: 250 Works from the Museum of Modern Art* (New York: The Museum of Modern Art, 2007), p. 18.

39 Dolores Vanetti, interview by Annie Cohen-Solal, January 27, 1996.

40 Emile de Antonio, Mitch Tuchman, *Painters Painting: A Candid History of the Modern Art Scene, 1940–1970* (New York: Abbeville Press, 1984), p. 39.

41 Florence Rubenfeld, *Clement Greenberg: A Life* (Minneapolis: University of Minnesota Press, 2004), p. 107.

42 Ibid.

43 Philip Pavia, oral history interview, January 19, 1965, Archives of American Art, Smithsonian Institution, Washington, D.C.

44 John Elderfield, Susan F. Lake, et al. *De Kooning: A Retrospective* (New York: The Museum of Modern Art, 2011), p. 243.

45 Stephen C. Foster, Bill Berkson, Frank O'Hara, and B. H. Friedman. *Franz Kline: Art and the Structure of Identity* (Barcelona: Fundació Antoni Tàpies, 1994), p. 45.

46 Greenberg, *Clement Greenberg: The Collected Essays and Criticism*, vol. 2, p. 166.

47 Clement Greenberg, "The Decline of Cubism," *Partisan Review*, no. 3 (1948), p. 369.

48 Greenberg, *Clement Greenberg: The Collected Essays and Criticism*, vol. 2, p. 228.

59 Philip Pavia, oral history interview.

50 Barnett Newman produced four copies of *Broken Obelisk* between 1963 and 1969. In 2003, with the permission of the Barnett Newman Foundation, a fourth *Broken Obelisk* was cast and temporarily installed in front of the Neue Nationalgalerie in Berlin.

51 "A Symposium: The State of American Art," *Magazine of Art* 42, no. 3 (March 1949), p. 92.

52 Margit Rowell, ed., *Joan Miró: Selected Writings and Interviews* (Boston: G. K. Hall, 1986), p. 204.

53 Greenberg, *Clement Greenberg: The Collected Essays and Criticism*, vol. 2, p. 322.

54 Ileana Sonnabend, interview by Annie Cohen-Solal, New York, November 26, 2005.

55 Deborah Solomon, *Jackson Pollock: A Biography* (New York: Cooper Square Press, 2001), p. 153.

56 Michel Seuphor, "Paris–New York 1951," *Art d'aujourd'hui*, June 1951.

57 Ibid.

58 Naifeh and Smith, *Jackson Pollock: An American Saga*, p. 658.

59 Ibid.

60 "18 Painters Boycott Metropolitan; Charge 'Hostility to Advanced Art,'" *New York Times*, May 22, 1950.

61 Ibid.

62 "The Metropolitan and Modern Art," *Life*, January 15, 1951, p. 34.

63 Barbara Hess, *De Kooning 1904–1997: Content as a Glimpse* (Cologne, Germany: Taschen, 2004), p. 7.

64 Thomas B. Hess, Review of the Ninth Street Show of 1951, *ARTnews* 50 (June 1951), p. 46.

65   Ibid.

66   Seuphor, "Paris–New York 1951."

67   Ashton, "The City and the Visual Arts," p. 146.

68   Frank O'Hara, 1957, in Marjorie Perloff, *Frank O'Hara: Poet Among Painters* (Chicago: University of Chicago Press, 1977), p. 102.

69   Rubenfeld, *Clement Greenberg: A Life*, p. 172.

70   Max Kozloff, "An Interview with Friedel Dzubas," *Artforum*, September 1965, p. 51.

71   Naifeh and Smith, *Jackson Pollock: An American Saga*, p. 713.

72   Harold Rosenberg, "American Action Painters," *Art News* 51, no. 8 (December 1952) p. 22. Reprinted in David Shapiro and Cecile Shapiro, eds., *Abstract Expressionism: A Critical Record* (New York: Cambridge University Press, 1990), pp. 75–84.

73   Clement Greenberg, "Introduction to an Exhibition of Ernest Lindner," in *Clement Greenberg: The Collected Essays and Criticism*, vol. 4, *Modernism with a Vengeance, 1957–1969* (1995), p. 144.

74   Fairfield Porter, *Art in Its Own Terms: Selected Criticism 1935–1975*, ed. Rackstraw Downes (Boston: Museum of Fine Arts, 2008), p. 235.

75   Clement Greenberg, "A Critical Exchange with Fairfield Porter on 'American-Type' Painting," *Partisan Review*, Fall 1955. Reprinted in *Clement Greenberg: The Collected Essays and Criticism*, vol. 3, *Affirmations and Refusals 1950–1956* (1993), p. 240.

76   Edwin Denby, "The Silence at Night," in David Lehman, ed., *Oxford Book of American Poetry* (New York: Oxford University Press, 2006), pp. 479–80.

77   Richard Kostelanetz, *Master Minds: Portraits of Contemporary American Artists and Intellectuals* (New York: Macmillan, 1969), p. 264.

78   Jasper Johns, *Jasper Johns: Writings, Sketchbook Notes, Interviews*, ed. Kirk Varnedoe and Christel Hollevoet (New York: Museum of Modern Art, 1996), p. 15.

79   Chris Granlund, dir., *Robert Rauschenberg: Man at Work*, BBC/RM Arts in association with the Guggenheim Museum and Ovation (Chicago: Home Vision Arts, 1997).

80   Ibid.

81   Ibid.

82   Robert Rauschenberg, oral history interview by Dorothy Seckler, December 21, 1965, Archives of American Art, Smithsonian Institution, Washington, D.C.

83   Mark Stevens and Annalyn Swan, *de Kooning: An American Master* (New York: Knopf, 2006), p. 359.

84   Ibid., p. 360.

85   Leo Castelli, interview by Annie Cohen-Solal, New York, November 5, 1995.

86   James Stourton, *Great Collectors of Our Time: Art Collecting Since 1945* (New York and London: Scala Publishers, 2007), p. 80.

87   Ibid., p. 81.

88   Jean Lipman, ed. *The Collector in America* (New York: Viking Press, 1970), p. 138.

89   Ibid., p. 140.

90   Stourton, *Great Collectors of Our Time*, p. 82.

91   Tom Wolfe, *The Purple Decades: A Reader* (New York: Berkley Books, 1983), p. 7; Marie Brenner, "The Latter Days of Ethel Scull: Fallen Angel," *New York* magazine, April 6, 1981, p. 22.

92   As reported in *New York* magazine, Nov 5, 1983, p. 80.

93   Stourton, *Great Collectors of Our Time*, p. 85.

94   Ibid., p. 84.

95   Tom Armstrong and Susan C. Larsen, *Art in Place: Fifteen Years of Acquisitions* (New York: Whitney Museum of American Art, 1989), p. 40.

96   Matthew Israel, "A Magnet for the With-It Kids: The Jewish Museum, New York, of the 1960s," *Art in America*, October 2007, p. 75.

97   Leo Castelli, interview by Annie Cohen-Solal, New York, November 5, 1995.

98   Jacob Baal-Teshuva, *Rothko* (Cologne, Germany: Taschen, 2003), p. 66; Esteban Vicente, oral history interview by Irving Sandler, August 26, 1968, Archives of American Art, Smithsonian Institution, Washington, D.C.

99   Dore Ashton, "The City and the Visual Arts," p. 149.

100 Allan Kaprow, *Essays on the Blurring of Art and Life*, expanded ed., ed. Jeff Kelley (Berkeley and Los Angeles: University of California Press, 2003), pp. 7, 9.

101 Ashton, "The City and the Visual Arts."

102 G. R. Swenson, "What Is Pop Art? Interviews with Eight Painters," *ARTnews* 62, no. 7 (November 1963); Ivan Karp, "Anti-Sensibility Painting," *Artforum* 2, no. 3 (1963), pp. 26–27; John Canaday, "Pop Art Sells On and On—Why?" *New York Times Magazine*, May 31, 1964, p. 7.

103 John Rublowsky, *Pop Art* (New York: Basic Books, 1965), p. 159.

104 Josh Greenfield, "Sort of the Svengali of Pop," *New York Times Magazine*, May 8, 1966, p. 34.

105 David Pagel, "The Wesselman Season," *Los Angeles Times*, September 2, 2003, accessed 08/03/2013, articles.latimes.com/2003/sep/02/entertainment/et-pagel2.

106 Ivan Karp, oral history interview by Paul Cummings, March 12, 1969, Archives of American Art, Smithsonian Institution, Washington, D.C.

107 Frayda Feldman and Jorg Schellman, eds., *Andy Warhol Prints: A Catalogue Raisonné 1962–1987* (New York: R. Feldman Fine Arts, 1989), p. 9.

108 James Edwards, David E. Brauer, Christopher Finch, Ned Rifkin, and Walter Hopps, *Pop Art: US/UK Connections, 1956–1966* (Ostfildern, Germany: Hatje Cantz, 2000), p. 44.

109 Ileana Sonnabend, interview by Annie Cohen-Solal, November 26, 2005.

110 Alain Jouffroy, "White Car Crash," in *Warhol* (Paris: Ileana Sonnabend Gallery, 1964).

111 John Ashbery, "Pop Artist's Horror Pictures Silence Snickers," *New York Herald Tribune*, January 15, 1964.

112 Thomas Crow, "Saturday Disasters: Trace and Reference in Early Warhol," in *Andy Warhol*, ed. Annette Michelson, October Files 2 (Cambridge, MA: MIT Press, 2001), p. 60.

113 Andy Warhol, *America* (New York: Harper & Row, 1985), p. 176.

114 Thomas E. Crow, *Rise of the Sixties: American and European Art in the Era of Dissent* (1996; London: Laurence King Publishing, 2004), p. 86.

115 Diana Crane, *The Transformation of the Avant-Garde: The New York Art World, 1940–85* (Chicago: University of Chicago Press, 1987), p. 38.

116 Ivan Karp, interview by Annie Cohen-Solal, New York, April 19 and 26, 2007.

ARCHITECTURE AND DESIGN

1 Robert A. M. Stern, Thomas Mellins, and David Fishman, *New York 1960: Architecture and Urbanism between the Second World War and the Bicentennial* (New York: The Monacelli Press, 1995), p. 613.

2 Lewis Mumford, "The Sky Line: United Nations Headquarters: The Ground Plan," *The New Yorker*, October 25, 1947, pp. 56, 58, 61–62.

3 Le Corbusier, *United Nations Headquarters Report* (New York: Reinhold Publishing Corp., 1947), p. 18.

4 Lewis Mumford, "The Sky Line: The Lesson of the Master," *The New Yorker*, September 13, 1958, pp. 143–44, 150.

5 John Canaday, "Wright vs. Painting," *New York Times*, October 21, 1959.

6 Ada Louise Huxtable, "That Museum: Wright or Wrong?" *New York Times Magazine*, October 25, 1959, pp. 16, 91.

7 Lewis Mumford, "The Sky Line: What Wright Hath Wrought," *The New Yorker*, December 5, 1959, pp. 118, 128.

8 Ada Louise Huxtable, *Will They Ever Finish Bruckner Boulevard?* (New York: The Macmillan Company, 1963), p. 97.

9 Robert Moses, quoted in Robert A. Caro, *The Power Broker: Robert Moses and the Fall of New York* (New York: Alfred A. Knopf, 1974), p. 1013.

10 Lewis Mumford, "The Roaring Traffic's Boom—II," *The New Yorker*, April 2, 1955, p. 97.

11 Memorandum, March 26, 1947, from Edgar Kaufmann Jr. to d'Harnoncourt, Wheeler, Abbott, Barr and Virich (Re: Sept. 16 "Memo to the Coordinating Committee").

12 Katherine Hiesinger and George Marcus, *Landmarks of Twentieth-Century Design* (New York: Abbeville Press, 1994), pp. 175–83.

13 Memorandum, Museum of Modern Art, on "Good Design" criteria, published January 1, 1953. www.moma.org/docs/press_archives/1669/releases/MOMA_1952_0091_81.pdf?2010

14 Olga Gueft, "The Flooded Cathedral," *Interiors* 125 (August 1965), p. 89.

15 Frank O'Hara, *Lunch Poems* (1964; reprint, San Francisco: City Lights Publishers, 2001).

16 Louis Skidmore, "Something to See," *Time*, August 31, 1953, p. 78.

17 Advertisement in *The New Yorker*, February 27, 1965.

18 Vincent Scully, *American Architecture and Urbanism*, rev. ed. (New York: Henry Holt and Company, 1988), pp. 142–43.

19 Ada Louise Huxtable, "Farewell to Penn Station," *New York Times*, October 30, 1963.

20 Stern, Mellins, and Fishman, *New York 1960*, p. 1140.

21 Edgar Kaufmann Jr., "The Biggest Office Building Yet . . . Worse Luck," *Harper's*, May 1960.

22 Vincent Scully, "The Death of the Street," *Perspecta* 8 (1963), p. 95.

23 Ada Louise Huxtable, "Architecture: Grotesquerie Astride a Palace," *New York Times*, June 20, 1968.

24 E. B. White, *Here Is New York* (New York: Harper & Brothers, 1949; New York: The Little Bookroom, 1999), p. 52.

SELECTED BIBLIOGRAPHY

Altshuler, Bruce. "Downtown, Ninth Street Show, New York, May 21–June 10, 1951." In *The Avant-Garde in Exhibition: New Art in the 20th Century.* New York: Harry N. Abrams, 1994.

Antonio, Emile de, and Mitch Tuchman. *Painters Painting: A Candid History of the Modern Art Scene 1940–1970.* New York: Abbeville Press, 1984.

Armstrong, Tom, and Susan C. Larsen. *Art in Place: Fifteen Years of Acquisitions.* New York: Whitney Museum of American Art, 1989.

Ashton, Dore. "The City and the Visual Arts." In Wallock, Leonard, and Dore Ashton, eds. *New York: Culture Capital of the World 1940–1965.* New York: Rizzoli, 1988, pp. 123–56.

———. *The New York School: A Cultural Reckoning.* Berkeley: University of California Press, 1992.

———. *About Rothko.* Cambridge, MA: Da Capo Press, 1996.

Augur, Julie, et. al. *Castelli and His Artists: Twenty-five Years.* Aspen, CO: Aspen Center for the Visual Arts, 1982.

Baal-Teshuva, Jacob. *Rothko.* Cologne, Germany: Taschen, 2003.

Barr, Alfred H., Jr. "Gorky, de Kooning, Pollock (7 Americans Open in Venice)." *ARTnews* 49, no. 4 (June–August 1950).

———, ed. *Fantastic Art, Dada, Surrealism.* New York: The Museum of Modern Art, 1936.

Bellamy, Richard. Oral history interview, 1963. Archives of American Art, Smithsonian Institution, Washington, D.C.

Béret, Chantal, ed. *Frederick Kiesler: Artiste-architecte.* Paris: Centre Georges Pompidou, 1996.

Boehm, Gero von. *Portrait de Pierre: L'enfant au chapeau rouge.* Documentary film, ZDF, 1995.

Cage, John. Oral history interview, May 2, 1974. Archives of American Art, Smithsonian Institution, Washington, D.C.

Canaday, John. "Wright vs. Painting." *New York Times,* October 21, 1959.

Caro, Robert A. *The Power Broker: Robert Moses and the Fall of New York.* New York: Alfred A. Knopf, 1974.

Castelli, Leo. Oral history interviews, May 14, 1969–June 8, 1973, May 22, 1997. Archives of American Art, Smithsonian Institution, Washington, D.C.

Chave, Anna C. *Mark Rothko: Subjects in Abstraction.* New Haven: Yale University Press, 1989.

Cohen, Jean-Louis, and Hubert Damisch, eds. *Américanisme et Modernité: L'Idéal américain dans l'architecture et l'urbanisme.* Paris: Flammarion/EHESS, 1993.

Cohen-Solal, Annie. *Painting American: The Rise of American Artists, Paris 1867–New York 1948.* New York: Alfred A. Knopf, 2001.

———. *Leo & His Circle: The Life of Leo Castelli.* New York: Alfred A. Knopf, 2010.

Collection Sonnabend: 25 années de choix et d'activités d'Ileana et Michael Sonnabend: du 6 mai au 21 août 1988. Bordeaux: Musée d'art contemporain, 1988.

Crane, Diana. *The Transformation of the Avant-Garde: The New York Art World, 1940–1985.* Chicago: University of Chicago Press, 1987.

Crow, Thomas E. *The Rise of the Sixties: American and European Art in the Era of Dissent.* New Haven: Yale University Press, 1996; London: Laurence King Publishing, 2004.

Duve, Thierry de. *Nominalisme pictural: Marcel Duchamp, la peinture et la modernité.* Critical edition. Paris, Editions de Minuit, 1984.

de Kooning, Elaine. Oral history interview, August 27, 1981, Archives of American Art, Smithsonian Institution, Washington, D.C.

———. *Elaine de Kooning: The Spirit of Abstract Expressionism, Selected Writings.* New York: George Braziller, 1994.

Duberman, Martin. *Black Mountain: An Exploration in Community.* New York: E. P. Dutton, 1972; Evanston, IL: Northwestern University Press, 2009.

Edgar, Natalie, ed. *Club Without Walls: Selections from the Journals of Philip Pavia.* New York: Midmarch Arts Press, 2007.

Elderfield, John, Susan F. Lake, et al. *De Kooning: A Retrospective.* New York: The Museum of Modern Art, 2011.

Feldman, Frayda, and Jorg Schellman, eds. *Andy Warhol Prints: A Catalogue Raisonné 1962–1987.* New York: R. Feldman Fine Arts, 1989.

Foster, Hal, Rosalind Krauss, Yve-Alain Bois, and Benjamin Buchloh. *Art Since 1900: Modernism, Antimodernism, Postmodernism.* 2 vols. London and New York: Thames & Hudson, 2005.

Foster, Stephen C., Bill Berkson, Frank O'Hara, and B. H. Friedman. *Franz Kline: Art and the Structure of Identity.* Exh. cat., Fundació Antoni Tàpies, Barcelona, March 18–June 5, 1994. Barcelona: Fundació Antoni Tàpies, 1994.

Gavin, James. *Intimate Nights: The Golden Age of New York Cabaret.* New York: Limelight Editions, 1992.

Geldzahler, Henry. *New York Painting and Sculpture, 1940–1970.* Exh. cat. New York: E. P. Dutton and The Metropolitan Museum of Art, 1969.

———. *Making it New: Essays, Interviews, and Talks.* New York: Turtle Point Press, 1994.

Gill, Anton. *Art Lover: A Biography of Peggy Guggenheim.* New York: HarperCollins, 2002.

Goldman, Judith. *Robert and Ethel Scull: The Portrait of a Collection.* Exh. cat. New York: Acquavella Galleries, 2010.

Goodnough, Robert. "Pollock Paints a Picture." *ARTnews* 50, no. 3 (May 1951).

Gordon, Max. *Live at the Village Vanguard.* New York: Da Capo Press, 1980.

Granlund, Chris, dir., *Rauschenberg: Man at Work.* BBC/RM Arts in association with the Guggenheim Museum and Ovation. Chicago: Home Vision Arts, 1997.

Greenberg, Clement. "The Present Prospects of American Painting and Sculpture." In *Arrogant Purpose, 1945–1949,* pp. 160–70. Vol. 2 of *Clement Greenberg: The Collected Essays and Criticism.* Edited by John O'Brian. Chicago and London: University of Chicago Press, 1986. First published in *Horizon* 16, nos. 93–94 (October 1947).

———. *Art and Culture: Critical Essays.* Boston: Beacon Press, 1961.

———. *Clement Greenberg: The Collected Essays and Criticism.* Edited by John O'Brian. 4 vols. Chicago and London: University of Chicago Press, 1986–1995.

Greenfield-Sanders, Timothy. *The Ninth Street Show.* Toronto: Lumiere Press, 1987.

Gruen, John. *The Party's Over Now: Reminiscences of the Fifties—New York's Artists, Writers, Musicians, and Their Friends.* Wainscott, NY: Pushcart Press, 1989.

Gueft, Olga. "The Flooded Cathedral." *Interiors* 125 (August 1965).

Guilbaut, Serge. *How New York Stole the Idea of Modern Art: Abstract Expressionism, Freedom, and the Cold War.* Translated by Arthur Goldhammer. Chicago: University of Chicago Press, 1983.

Hall, Lee. *Betty Parsons: Artist, Dealer, Collector.* New York: Harry N. Abrams, 1991.

Harrison, Helen A., ed. *Such Desperate Joy: Imagining Jackson Pollock.* New York: Thunder's Mouth Press, 2000.

Herrera, Hayden. *Arshile Gorky: His Life and Work.* London: Bloomsbury Publishing, 2003.

Hess, Barbara. *De Kooning 1904–1997: Content as a Glimpse.* Cologne, Germany: Taschen, 2004.

Hess, Thomas B. *Barnett Newman.* New York: Museum of Modern Art, 1971.

Hiesinger, Katherine, and George Marcus. *Landmarks of Twentieth-Century Design.* New York: Abbeville Press, 1994.

Hindry, Ann. *Claude Berri rencontre (meets) Leo Castelli.* Paris: Renn, 1990.

Hoving, Thomas. *Making the Mummies Dance: Inside the Metropolitan Museum of Art.* New York: Simon & Schuster, 1993.

Hughes, Robert. *American Visions: The Epic History of Art in America.* New York: Museum of Modern Art and Alfred A. Knopf, 1997.

Huxtable, Ada Louise. "That Museum: Wright or Wrong?" *New York Times Magazine,* October 25, 1959.

———. "Farewell to Penn Station." *New York Times,* October 30, 1963.

———. *Will They Ever Finish Bruckner Boulevard?* New York: The Macmillan Company, 1963.

———. "Architecture: Grotesquerie Astride a Palace." *New York Times,* June 20, 1968.

Israel, Matthew. "A Magnet for the With-It-Kids: The Jewish Museum, New York, of the 1960s." *Art in America* 95, no. 9 (October 2007), pp. 72–83.

Janis, Sidney. Oral history interview, March 21–September 26, 1972. Archives of American Art, Smithsonian Institution, Washington, D.C.

Jewish Museum. *Artists of the New York School: Second Generation.* Curated by Meyer Schapiro. Introduction by Leo Steinberg. Exh. cat. New York: Jewish Museum of the Jewish Theological Seminary of America, 1957.

Johns, Jasper. *Jasper Johns: Writings, Sketchbook Notes, Interviews.* Edited by Kirk Varnedoe and Christel Hollevoet. New York: Museum of Modern Art, 1996.

Kaprow, Allan. *Essays on the Blurring of Art and Life.* Expanded ed. Edited by Jeff Kelley. Berkeley and Los Angeles: University of California Press, 2003.

Karmel, Pepe, ed. *Jackson Pollock: Interviews, Articles, and Reviews.* New York: Museum of Modern Art, 1999.

———. *New York Cool: Painting and Sculpture from the NYU Art Collection.* New York: Grey Art Gallery, New York University, 2008.

Karmel, Pepe, and Kirk Varnedoe, eds. *Jackson Pollock: New Approaches.* New York: Museum of Modern Art and Harry N. Abrams, 1999.

Karp, Ivan. Oral history interview, 1969. Archives of American Art, Smithsonian Institution, Washington, D.C.

Kaspi, André. *New York: 1940–1950. Terre promise et corne d'abondance: l'emblème du rêve américain.* Paris: Autrement, 1995.

Kaufmann, Edgar, Jr. "The Biggest Office Building Yet . . . Worse Luck." *Harper's,* May 1960.

Kirschenbaum, Baruch D. "The Scull Auction and the Scull Film." *Art Journal* 39, no. 1 (Autumn 1979), pp. 50–54.

Kleeblatt, Norman L., ed. *Action/Abstraction: Pollock, de Kooning, and American Art 1940–1976.* New York: The Jewish Museum, 2009.

Kostelanetz, Richard. *Master Minds: Portraits of Contemporary American Artists and Intellectuals.* New York: Macmillan, 1969.

Krasner, Lee. Oral history interviews, 1964, 1967, 1968, 1972. Archives of American Art, Smithsonian Institution, Washington, D.C.

Larson, Gary O. *The Reluctant Patron: The United States Government and the Arts, 1943–1965.* Philadelphia: University of Pennsylvania Press, 1983.

Le Corbusier. *United Nations Headquarters Report.* New York: Reinhold Publishing Corp., 1947.

Levy, Julien. *Memoir of an Art Gallery.* Boston: MFA Publications, 2003.

Lipman, Jean, ed. *The Collector in America.* New York: Viking Press, 1970.

Marquis, Alice Goldfarb. *Alfred H. Barr Jr.: Missionary for the Modern.* Chicago: Contemporary Books, 1989.

Matossian, Nouritza. *Black Angel: The Life of Arshile Gorky.* New York: Overlook Press, 2000.

Miller, Dorothy C., ed. *14 Americans.* New York: Museum of Modern Art, 1946.

———. *15 Americans.* New York: Museum of Modern Art, 1952.

———. *12 Americans.* New York: Museum of Modern Art, 1956.

———. *16 Americans.* New York: Museum of Modern Art, 1959.

Motherwell, Robert. Oral history interview, November 24, 1971. Archives of American Art, Smithsonian Institution, Washington, D.C.

Motherwell, Robert, and Ad Reinhardt, eds. *Modern Artists in America.* First series. New York: Wittenborn Schultz, 1951. Particularly "The Western Round Table on Modern Art," San Francisco, April 8–10, 1949, pp. 25–38, and "Artists' Sessions at Studio 35," New York, April 21–23, 1950, pp. 10–21.

Moulin, Raymonde. *L'artiste, l'institution et le marché.* Champs series. Paris: Flammarion, 1999.

Moynihan, Danny. *Boogie-Woogie.* London: Duck Editions, 2000.

Mumford, Lewis. "The Sky Line: United Nations Headquarters: The Ground Plan." *The New Yorker,* October 25, 1947.

———. "The Roaring Traffic's Boom—II." *The New Yorker,* April 2, 1955, p. 97.

———. "The Sky Line: The Lesson of the Master." *The New Yorker,* September 13, 1958, pp. 143–44, 150.

———. "The Sky Line: What Wright Hath Wrought." *The New Yorker,* December 5, 1959, pp. 118, 128.

Myers, Jerome. *Artist in Manhattan.* New York: American Artists Group, 1940.

Naifeh, Steven, and Gregory White Smith. *Jackson Pollock: An American Saga.* New York: Clarkson N. Potter, 1989.

O'Hara, Frank. *Lunch Poems.* San Francisco: City Lights Books, 1964. Reprint, San Francisco: City Lights Publishers, 2001.

———. "What Appears to Be Yours." In *Poems from the Tibor de Nagy Editions, 1952–1966.* New York: Tibor de Nagy Editions, 2006.

Panza di Biumo, Count Giuseppe. Oral history interview, April 2, 1985. Archives of American Art, Smithsonian Institution, Washington, D.C.

Paris–New York, 1908–1968. Exh. cat. Paris: Gallimard and Centre Georges Pompidou, 1991.

Partouche, Marc, ed. *Jardin Secret, ou la collection privée de quatre marchands de tableaux: Bruno Bischofberger, Konrad Fischer, Pierre et Marianne Nahon, Ileana Sonnabend.* Marseilles: ARCA centre d'art contemporain, 1986.

Pavia, Philip. The Club records kept by Philip Pavia, 1948–1965. Archives of American Art, Smithsonian Institution, Washington, D.C.

La Peinture Americaine: 1900–1970. Translated by Dominique Le Bourg. New York: Time Life International, 1973.

Perl, Jed. *New Art City: Manhattan at Mid-Century.* New York: Alfred A. Knopf, 2005.

Perloff, Marjorie. *Frank O'Hara: Poet Among Painters.* Chicago: University of Chicago Press, 1977.

Phillips, Lisa. *Frederick Kiesler.* New York: Whitney Museum of American Art, 1989.

Pisano, Ronald G. *17 Abstract Artists of East Hampton: The Pollock Years, 1946–1956.* Southampton, NY: The Parrish Art Museum, 1980.

Rauschenberg, Robert. Oral history interview, December 21, 1965. Archives of American Art, Smithsonian Institution, Washington, D.C.

Rauschenberg, Robert, Alain Jouffroy, and John Cage. *Rauschenberg.* Paris: Ileana Sonnabend, 1963.

Rosenberg, Harold. *Arshile Gorky: The Man, the Time, the Idea.* New York: Horizon Press, 1962.

———. "American Action Painters." In Shapiro, David, and Cecile Shapiro, eds. *Abstract Expressionism: A Critical Record.* New York: Cambridge University Press, 1990, pp. 75–84. First published in *ARTnews* 51, no. 8 (December 1952).

Rowell, Margit, ed. *Joan Miró: Selected Writings and Interviews.* Boston: G. K. Hall, 1986.

Rubenfeld, Florence. *Clement Greenberg: A Life.* Minneapolis: University of Minnesota Press, 2004.

Rubin, William S. *Dada, Surrealism, and Their Heritage.* New York: Museum of Modern Art, 1968.

Rublowsky, John. *Pop Art.* New York: Basic Books, 1965.

Russell, John. *Matisse: Father and Son.* New York: Harry N. Abrams, 1999.

Sandler, Irving. "The Club: How the Artists of the New York School Found Their First Audience—Themselves." *Artforum* 4 (September 1965), pp. 27–31.

———. *The Triumph of American Painting: A History of Abstract Expressionism.* New York: Harper & Row, 1976.

———. "Tenth Street Then and Now." In Kardon, Janet, ed. *The East Village Scene.* Philadelphia: Intstitute of Contemporary Art, University of Pennsylvania, 1984.

———, ed. *Defining Modern Art: Selected Writings of Alfred H. Barr, Jr.* New York: Harry N. Abrams, 1986.

Sawin, Martica. *Surrealism in Exile and the Beginning of the New York School.* Cambridge, MA: The MIT Press, 1995.

Schapiro, Meyer. "The Introduction of Modern European Art in the United States: The Armory Show (1913)." In *Style, Artiste et Société.* Paris: Gallimard, 1982, p. 390.

Schimmel, Paul, ed. *Robert Rauschenberg: Combines.* Los Angeles: The Museum of Contemporary Art, 2005.

Scull, Robert. Oral history interviews, June 15–28, 1972. Archives of American Art, Smithsonian Institution, Washington, D.C.

Scully, Vincent. "The Death of the Street." *Perspecta* 8 (1963), p. 95.

———. *American Architecture and Urbanism.* Revised edition. New York: Henry Holt and Company, 1988.

Seuphor, Michel. "Paris–New York 1951." *Art d'aujourd'hui,* June 1951.

Shaw, Arnold. *52nd St.: The Street of Jazz.* New York: Da Capo Press, 1977.

Skidmore, Louis. "Something to See." *Time,* August 31, 1953, p. 78.

Solomon, Alan R. *Robert Rauschenberg.* New York: The Jewish Museum, 1963.

———. *Jasper Johns.* New York: The Jewish Museum, 1964.

———. Report on the American Participation in the XXXII Venice Biennale 1964, June–October 1964. Archives of American Art, Smithsonian Institution, Washington, D.C.

Solomon, Deborah. *Jackson Pollock: A Biography.* New York: Cooper Square Press, 2001.

Spender, Matthew. *From a High Place: A Life of Arshile Gorky.* New York: Alfred A. Knopf, 1999.

Steinberg, Leo. *Jasper Johns.* New York: George Wittenborn, 1963.

Stern, Robert A. M., Thomas Mellins, and David Fishman. *New York 1960: Architecture and Urbanism between the Second World War and the Bicentennial.* New York: The Monacelli Press, 1995.

Stevens, Mark, and Annalyn Swan. *de Kooning: An American Master.* New York: Alfred A. Knopf, 2004.

Stourton, James. *Great Collectors of Our Time: Art Collecting since 1945.* London: Scala Publishers, 2007.

Sylvester, David. *Interviews with American Artists.* New Haven: Yale University Press, 2001.

"A Symposium: The State of American Art." *Magazine of Art* 42, no. 3 (March 1949), pp. 82–102.

Tomkins, Calvin. *The Bride and the Bachelors: Five Masters of the Avant-Garde.* New York: Viking Press, 1965.

———. *Off the Wall: Robert Rauschenberg and the Art World of Our Time.* New York: Doubleday, 1980.

Turner, Elizabeth Hutton, Guy Davenport, and Elizabeth Garrity Ellis. *Americans in Paris (1921–1931): Man Ray, Gerald Murphy, Stuart Davis, Alexander Calder.* Washington, DC: Counterpoint, 1996.

Vail, Karole P. B. *Peggy Guggenheim: A Celebration.* New York: Solomon R. Guggenheim Foundation, 1998.

Varnedoe, Kirk. *Jasper Johns: A Retrospective.* New York: Museum of Modern Art, 1996.

———, ed. *Jasper Johns: Writings, Sketchbook Notes, Interviews.* New York: Museum of Modern Art, 1996.

Wadsworth Atheneum. *The Tremaine Collection: 20th Century Masters. The Spirit of Modernism.* Hartford, CT: Wadsworth Atheneum, 1984.

Wallach, Alan. *Exhibiting Contradiction: Essays on the Art Museum in the United States.* Amherst, MA: University of Massachusetts Press, 1998.

Warhol, Andy. *America.* New York: Harper & Row, 1985.

Weld, Jacqueline Bogard. *Peggy: The Wayward Guggenheim.* New York: E. P. Dutton, 1986.

White, E. B. *Here Is New York.* New York: Harper & Brothers, 1949. Reprint, New York: The Little Bookroom, 1999.

Wilkin, Karen. "Becoming a Modern Artist, 1920." In Sims, Lowery Stokes, et al. *Stuart Davis: American Painter.* New York: The Metropolitan Museum of Art, 1991, p. 54.

Wolfe, Tom. "Bob and Spike." In *The Pump House Gang.* New York: Farrar, Straus & Giroux, 1968, pp. 195–97.

Zelevansky, Lynn. "Dorothy Miller's 'Americans,' 1942–1963." *Studies in Modern Art* 4 (1994), pp. 57–107.

INDEX

Page numbers in *italics* refer to illustrations.

ACKNOWLEDGMENTS

First of all, I am very grateful to Georges Borchardt, my agent, who wholeheartedly endorsed my participation in this magnificent project. It has been a pleasure to work with the whole Vendome team, especially Alexis Gregory, Mark Magowan, and Jackie Decter, and to benefit from their impeccable professionalism and the magical input of the illustrations they compiled. I am also indebted to Robert Smith, who assisted me early on, when I was writing the first draft of the project. But it was with the support of Lillian Davies that I was truly able to develop the aesthetic commentary on the art of the period. With unbounded enthusiasm, Lillian brought her impressive expertise, sensitivity, energy, balance, and erudition to the project, and I am infinitely grateful to her for her generous help.

—ANNIE COHEN-SOLAL

I was not yet born in 1945, the beginning of the time span documented in this book, and I was a young teenager in 1965, the end of it. But I have vivid memories of New York in the 1950s and 1960s that surely form the foundation of the Architecture and Design section of this book. I remember the amazement of staring down into the vast excavation that was to become the Time & Life Building in Rockefeller Center, and the excitement of seeing the Guggenheim Museum poking out from the line of apartment houses as my father drove up Fifth Avenue—it was two-way then—toward Frank Lloyd Wright's great creation. I remember sensing an energy and excitement that were beyond anything I had ever experienced in any other place before. New York in the late 1950s was beautiful, and exhilarating, and those recollections compounded the pleasure of working on this project. They are no more than a starting point, of course, and when the time came for more formal research, Katie Dubbs helped me at the beginning of the process. Later, as this book was coming together, Patrick Corrigan graciously took time away from research he was doing for me on another project to provide some additional research on this one. I am grateful to them both, as I am to the encyclopedic work of Robert A. M. Stern, Thomas Mellins, and David Fishman, *New York 1960* (Monacelli Press, 1995), which proved itself yet again to be a reference guide beyond compare to the architecture and design of this period.

It is common for an author to note that others have contributed to his or her effort, but in this case it is more than a courtesy—this book has been a true act of teamwork. It is both a pleasure and an honor to be one-third of a writing trio when the other two writers are Bob Gottlieb and Annie Cohen-Solal, extraordinary colleagues to have. But none of us would have gotten much beyond a manuscript had this project not been brought to publication with care and understanding by Alexis Gregory and Jacqueline Decter of Vendome Press, whose enthusiasm for the subject, I think it is fair to say, equals our own.

—PAUL GOLDBERGER

First and foremost, Ron Mandelbaum and his colleagues at Photofest. They've been supplying me with illustrative material for at least a quarter of a century, and for this book they went beyond the call of duty.

As is always the case where dance is concerned, the Dance Division of the Library of Performing Arts at Lincoln Center was crucial. Fond thanks to its director, Jan Schmidt, and her stalwart staff, especially the indefatigable Alice Standin. For other dance images, I'm grateful to my friends Robert Greskovic and Twyla Tharp.

To the powers that be at Vendome Press, beginning with Alexis Gregory, who offered me this opportunity (thanks to Bob Silvers), and including my pal (and occasional co-conspirator) Jackie Decter. They not only held my hand but put up with my bursts of grumpiness (justified, of course).

—ROBERT GOTTLIEB

PHOTO CREDITS

bottom, 68, 70, 81, 82, 94, 106, © 2014 The Andy Warhol Foundation for the Visual Arts, Inc./ARS p. 118; George Karger/The LIFE Images Collection p. 373; Gordon Parks/The LIFE Picture Collection pp. 241, 374–75; Herbert Gehr/The LIFE Picture Collection pp. 354–55; James Burke/The LIFE Picture Collection pp. 37, 57 top; Lipnitzki/Roger Viollet p. 240; Michael Rougier/The LIFE Picture Collection p. 164; Mondadori pp. 92 bottom, 111 bottom; New York Daily News Archive/New York Daily News p. 163; Nina Leen/The LIFE Picture Collection p. 62; Tony Vaccaro/Archive Photos p. 12 top; Weegee (Arthur Fellig)/International Center of Photography p. 212 | Granger Collection, NY p. 90 | Herbert Gehr p. 364 | Herman Miller, Inc. p. 191 center right and bottom left | Heyman Collection: © 2014 The Andy Warhol Foundation for the Visual Arts, Inc./ARS p. 123; © 2014 The Arshile Gorky Foundation/ARS p. 18; © 2014 The Barnett Newman Foundation, New York/ARS p. 49; © 1998 Kate Rothko Prizel & Christopher Rothko/ARS p. 35; © 2014 The Pollock-Krasner Foundation/ARS pp. 12–13; © 2014 The Willem de Kooning Foundation/ARS p. 55 top; p. 110 | The Image Works: © AKG Images p. 29 left; © Jack Nisberg/Roger-Viollet p. 30 bottom; ©NMeM/Tony Ray-Jones/SSPL/© 2014 Carolee Schneemann/ARS p. 98 top | © Estate of Jack Mitchell/Highberger Media, Inc. pp. 86 bottom, 268–69 | Joan Mitchell Foundation p. 63 bottom | JPMorgan Chase History Program, Arthur Lavine photographer, 1978 p. 140 | Judy Cameron p. 263 | Kevin Roche John Dinkeloo and Associates LLC pp. 178, 179 top | Knoll, Inc. p. 191 top left, top right, bottom right | Jens Heilmeyer/The La MaMa Archive/Ellen Stewart Private Collection p. 313 | © Leslie E Spatt p. 245 | LOC: Cervin Robinson p. 225; Gottscho-Schleisner Collection pp. 184, 194, 195; Historic American Buildings Survey 219; Prints and Photographs Division p. 224 top; New York World-Telegram and the Sun Newspaper Photograph Collection p. 172; William P. Gottlieb Collection pp. 350, 351 top, 353, 356 | Limón Dance Company p. 262 | Louise Lawler and Metro Pictures, New York p. 88 | Magnum Photos: © Burt Glinn pp. 358–59; © Bruce Davidson p. 122 top; © Inge Morath © The Inge Morath Foundation p. 301 bottom | Marvin Lazarus p. 42 top | Maurice Berezov Photograph. © A.E. Artworks p. 36 | Metropolitan History p. 155 left | The Milton Resnick and Pat Passlof Foundation, Courtesy Cheim and Read p. 59 | MCNY: Aaron Rose p. 227; Wurts Bros. pp. 131, 134–35, 218, 228 | National Gallery of Art, Washington/© Board of Trustees p. 111 top | NPG/AR/© Elaine de Kooning p. 73 right | New York City Ballet Archives: Photograph by Walter E. Owens p. 253 | NYPL Astor, Lenox, and Tilden Foundations: Wurts Brothers/Milstein Division of United States History, Local History & Genealogy p. 182 | NYPL for the Performing Arts, Astor, Lenox, and Tilden Foundations: Jerome Robbins Dance Division: Bill Sauro/New York Herald Tribune/The New York Times/Redux p. 244; Herbert Midgoll p. 266; Oscar Bailey p. 267 bottom; Fred Fehl courtesy of Gabriel Pinski pp. 246, 249 bottom; Martha Swope/©The New York Public Library p. 248, 249 top, page 250–51, 254 | Pace Gallery: Bill Jacobson/© 2014 Estate of Ad Reinhardt/ARS p. 58; Fred W. McDarrah/Premium Archive/Getty Images/© 2014 Jim Dine/ARS p. 96 bottom;

Martha Holmes/The LIFE Images Collection/Getty Images p. 97; Photo © Estate of Robert R. McElroy/VAGA p. 98 bottom, © 2014 Jim Dine/ARS 96 top | Pavia 981, Manuscript, Archives, and Rare Book Library, Emory University p. 60 bottom left | Pamela D. Ellis/Alan Dunn Estate p. 221 | Peggy Guggenheim Collection, Venice (Solomon R. Guggenheim Foundation, N.Y.): Berenice Abbott Estate/Getty Images p. 15; © Estate of George Platt Lynes p. 16 | Photofest: ABC page p. 238, © Alix Jeffry p. 304 bottom; CBS p. 277 top right; Cecil Beaton p. 237; © Cranston & Jacino pp. 370–71; © Friedman-Abeles pp. 315 top, 341 top; © George Karger p. 291; © Jerome Zerbe p. 311 left; © John Vickers p. 277 left; © Julie Hamilton p. 286; NBC p. 280 left, © Vandamm Studio p. 280 right; pp. 232–33, 236 top left, 239 top, 242–43, 255, 257, 258, 260–61, 272–73, 275, 276, 277 bottom right, 278–79, 281, 282–83, 284 top, 285, 287, 288–89, 290, 292–93, 294, 295, 296–97, 298, 299, 300–301, 301 top, 302 top, 303, 304 top, 305, 307, 308, 309, 310, 312, 314, 315 bottom, 316, 317, 318, 319, 320–21, 322–23, 324–25, 326 bottom, 327, 328, 329, 330–31, 332–33, 334–35, 336–37, 338–39, 340–41, 342, 343, 344, 345, 346–47, 351 bottom, 360, 361, 371, 372 bottom, 377, 378–79 | Phyllis Lambert Fonds/Collection Centre Canadien d'Architecture/© United Press International p. 139 | The Pierpont Morgan Library, New York pp. 22–23 | Philip Pearlstein/From the Shelby White and Leon Levy Archives Center, Institute for Advanced Study, Princeton, NJ, USA. p. 73 left | Queens Museum, New York p. 176 top | Rachel Rosenthal/Art © Robert Rauschenberg Foundation/VAGA p. 77 | © Robert Barry/Tharp Productions p. 273 | Robert Gottlieb: Vandamm p. 284 bottom; pp. 234, 236 bottom left, right, 338, 239 bottom, 274 | Robert Greskovic pp. 242 left, 259 | © Roger Wood/ArenaPAL p. 265 | Rudolph Burckhardt/© YAYOI KUSAMA p. 99 bottom | Scott Bowron/© 2014 Helen Frankenthaler Foundation, Inc./ARS p. 66 | Seattle Art Museum: Eduardo Calderon/Art © Adolph and Esther Gottlieb Foundation/VAGA p. 43; Paul Macapia: © 2014 The Franz Kline Estate/ARS p. 40 bottom, Art © Jasper Johns/VAGA 80, © 2014 Robert Morris/ARS pp. 6–7, Art © Robert Rauschenberg Foundation/VAGA pp. 47, 76 | Sotheby's: © 2014 The Arshile Gorky Foundation/ARS p. 19 top; © 2014 Frank Stella/ARS p. 85; © 2014 The Franz Kline Estate/ARS pp. 40 bottom, 41; © 1998 Kate Rothko Prizel & Christopher Rothko/ARS p. 34; Art © Dedalus Foundation/VAGA p. 44; Art © James Rosenquist/VAGA p. 108 bottom; Art © Jasper Johns/VAGA p. 93; p. 51 | Stork Club Enterprises LLC p. 376 top right, bottom | Sam Falk p. 352 top | The Solomon R. Guggenheim Museum, New York. ©The Hilla von Rebay Foundation Archive p. 147 top | Southeastern Architectural Archive, Special Collections Division, Tulane University Libraries. p. 155 right | © 2014 Stephen Flavin/ARS, courtesy David Zwirner, New York/London p. 103 | Tectonic Photo/Emporis p. 181 | Ugo Mulas © Ugo Mulas Heirs. All rights reserved p. 125 | UN Photo p. 132 right | Vitra Design Museum pp. 191 center left, 192 | Walker Art Center, Minneapolis/Harold D. Field Memorial Acquisition, 1966/Art © Judd Foundation, Licenses by VAGA, New York, NY p. 101 top | Whitney Museum of American Art: © Estate of William Baziotes p.14 bottom; © 1963 Claes Oldenburg pp. 104–5 | William Rayner Leon R. Lewandowski p. 30 top right | Zoë Dominic/Alvin Ailey Dance Foundation, Inc. p. 271

First published in the United Kingdom in 2014 by
Thames & Hudson Ltd, 181A High Holborn,
London WC1V 7QX

Copyright © 2014 The Vendome Press
Visual Arts text copyright © 2014 Annie Cohen-Solal
Architecture & Design text copyright © 2014 Paul Goldberger
Performing Arts text copyright © 2014 Robert Gottlieb

British Library Cataloguing-in-Publication Data
A catalogue record for this book is available from the British Library

ISBN 978-0-500-51772-7

PRINTED AND BOUND IN CHINA

To find out about all our publications, please visit **www.thamesandhudson.com**.
There you can subscribe to our e-newsletter, browse or download our current
catalogue, and buy any titles that are in print.